D0866172

mission and place

Strengthening Learning and Community through Campus Design

Daniel R. Kenney Ricardo Dumont Ginger Kenney

AMERICAN COUNCIL ON EDUCATION
PRAEGER
SERIES ON HIGHER EDUCATION

Library of Congress Cataloging-in-Publication Data

Kenney, Daniel R.
    Mission and place: strengthening learning and community through campus design /
    Daniel R. Kenney, Ricardo Dumont, and Ginger Kenney.
        p. cm. – (ACE/Praeger series on higher education)
    Includes bibliographical references and index.
    ISBN 0-275-98123-1 (alk. paper)
    1. Campus planning–United States. 2. College environment–United States.
I. Dumont, Ricardo. II. Kenney, Ginger III. Title. IV. American Council on
Education/Praeger series on higher education.
LB3218.A1K46 2005
378.1'962—dc22   2004015964

Formerly ACE/Oryx Press Series on Higher Education

British Library Cataloguing in Publication Data is available.

Library of Congress Catalog Card Number: 2004015964
ISBN: 0-275-98123-1

First published in 2005

Praeger Publishers, 88 Post Road West, Westport, CT 06881
An imprint of Greenwood Publishing Group, Inc.
www.praeger.com

Printed in the United States of America

The paper used in this book complies with the
Permanent Paper Standard issued by the National
Information Standards Organization (Z39.48-1984).

10 9 8 7 6 5 4 3 2 1

To Hideo Sasaki, pioneer in campus design and planning and creator of the collegial, inclusive design process still at the heart of Sasaki Associates' practice. He continues to be an inspiration.

Table of Contents

Chapter Lead-in Photographs

Leading a university has grown increasingly complex since I first served as president of West Virginia University some twenty-four years ago. Once a position seemingly populated by thinkers of big thoughts who were looked to by society for help in shaping the intellectual climate of the country, today's college and university presidents are more accurately likened to mayors of small cities or to CEOs. For in addition to concerning ourselves with the education of students and the creation of new knowledge, we must also fill such roles as union arbitrator, public relations guru, fundraiser, and campus architect and general contractor, among other things. These new expectations and responsibilities for leaders in higher education, while significant and rewarding, are not always congruous with a focused style of management.

This is particularly unfortunate now, at a time when colleges and universities—much like those at their helms—increasingly struggle to stay the course of fulfilling both mission and agenda. Just as chancellors and presidents are pulled in numerous directions, so, too, are the institutions themselves subjected to the siren call of such current, popular undertakings as distance learning, core curriculums, high-end residence halls, and the ever-present concern with parking.

Because of the challenges facing presidents and schools alike, times demand of those of us in higher education most serious reflection upon the missions of our institutions. Times require that deliberations be made in order to ensure our actions appropriately convey our goals and values. This is not so easily done, I know. But we must begin to designate time as generously to the planning process as we do to the execution of ideas. We must develop and guard preciously our plans for the future.

As resources are stretched ever thin and space on and around our campuses is at an increasing premium, those of us in higher education will soon—if not already—find it detrimental to fail to seriously consider and explore the long-term ramifications of our decisions.

It is in the area of our physical campuses that a particular vulnerability exists when long-range planning is not undertaken. For here the rash decision about paving a green space or the incorporation of the latest building fad into the "geography of the heart" is clearly evident. Only a few shortsighted decisions need be made before the physical quality of a campus soon reflects the scattered and distracted spirit—and administration—of the institution.

All is not lost, though, if we come late to understanding the significance of the interlocking nature of planning and space and mission. Inroads must constantly be made in order to realign what a university looks like and what it believes. And while the undoing of damage to the campus is difficult, the significance of focus and the return to core values this undoing requires of us can hardly be measured.

At my own institution—Vanderbilt University—our threefold mission includes a commitment to scholarly research, creative teaching and service to the community and society. In keeping this triad at the forefront of every decision we make—every grant for which we apply, every course we offer, every event we sponsor—we also allow ourselves a matrix by which to weigh changes to our physical campus. In accepting the significance of how decisions regarding bricks and mortar affect not only individual programs but also our ability as an institution to sustain our mission, we begin to fulfill our highest potential.

A belief prevails at an increasing number of institutions—including Vanderbilt—that space and mission are synonymous. This philosophy, coupled with a commitment to carefully weigh decisions and how they will impact the whole university for years to come, can set higher education on a newly focused path that will surely result in improvements for us all.

Here is a book that will help us make these decisions wisely.

Gordon Gee
Chancellor
Vanderbilt University

Acknowledgments

A member of the leadership team of a highly regarded medium-sized university once advised us that charging full cost for parking was a "sleeping dog," implying that we would be well advised to let it lie. We did not heed that advice, as you can see in Chapter 13 – Taming the Automobile. But we are deeply grateful for his willingness to tell us what he really thought, and for all the insights shared with us by presidents and other leaders of a number of colleges and universities, large and small, public and private, during roundtable discussions held at the annual meetings of the American Council on Education and the National Association of College and University Business Officers. The participants to whom we are indebted include David Christiansen, University of Scranton; Richard M. Freeland, Northeastern University; Jo Ann Gora, University of Massachusetts Boston; Kermit L. Hall, Utah State University; Bernard A. Mackey, University of South Florida–Lakeland Campus; Roy Merolli, Marist College; Betsy Muhlenfeld, Sweet Briar College; Elsa Nunez, Lesley University; Peter Smith, California State University-Monterey Bay; Sally Smith, California State University-Monterey Bay; Blanche Touhill, University of Missouri St. Louis; Gerald Whittington, Elon University; Peggy Williams, Ithaca College; Dave Wilson, University of California at Los Angeles; and Roland Yoshida, Lehigh University.

Sasaki Associates and its chief executive officer, Jim Sukeforth, deserve special thanks. They have supported us completely to make this book possible. Some of this support appeared in the form of hard-working and dedicated people: Kris Waldman and Anne Dauchy for their creative energy and graphic design, Allyson Solorzano for her great research and overall management, Jantrue Ting's initial research and Roberta Doocey for her thorough editing. But more than anything, we owe thanks to our colleagues at Sasaki for their collaboration, discussion, debate, and sharing of ideas.

Many people reviewed one or more chapters of this book. We are grateful for their time and their suggestions, for you are reading a much better book because of them. Our reviewers included Perry Chapman, Ken Bassett, Joe Hibbard, Scott Smith, and Vincent Giuliano. We especially thank Philip Parsons, who reviewed the entire book and took the time to let us know in detail how we might improve it.

We also want to acknowledge Archie Brodsky, who helped us learn how to express our passion for creating enduring, lively campuses in the form of a book, and to Susan Slesinger, who believed in that book's importance enough to publish it.

Of course we've saved the most important acknowledgment for last. Our families saw less of us on nights and weekends, and heard from us less than they might have liked, for a year and a half. They were, through all this, always supportive. They gave us articles, suggestions, dinners, and encouragement—whatever it took. Our heartfelt thanks go to Margot and Adam Kenney, Sarah Forrester, Sage and India Dumont, Janice Kenney, Elvira Nado, and Annette Singer.

Part I.
Introduction

Meeting Today's Challenges

All across the country, American institutions are reevaluating their identities and how best to express them, their missions, and their fundamental charge to deliver a high-quality education. Professional preparation has never been more important to students, while a liberally educated citizenry has never been more critical to society. Greater numbers of people of increasingly diverse backgrounds are enrolling in colleges and universities. Competition for the best students and faculty is stiff, while financial constraints continue unabated; in fact, costs continue to increase more rapidly than the rate of inflation. Sometimes, institutions can barely manage to keep up with critical campus maintenance, much less accommodate needed growth. While technology is transforming the teaching and learning experience, the social experience is also changing. Institutions everywhere are concerned about loss of community and loss of a sense of place.

The American institution of higher education today is truly facing formidable challenges.

This book will help institutional leaders and the planners and designers who work with them to leverage one of the most powerful resources they have to change formidable challenges into resounding opportunities: the campus and its environs—what we refer to as *place*—and the act of making physical decisions about these—*placemaking*. Some of the points addressed in this book may seem obvious. Many have been discussed in the press and at conferences. Nevertheless, most institutions could be doing more effective placemaking than they are.

Education is an endeavor that is most sensitive to ambience; students respond all their lives to memories of the place that nourished their intellectual growth.[1]

- THOMAS A. GAINES

Addressing institutional challenges

Most of the challenges facing today's institutions are not about place. They are about learning and teaching, about community and communication, about leadership and vitality. But having visited over 250 institutions in our careers as institutional campus planners and designers, the authors have found that in most cases, the campus mirrors the issues that an institution faces.

Is the institution struggling to achieve better cross-disciplinary communication among its sciences faculties? How far apart, then, are their offices and classrooms?

Does the spark of vitality seem missing from the college these days? What, then, does the campus offer to students so that they will linger when classes are over?

Is recruiting hindered by a run-down neighborhood? How, then, can the institution rethink its own campus edge in a way that contributes to the neighborhood?

Do students complain of isolation and lack of community? How much, then, do they have to drive from one place to the next—a solitary activity—as opposed to walking—often with friends?

This is a book about transforming challenges into exciting opportunities. The physical campus offers the potential for changes that can address and improve most of the issues that many institutions struggle with. Often, these improvements can be made without higher expenditure, and often, too, these changes can accomplish multiple objectives at the same time.

Because it is easy to see and grasp, physical change is a powerful way to stimulate change along other dimensions as well. A university's new sciences quadrangle with its arcaded walkway that unites the biology and chemistry buildings may be an exciting space that speaks to the university's vision of the importance of the sciences in its curriculum. It may also spark more interdisciplinary communication between these two departments, leading to more creative research and new, leading-edge course offerings. The dictum "form follows function" has been considered a fundamental truth in the field of architecture since it was first stated by the famous architect Louis Sullivan in 1896. But it is also true that function follows form. If we design our buildings and spaces in certain ways, we can cause certain things—more effective learning, more vibrant community—to happen there. Physical changes can be a powerful tool in facilitating social and organizational change in an institution's culture. We can also shape perceptions, opinions, and memory.

The campus planning process itself can often facilitate change. Constituents have an opportunity to express what they value about an institution and its campus as well as what improvements they'd like to see. Through promoting an understanding of social and educational consequences of physical decisions, the planning dialog provides an opportunity to build consensus for positive change.

Reflecting the geography of the heart

People want to be in places that feel good to them. They prefer nicely appointed places with beautiful views rather than adequate but uninteresting places. Further, people want to feel good about the physical places they are affiliated with: their home, their workplace, sometimes their city and state. Why should it be any different on campus?

The goal is to use the campus's entire physical environment—its neighborhood, buildings and landscape, paths and roadways, parking lots, fountains, and bell-towers—to promote institutional goals. Physical decisions that are not made specifically to forward the institutional agenda may inadvertently be working against it. Furthermore, every decision and action taken regarding the campus may have multiple effects—some for the good and others not—that reflect back on the institution itself.

The heart of the campus:
Rice University

By realizing the interconnection between their strategic goals and their campus, institutional leaders have an opportunity to take control of institutional direction by making wise physical decisions about the campus.

Expressing vision

The campus should reflect the vision and the values of the institution. Campuses need "meaningful places"—places that actually feel like the idea of the institution to students, faculty, and visitors. A television program about a remarkable student who, despite being homeless, became her high-school class valedictorian describes her first visit to Harvard Yard on a high-school field trip. Her reaction to Harvard Yard was strong and immediate: she wanted to go there. The authors have seen prospective students react this way on other campuses as well. Love at first sight is not unusual on campuses where the place expresses the vision of the university or college.

All too often, physical decisions are divorced from the institutional mission. The campus decision makers don't fully see how a physical decision (to add more parking, perhaps, or to locate a building in a certain place) can manifest—or contradict—an essential part of the institutional mission. Investing more money in more construction does not necessarily make campuses better places.

The next section of this book, *Foundations*, describes in detail how the campus can reinforce the three fundamental components of institutional mission—teaching and learning, creating community on campus, and acting as responsible citizens of society and the world.

Teaching and learning

Learning occurs everywhere on campus

As the educational emphasis shifts from teaching to learning, the size, number, arrangement, and mix of classroom types needed on campus has also been changing. An increased focus on interdisciplinary study and research brings new importance to the physical arrangement of spaces for these activities on campus. But this focus is still too narrow. On average, students spend only fifteen hours per week in class. Even considering academic subjects alone, the rest of students' learning time is spent in an astonishing array of locations on campus. Add in the nonacademic but vital learning that most institutions consider part of their missions, and truly every part of a campus must be considered a learning environment. Anything less is a missed opportunity.

Creating community

On many of the campuses we visit, educators and students alike lament the loss of community. We hear this so often that we have come to understand loss of community as a manifestation of today's fast-paced television- and automobile-centric American culture. Nevertheless, institutions of higher education demand of themselves leadership in counteracting this trend, in creating an environment in which community can flourish. Some institutions have made unfortunate physical decisions that may have accelerated loss of community—such as building off-campus or remote housing on campuses that already lack vitality. But most campuses offer many opportunities to further a feeling of community.

Acting responsibly in society and the world

The campus contributes at many levels to an institution's ability to teach social responsibility. First, the campus itself is a microcosm of society. In a tradition stretching back to the ancient Greek *agora*, the campus provides public spaces for people to meet, to post notices, and to engage in the activities of an aware citizenry. It also provides a small (or sometimes, not so small) piece of the natural world—one that before the eyes of all the institution can squander or can nurture and protect. An institution teaches social responsibility by its actions on campus, and the results of these actions are emblazoned in the campus landscape for all to see—sometimes in green spaces that have been turned into parking lots, but sometimes in proudly displayed environmental certifications on buildings.

Institutions also have neighborhoods. Many are fortunate to find themselves adjacent to charming urban areas, but others are challenged by neighborhoods in decline. When they barricade themselves off from these neighborhoods—whether by fences, by parking lots, or by the turned backs of buildings—they may be contributing to this decline. Conversely, many institutions have found ways to work with their neighborhoods to the benefit of all.

Integrating the institution

Overall planning is necessary for an institution. When an institution allows individual departments to make their own decisions, not all decisions benefit the institution as a whole. Individual decisions tend to solve one need at a time, without sufficient consideration of the long term and the big picture.

The same is true for the campus. Although American colleges and universities typically began with a strong, even visionary, plan for their campus environments, many have evolved over the years not through a consciously planned process but rather by making single decisions to solve one problem at a time. These campuses are composed of buildings and facilities created as individual entities rather than as part of a greater whole.

Unified initial plan at Texas A&M University

CUSHING LIBRARY, TEXAS A&M UNIVERSITY

Campuses, like cities, should grow according to a particular hierarchy. They should be considered first as manifestations of a single *plan or idea,* then second, united by their *landscape and open space structure,* and finally, framed by *buildings.* Recent years have seen a loss of understanding of this hierarchy. Today, we more often see campuses comprised of seemingly random collections of *buildings* served by *parking* tied together with *roads.* When the institution comes to understand the need for a campus plan, they and their planners have to work back through these layers to excavate—or sometimes to create—a vision of the campus as a whole.

Whether a campus is already unified or is in need of integrating components, it will benefit through the application of certain principles to physical campus decisions. These include:

· Precedence of the overall plan over individual buildings and spaces
· Use of compactness (density) and mixing campus uses to create vitality and interaction
· Creating a language of landscape elements that expresses the campus's individuality and relationship to its regional context
· Embracing environmental considerations
· Taming the automobile
· Utilizing campus architecture to further placemaking
· Integrating technology
· Creating a beneficial physical relationship with the neighborhood
· Bringing meaning and beauty to the special places on campus

These topics are discussed in detail in the *Principles* section of this book.

Managing change

Things change. The stories of many institutions are stories of change.

Today, growth in enrollment, growing competition, increased student diversity, and mind-bogglingly-rapid advances in technology continue to drive change. The choice is not whether to change, but whether to drive change or be driven by it. Just as the campus is affected by changes to the institution, so too can it be a powerful instrument to effect change. This book concludes by providing a planning-based methodology for making desired changes real.

two

A Changing Context

Current planning issues

Higher education has always changed and evolved to meet society's needs. And now society is changing more rapidly than ever. Institutions are under pressure to change faster and in more ways to keep up. Today's institutions face more issues than ever before, sometimes with conflicting priorities. To succeed, institutions must in one way or another respond to all of them. In many cases, the institution's *place*—its campus or campuses or other physical locations—if properly leveraged can make a key difference in meeting today's challenges.

Changing constituencies

Colleges and universities are competing for an increasingly diverse student body. Because of this competition, they have to be sensitive to the needs of different groups to attract and retain the best students. Reflecting the growing diversity of college and university students, requirements for physical facilities are changing. As each institution comes to terms with its own approach to diversity, the solutions it reaches may have an impact on how the spaces of the campus are organized.

The population of the United States is increasingly non-middle-class and nonwhite. Like their white middle-class counterparts a generation earlier, many of these new populations look to a college education to provide them with increased opportunity and upward mobility. The United States Department of Education reports that American college and university students who are minorities increased from 16 to 27 percent in the twenty-one-year period from 1976 to 1997.[2]

Globalization has created an unprecedented worldwide demand for the intellectual capital that American colleges and universities can provide, and many colleges and universities want to increase the diversity of their

The pessimist complains about the wind;

The optimist expects it to change;

And the realist adjusts the sails.[1]

- WILLIAM ARTHUR WARD

student bodies by recruiting students from other countries. Between 1960 and the late 1980s, the number of foreign students increased more than elevenfold to more than 450,000.[3] This rate was more than double the general increase in numbers of students. Although they comprise overall only about 3 percent of the entire student population, foreign nationals are disproportionately represented in graduate schools. Many institutions with larger foreign student populations are discovering unexpected physical implications. George Mason University, for example, responded to the needs of its Moslem students by installing foot-washing facilities in its student-center bathrooms. Others find they must provide more diverse meal alternatives or accommodate cooking in residence-hall rooms.

In addition, growing numbers of adults with families, single parents, working students, and others are attending college. The Department of Education tracks postsecondary enrollments of non-traditional students who have one or more of the following characteristics: "delayed enrollment into postsecondary education, attended part time, financially independent, worked full time while enrolled, had dependents other than a spouse, was a single parent, or did not obtain a standard high school diploma."[4] Even over the relatively short period from 1986 to 1992, such students increased from 65 to 70 percent of the student population. Thus, the traditional eighteen- to twenty-five-year-old resident full-time students are a minority of all those pursuing undergraduate study. "By 1995," wrote Arthur Levine, president and professor of education at Teachers College at Columbia University, and Jeanette Cureton, "44 percent of all college students were over 25 years old; 54 percent were working; 56 percent were female; and 43 percent were attending part-time. Currently, fewer than one in six of all undergraduates fit the traditional stereotype of the American college student attending full-time, being 18 to 22 years of age, and living on campus."[5]

Many nontraditional students are unable to afford or uninterested in a traditional four-year residential college experience. The needs of these growing nontraditional student populations will have increasing influence on how we plan and design our campuses. Commuting, working adults may use classrooms, laboratories, and other facilities at different times and in different ways than resident students. Commuter students also want to feel part of the student community but cannot do so through residence-hall life. Some schools have accommodated them through providing lockers and "hang-out" spaces in the student centers, where they are encouraged to linger. Others engage them in group projects, but then find they need to provide more group study facilities in libraries and computer areas. Institutions are experiencing physical impacts ranging from the types of services they provide in student centers to the number and location of parking spots.

Changing learning needs

Students are generally less prepared for college than ever. In 1997, nearly three quarters of the deans in one survey reported that the proportion of students needing remedial work had increased over the last decade. Nearly one-third of the undergraduates who were surveyed reported taking a basic skills or remedial course.[6] Students with different learning needs also require different kinds of spaces on campus, including better student educational support facilities and smaller classrooms. Some institutions are providing more learning-center facilities in libraries and classrooms in dormitories to encourage community and support the educational needs of different student populations. The need for different kinds of spaces to support these learning communities will continue to evolve.

Financial resource constraints

Even after adjusting for inflation, the cost in constant dollars of tuition, room, and board rose 71 percent at private four-year colleges and 48 percent at public institutions between 1980 and 1995. In 1994, the cost of tuition, room, and board at a private four-year college was a staggering 43 percent of median family income, up from just over 25 percent in 1980.[7] Between 1994 and 1999—not a period of great inflation—the cost of tuition, room, and board rose between 25 percent (for in-state students at public institutions) and 30 percent (at private institutions).[8]

Increased pressure for accountability

During this same period, social pressure began demanding that education be made accessible to people of lower income by reducing its price. The structure of work in American society increasingly required at least some college education for its better-paying jobs. Parents and students—the customers of the education industry—generally perceive the average cost of a college education as high, while realizing its growing necessity.

Board members and potential donors added to the pressure on institutions to keep costs down and to justify expenditures. Institutions have had to reduce their cost structures or find other sources of revenue—or both—to close the gap between the cost of delivering an education and what students could pay.

Reflecting the persisting demand for accountability, over 60 percent of institutions polled by the Institute for Research on Higher Education had by the year 2000 developed *formal plans* to increase accountability to governmental or regulatory agencies, to students, to funding agencies, to their local communities, and to the general public.[9]

Limited financial resources

Except for a small number of institutions that have ample per-student endowments, limited financial resources are a critical factor in an institution's ability to meet its goals. Even in the "second golden age" of the 1990s, institutions rarely seemed to have the financial resources to create the physical environment necessary to support needed learning environments and community. In periods of recession, even fewer resources are available. In fact, since the mid-1970s, public funding of higher education has not kept pace with rising enrollments and costs, barely keeping up with inflation in a period when real costs per student rose by about 40 percent.[10]

The increases in tuition described above partly reflect a steady erosion of government funding. From 1981 to 1993, government funding fell from almost 50 percent of all funding to less than 40 percent.[11] Overall, the shortfall between the actual cost of providing a postsecondary education and the funds available from all sources is expected to increase, with forecasters at the Commission on National Investment in Higher Education grimly predicting a shortfall of some 25 percent by the year 2015.[12]

The economic downturn of the early 2000s has forced many states to decrease funding of public education while enrollment is still increasing. Public institutions are responding with tuition increases, hiring freezes, delayed equipment purchases, and reduced building maintenance. In some cases, furloughs and program cuts are contemplated.[13] Private institutions—especially those below the top tier but with high tuition, room, and board costs—may have to offer less financial aid while costs increase.

One factor in the increase in the cost of higher education has been the increase in the square feet of building space per student. In planning facilities for higher education, institutions are required to demonstrate that the investment in new buildings or renovations is sound. At many institutions, the soundness of the investment is measured only in cost per square foot. There is no easy way to measure the other benefits the investment might provide for the campus: Does it create places for engagement, enhance the image and identity of the school, or provide a symbol of the school's mission and future? A cost-effective solution (narrowly conceived) may look cheaper in cost per square foot but be detrimental in achieving the institution's other goals.

Funding campus facilities needs

Many institutions cannot keep up with the cost of maintaining their existing physical facilities. During the financially tight times of the late 1980s and early 1990s, many cut back on maintenance funding to balance their budgets. Using data from four hundred colleges and universities, a 1995 survey by the Association of Higher Education Facilities Officers (APPA), the National Association of College and University Business Officers (NACUBO), and Sallie Mae showed a backlog of over $26 billion in deferred maintenance on campuses nationwide, of which $6 billion were deemed urgent. Urgent maintenance needs are those that, if not attended to, will become even more costly in the future. According to this survey, the average public research university spends about $2.3 million per year on deferred maintenance, but the backlog on campus is about $64 million, $15 million of it urgent.[14] This bleak trend, if unchecked, presages widespread decay on American campuses. Since most deferred maintenance is on older buildings, which tend to be located in the core part of the campus, foregoing urgent maintenance can also have a devastating impact on campus image and identity.

Providing access for all to all buildings is also a priority in maintenance budgets, directly affecting institutions' missions to provide education to a diverse student body.

Yet funding for needed maintenance projects is hard to come by. Private donations for new buildings are easier to obtain because donors can see something for their money. Observes Alan G. Merten, president of George Mason University, "It is hard to put your name on a new plumbing system. There is a large backlog of maintenance projects because they are hard to sell."[15]

If there is a bright side to the maintenance issue, it is that creative planning can often make a difference. Needed maintenance can sometimes be combined with building reuse as a way of invigorating the older parts of the campus and increasing support for renewal of older facilities while bringing new uses and new life to the campus core.

With growing enrollments and space needs, funding long-term building and campus infrastructure investments for new construction is also more challenging than ever. Not only are more facilities needed to support increasing enrollment, but the new facilities frequently also require expensive new equipment and information-technology infrastructure. Financial constraints respond to many forces—political, economic, and social—that may not reflect the educational goals and priorities of the institution. Even in the best of times, the challenge of raising money for capital projects makes every available dollar important. What compromises are acceptable?

Since the impact of long-term capital decisions could last for centuries, the larger issues on campus, such as identity, community, and mission, must illuminate these decisions. The institutions that are most successful in implementing their vision for the campus are those that arrange finances to support their mission, compromising where necessary on *how much* is done rather than on *how well*.

Competition

By 1990, with changing demographics and development of greater capacity in higher education, all but an elite few institutions found themselves in a highly competitive market. New types of institutions, such as for-profit institutions, virtual universities, and corporate universities, are changing the ways in which more established institutions must compete. Phoenix University, for example, grew more than tenfold, from an enrollment of some 4,700 students to over 49,000 students in the five years from 1997 to 2002.[16]

Many institutions compete for the same pool of students. Providing a quality education continues to be essential in attracting the best students—but it is no longer enough. Even the idea of what constitutes a quality education seems to be changing because of market influences. More and more, students want their education to give them the credentials to get a good-paying job. The much-noted "vocationalization" of a college education has led more than one pundit to declare that the core liberal arts curriculum is dead. "The curriculum will be more and more market- [not mission-] driven," declared Anthony Carnevale, ETS Vice President for Public Leadership, "unless our sense of urgency on the broader project known as Western Civilization gets stronger."[17]

Marketing the campus

Naturally, a focus on marketing has an impact on the campus, which is, after all, perhaps the single most effective marketing tool.

The campus visit. The campus visit is increasingly important. A front-page story in the *Boston Globe* reports that "a study…presented at a national conference of college admissions counselors ranked the campus visit first among fifteen 'influential information sources' considered by college applicants."[18] Not surprisingly, many institutions are spending significant amounts of money to ensure that the visit is a memorable experience. Many schools, such as Harvard, have begun to invest in making the tour more professional by training tour guides. Others supply tour busses so that visitors don't have to walk too much. Visitors commonly receive lagniappes such as bottled spring water, disposable cameras, and coupons for free lunches. Some institutions, such as the University of Connecticut, have built new visitor centers on campus, or have, like Boston University, established visitor centers in impressive on-campus buildings.

Branding. The campus can play a significant role in establishing the recognition that many institutions crave. Uniquely beautiful spaces, such as the central space at the University of Chicago, or significant buildings or constellations of buildings, such as the old central buildings at MIT, come to symbolize the institution as a whole. How many catalogues, brochures, and promotional flyers feature attractive views of buildings and quadrangles?

A number of institutions have commissioned internationally famous architects to build signature buildings to enhance their identity and demonstrate their leading-edge position to prospective students, parents, faculty, and alumni. Signature buildings can sometimes be used as a symbol of the institution. Trustees find these buildings dazzling, and sometimes donors can be found who would not give as generously for a less distinctive building. However, the creation of signature buildings on campus is not without its risks.

The country club factor

Promoting the campus image

In addition to the academic curriculum, more students are looking for amenities from the college or university they choose, and most institutions feel compelled to provide them. "Colleges hope perks can boost enrollment," declares the headline of a front-page article in the *Boston Globe*.[19] The offered perks reported in the article include gourmet food courts, sushi stations, and cyber cafés; personal trainers, weight rooms, climbing walls, and squash courts; cable television, high-speed Internet access, and additional electrical outlets for DVD players, televisions, printers, refrigerators, and other student appliances in the dorm rooms. As more institutions add perks to the admissions offer, others are compelled to compete. Joan Schmidt, associate director of residential life at Central Michigan University, observes, "The students say, 'What can you offer me? So everybody's building new facilities to keep up with the Joneses.'"[20]

The need to offer increasingly luxurious perks has had a major impact on the campus environment, and upgrading facilities to provide competitive amenities has become a significant expense for many institutions. In 2000, 64 percent of the money spent on facilities construction by institutions of higher education nationwide—approximately $9.4 billion—was spent on nonacademic facilities.[21] Campuses across the country are improving recreational facilities, building larger and more luxurious housing, and providing more (and more convenient) parking.

Student recreation centers, field houses, and improved athletic facilities.
Today's students, residents and commuters alike, look upon a school's
recreation center as an essential part of the college experience, both as
a social amenity and as a wellness facility. "These revamped centers are
increasingly seen as the new student unions, the largest and swankiest
meeting places on campus and the schools' biggest magnets for recruitment and retention."[22] A good recreation center has become an essential
selling point.

New large-scale recreation centers can easily comprise a quarter of a million square feet or more and cost $50 million. The University of Denver's
490,000 square-foot facility cost $77 million; the renovation and expan-
sion of Larkin Hall at Ohio State University will provide 648,000 square
feet and cost $97 million.[23]

At issue is how recreation centers can contribute to the overall synergy of
campus life. Large, bulky buildings, they are often planned at the fringe
of the campus where students drive rather than walk, decreasing overall
campus vitality. Located more centrally, perhaps in a number of smaller
buildings, student recreation facilities can have a major influence in promoting community on campus and a healthy lifestyle.

What students want

Larger and more luxurious rooms and housing types. Many institutions are
finding they must now offer larger and more luxurious housing to the
students they are eager to attract. Many students also want more housing choices. To be competitive, institutions have responded by building
more single rooms, suite-style units, and on-campus apartments, and by
providing them with more amenities.

What students get

Providing this type of housing costs significantly more per student than
traditional residence halls. In 1998, the median new residence hall had
almost 300 square feet per student and cost an average of $37,662 per
student. According to *American School & University*'s 10th Annual Residence Hall Construction Report, "Colleges and universities realize the
benefits of providing quality, sought-after housing on campus—and are
sparing little expense."[24]

Renovation of a residence hall at Northern Illinois University shows
clearly the cost of providing competitive housing. The university replaced
old cafeteria-style dining halls with food courts, upgraded telephone systems, provided individual thermostats, and improved the students per
bathroom ratio by a factor of two. All the rooms were renovated and
improved to accommodate computers and other devices students might
bring. Upon completion of this $10.6 million project, the renovated resi-
dence hall housed 1,280 students in the same space that had previously
housed 2,000.

Not only is the more luxurious housing more expensive, but it also encourages students to stay in their rooms. With food, TV, cable, Internet access, and music, why go out? We hear from student-life directors all over the country that this trend is one cause of loss of community and lack of student engagement on campus. Have we gone too far in responding to the market?

Suburbanization

Like their suburban counterparts, students, faculty, and staff on almost every campus lament the loss of community and social interaction. Yet many administrators don't realize that their decisions to suburbanize the physical campus environment are contributing to this loss of community. Like the suburbs, the new campus districts are characterized by sprawl and automobile dominance; they lack a sense of place, connection, and human scale. While some loss of community is symptomatic of larger societal issues, the role of the campus physical environment should not be underestimated.

Automobile dominance erodes campus quality

Becoming part of city life

Ironically, as suburban-like sprawl is growing on many campuses, the amenities of city life are more in demand than ever. Most students and faculty want to be in vital, vibrant urban environments, where they can enjoy a fast-paced, exciting city life. They don't want their choice of a college or university to isolate them. Faculty, too, want the intellectual and cultural resources of a city. Perhaps, along with other factors, urban locations contribute to the popularity of such diverse institutions as Boston University, Boston College, Brown University, New York University, and Columbia.

Even well-regarded non-urban schools, from Oberlin College to Sweet Briar College, report that students leave the campus in large numbers on weekends, seeking the excitement of nearby cities. Institutions that aren't in urban environments or are in second- or third-tier cities strive to find a way to compensate.

Technology

Technology can be an enabler of community and education as well as a factor in increasing isolation. Colleges and universities must face the opportunities and threats of new technologies with imagination and vision.

Having grown up with computers, students are more comfortable than ever before with access to information and communication via computer. Yet, this access is generally achieved in a private way—often through a network connection in the student's room. Because of this isolating tendency, student-life professionals are putting a higher priority on places where people can interact, develop social skills, and build community.

On the other hand, technology also supports the building of community. Much of the time that students are spending on computers is used in social ways. They keep in touch with family, friends on distant campuses, and friends on the same campus via email and instant messaging. They use publicly available computers in a group or working side by side. They may also have good friends met in gaming or other online environments—friends they may have never met in person.

Technology may require some changes in teaching style. As access to education increases, students can often get information on the World Wide Web or at their jobs that is better or more current than the professor's.

I *A Changing Context*

In this environment, disseminating information is less important educationally than learning how to manipulate information and discussing what it means. This kind of education is more interactive than lecturing, and it affects the kinds of classrooms and learning environments that are needed. Some educators are also experimenting with classes that sometimes meet online. To the extent that their success takes hold, existing physical facilities may be able to support a greater number of classes—but the demand will increase for good virtual facilities and support.

Distance learning is a technology-enabled trend that provides educational opportunities for traditionally underserved constituents. Single parents, older people, and students in distant locations can now enroll in programs and get their degrees without ever setting foot on campus. While this group may not need an on-campus community as much as the traditional, younger constituency, schools are grappling with how to provide some of the same social and group-learning benefits as place-based education, and to provide the same sense of identity with the institution that more traditional students have.

Because computer technology is so new and still changing so rapidly, not enough attention has yet been paid to its impact on campus community and what this means for the physical environment. We expect that new models will emerge for group learning and for interactivity, and that these models will drive new requirements for the campus and its spaces.

Concern about loss of community

All of these trends and challenges have an impact on the feeling of community on campus—some positive and some negative. Overall, most institutions have a sense that community on campus has diminished. "We can't get them out of their rooms!" is a grievance we often hear from directors of student life and other administrators on campus. "There's nowhere to go!" complain the students, and "I don't feel connected here."

Sometimes these trends are at odds with one another. Marketing in a more competitive environment, for example, leads to the offering of luxuries and services that may, ironically, decrease community. The conflict among these trends may not always seem so obvious. Providing a parking space for every student and faculty member close to every destination is an attractive convenience, but it forces construction of new facilities ever farther apart, thereby making walking less feasible. With fewer pedestrians, the emptier-feeling campus erodes both a feeling of safety and a sense of community. In addition, the cost of maintaining roadways and parking facilities, often not clearly itemized in budgets, reduces the funds available for professors, courses, and other needed facilities.

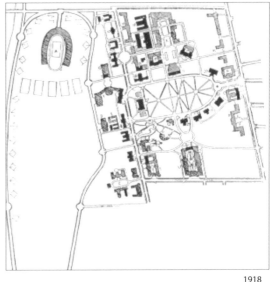

1888

1918

Growth

Enrollment at America's colleges and universities increased by a factor of six from 1950 to 1995, with a threefold increase (from 7.7 to 23 percent) in the percentage of people aged twenty-five to twenty-nine who had attended at least four years of college. During this same period, colleges and universities increased their facilities space by a factor of seven. Between 1997 and 2003, total facilities spending on campus almost doubled from $5.78 billion to $11.06 billion. Enrollment is projected to grow by almost 20 percent from 2000 to 18.2 million in 2013.[25]

The impact of this huge physical growth and resulting changes in the character of American campuses has not all been positive. By 1994, the median age of campus buildings was twenty-eight years, and many were in need of major renovation or replacement.[26]

The issues around dealing with these difficult and often-conflicting trends are discussed in greater detail in later chapters of this book.

present

Opportunities

Higher education has always changed and evolved to meet society's needs. And now society, too, is changing. Institutions are under pressure to change faster, and in more ways, to keep up. Today's institutions face more challenges and diverse issues than ever before, sometimes with conflicting priorities. To succeed, institutions must avail themselves of every possible resource.

In many cases, the institution's *place*—its campus or campuses or other physical locations—if properly leveraged can make a key difference in meeting today's challenges. Many campuses have some splendid historical and new buildings, rich original plans, fine open spaces, and beloved places that can be used as a basis for future growth and change.

Institutions increase their total space by ¾ to 1½ percent per year on average, even if enrollment doesn't grow. At a growth rate of 1½ percent, campuses double their building areas in less than fifty years. In coming years, we have the opportunity to use needed building renovations and replacements, as well as continuing expansion, to achieve institutional missions and physically transform our campuses to better accommodate a growing and more diverse student body. This growth, if channeled correctly, can, over time, create on campus the memorable environments that support a rich learning community.

Part II.
Foundations

three

Linking an Institution's Mission and Its Place

The mission and values of higher education shared by most colleges and universities bind them to society and to each other. An institution's mission, expressed in its mission statement, is the foundation to which that institution's every decision and action should be held accountable. Upon this bedrock of institutional values, the entire edifice of educational and co-curricular programs, student life, faculty interaction, and community relations is built. The campus plan, architecture, and landscape architecture facilitate the realization of fundamental values in all these areas.

> The American campus is a world in itself, a temporary paradise, a gracious stage of life.[1]
>
> - LE CORBUSIER

A closer look at mission

Washington University in St. Louis has an ambitious mission and inspiring goals. In this, it is not unusual. "Central to our mission are our goals, which are to foster excellence in our teaching, research, scholarship, and service; to prepare students with the attitudes, skills, and habits of lifelong learning and with leadership skills, enabling them to be useful members of a global society; and to be an exemplary institution in our home community of St. Louis, as well as in the nation and in the world."[1]

Other mission statements, each with its unique quality, express much the same central foci. Here are a few more examples from a diverse selection of institutions:

· "Texas A&M University is a public institution dedicated to the development and dissemination of knowledge in many and diversified academic and professional fields. The University is committed to assist students in their search for knowledge, to help them understand themselves and their cultural and physical environments, and to develop in them the wisdom and skills needed to assume responsibility in a democratic society."[2]

- "The University of Miami's mission is to educate and nurture students, to create knowledge, and to provide service to our community and beyond. Committed to excellence and proud of the diversity of our University family, we strive to develop future leaders of our nation and the world."[3]

- "Duquesne [University, in Pittsburgh, Pennsylvania] serves God by serving students–through commitment to excellence in liberal and professional education, through profound concern for moral and spiritual values, through the maintenance of an ecumenical atmosphere open to diversity, and through service to the Church, the community, the nation and the world."[4]

- "Marlboro College's mission is to help students think clearly, learn independently, strive for academic excellence and take part in a community that values democratic participation."[5]

Most mission statements in their broadest terms identify education (and often research), productive social and personal development of the students, and service to community and society as institutional core values.

The link between mission and place

An institution's physical campus environment plays a key role in expressing—and in helping to achieve—that institution's mission and strategic objectives.

Teaching and research

The campus supports an institution's fundamental mission of education and research in both obvious and subtle ways. Clearly, the campus provides the classroom and laboratory spaces needed for formal teaching and learning. But on campus, the spaces that are used for learning activities include less formal but equally critical areas. These less formal areas can be a widened space at the bend of a corridor where a student can sit on a chair with a book while waiting to meet a friend, a busy coffee shop, the front steps of the library on a sunny day, or a sheltered quad where an inspired teacher brings a class to discuss Plato in the fresh air. They can also include the open and undeveloped areas of the campus where native ecosystems can be observed and natural environments enjoyed.

Students can learn wherever they have opportunities for interaction; and the more chance for running into friends, teachers, fellow students, or colleagues, the better.

Strengthening interdisciplinary programs and sharing academic experiences across departments is often a high-priority strategy for advancing knowledge as well as for providing a meaningful educational experience. Today, faculty and students want a campus that fosters a sense of collegiality and supports the open exchange of ideas, free inquiry, exposure to many disciplines, and collaboration. The layout of the campus—including the adjacency and proximity of programs—can foster the exposure and interactions that lead to successful interdisciplinary collaboration, or it can stymie them.

The classroom moves outdoors at Creighton University

Productive social development

Institutions have long viewed developing and preparing the whole individual for a productive life and meaningful contribution to society as central to their missions. In his seminal book *A University for the 21st Century,* James Duderstadt, President Emeritus and University Professor of Science and Engineering at the University of Michigan, expressed this role of the university well. "Beyond formal education in the traditional academic disciplines and professional fields, the university has been expected to play a far broader role in the maturation of students…The campus experience we tend to associate with undergraduate education does a remarkable job in preparing the student for later life, and clearly it does so through a complex social experience extending far beyond the classroom and the curriculum."[6]

In an increasingly individualistic yet diverse society, this aspect of most college and university missions is more critical than ever. We must use every part of the public realm on campus—every place two paths intersect, every stairway, every lobby, every lawn and garden—as an opportunity for encouraging communication and engagement. Conversely, without comfortable, human-scaled common spaces for people to get together, social interaction is stifled. A plan that provides "front-door" access to automobiles can encourage students and faculty to leave campus quickly when their formal work is done, limiting opportunities for collegial exchange.

Service to society

"If the condition of man is to be progressively ameliorated, as we fondly hope and believe, education is to be the chief instrument in effecting it," wrote Thomas Jefferson in 1818.[7] From Jefferson's time on, the American university has taken this responsibility to heart. Today, institutions of higher education are concerned with improving society at every scale, from local to planetary.

"I know no safe depositary of the ultimate powers of the society but the people themselves," Jefferson wrote in September, 1820, "and if we think them not enlightened enough to exercise their control with a wholesome discretion, the remedy is not to take it from them, but to inform their discretion by education."[8] Jefferson was referring both to "knowledge of those facts which history exhibits"—dissemination of information—but also to the development of habits of mind and virtue of character appropriate to those who must take responsibility for making decisions that affect the governance of their nation.

Colleges and universities are a microcosm of society whose every member has the opportunity to practice social values ranging from simple neighborliness to good citizenship to governance. The public spaces—large and small, indoors and out—of the university provide a forum in which all of these activities can be engaged.

Most institutions today include education about promoting a sustainable world and direct action to further environmental stewardship as part of their essential values. Institutions' actions on campus in managing the built environment provide an opportunity to demonstrate their commitment to this value.

Above all, to be true to their mission of serving society, colleges and universities must themselves be willing to act as role models to educate our young citizens and future leaders on the meaning and importance of fostering the economic and social well-being of the neighborhood, city, and region in which they are located.

Place as an expression of the institution

Most institutions start as an idea, but as soon as a place is created to house the institution, the idea becomes grounded in the place. The idea and the place of the institution have a mutual and enduring impact on one another. Harvard Yard, for example, means something to most people. But even if a person is not familiar with the institution, its place says something about it—whether that place is the great playing field at the heart of Wesleyan University in Connecticut or the seven-story atrium of Hartford Community College's downtown former-department-store building.

One high-school junior, strolling the gracious campus of Rollins College in Winter Park, Florida, decided that she wanted to attend the college without talking to a single student. She felt the quality and character of the institution in the place, and later conversations with students and admissions representatives confirmed this impression for her.

When a brand-new campus is created, university leaders frequently feel the need to express the essence of the institution in how it is built. The campus is physically designed to meet the pedagogical model. Although its inspiration came from a number of influences, the overall form of

Stanford University owes much to Leland Stanford's vision of a great but uniquely Californian institution whose role was to produce citizens who would be both cultured and "useful." The combined use of arcaded walkways, interconnected, formal courtyards, and native building styles and materials was revolutionary. In 1913, Stanford University's first president, David Starr Jordan, wrote of the twenty-two-year-old school: "The yellow sandstone arches and cloisters, the 'red-tiled roofs against the azure sky,' make a picture that can never be forgotten, itself an integral part of a Stanford education."[9]

As institutions grow, expand, and change, the connection between the physical layout and the pedagogical model typically becomes weakened. Pedagogical models change, as does society as a whole. New needs develop. New buildings are added to old, new functions appended to existing, wherever there seems to be room. With the pressure to add new building space and accommodate an increasing number of cars on campus, many institutions appear to have lost altogether the connection between their physical campus and their mission and vision.

We're not creating a lot of great new spaces on our campuses today. In fact, we're lucky to preserve the old ones undamaged by automotive encroachment and inappropriately scaled buildings. On many campuses today, projects are carried out to meet discrete needs—more classroom space, more parking, a new student center—until the overall sense of unity and harmony on the campus as a whole is destroyed. Campus leaders, planners, architects, and landscape architects need to help institutions reveal the connection between their visions and their campus as they help these institutions grow.

Looking toward the future

Attracting the best

Every college and university wants to attract the most talented scholars, researchers, and teachers, as well as a bright, diverse, and intellectually vibrant student body. The mission of each institution reflects its vision in a way that can inspire potential students, faculty, and staff. An attractive campus with facilities that support an active and vital campus life is a well-documented critical factor in attracting both students and faculty. Thomas Gaines reports, "Sixty percent of college-bound students told the Carnegie Foundation that visual environment was the most important factor in choosing a college."[10] *Mission-driven planning and design* provide institutions with a method for implementing campus facilities and open spaces with a view toward supporting the mission of the institution and providing this kind of attractive environment.

Laying the groundwork for tomorrow's education

Does the physical campus play a pivotal role in helping to realize all kinds of institutional missions? Clearly, it makes a difference for some more than others. A storefront campus makes sense for Heald College, with its no-nonsense approach. "Get in. Get out. Get ahead," states its storefront window in downtown San Francisco. "Heald College," the institution declares unequivocally in its mission statement, "provides focused programs in business, technology, and healthcare that prepare students for success in the workplace in the shortest practical time." The institution has selected a location to reinforce its businesslike approach and perhaps needs only sufficient and well-designed classroom and laboratory space.

Educational values of most students have changed over the last few decades, placing a greater emphasis on vocational preparation and training.[11] Arthur Levine and Jeanette Cureton observe, "Even more dramatic than this continuing trend toward vocationalism…is the plummeting value placed on nonmaterial goals, such as learning to get along with people and formulating the values and goals of one's life. Whereas these personal and philosophical goals were the principal reasons for attending college in the 1960s, today they are at the bottom of the list."[12]

Many of the more visionary educators today lament these changes in student values. They are calling for changes in undergraduate education and new visions for learning to meet the needs of students and of society in the rapidly changing culture and global environment of the early 21st century. The historical mission of educating the whole individual has never been more important. Levine and Cureton, for example, propose an educational curriculum woven around five critically needed elements:

communication and thinking skills; human heritage; the natural and human-made environments; the variety of individual roles that people will play in their lives and how these interact to create a full and complete life; and civic and personal values. Calling this "a curriculum for living," Levine and Cureton describe it as "grounded in the life needs of students...designed specifically to prepare current undergraduates for the life they will lead and the world in which they will live."[13]

To rise to the opportunities, face the challenges, and meet the diverse needs of widening American college enrollment demographics, the Association of American Colleges and Universities (AACU) created the Greater Expectations Initiative. The AACU's rational for Greater Expectations declares that "capacities traditionally developed through a liberal arts education, that include but go beyond a body of factual knowledge, will be required of most Americans as they live and work in the twenty-first century."[14] While acknowledging that students will pursue specializations in college, Greater Expectations calls for higher education *across all fields* to "help college students become intentional learners who can adapt to new environments, integrate knowledge from different sources, and continue learning throughout their lives." Students must master intellectual and practical skills; learn about the natural and social worlds and about how to continue learning in these areas; and take responsibility for their personal actions and for civic values.[15]

The requirements for a high-quality education, one that meets the needs of a widely diverse and growing student body in the twenty-first century, go well beyond vocational training. Students need to learn civic and moral values as well as the qualities that will enable them to become life-long enthusiasts of learning. The campus plays a key role in establishing, reinforcing, and facilitating the realization of this mission.

Planning our campuses to meet these broad challenges and establish effective learning communities is fundamental to the mission of higher education. Since most educators agree that learning occurs best with a combination of instruction (in a classroom or on the computer), peer group interaction, and "real-world" hands-on experience, campus and building spaces should be designed to support all three of these learning modalities.

The following chapters in the *Foundations* section of this book describe the significant role of the campus's physical environment in supporting a college or university to realize its goals in the areas of teaching and research, productive social development of students, and service to the world outside of the campus. Later chapters in the *Principles* section of the book go into greater detail on the campus planning and design principles that should be followed in support of the institutional mission.

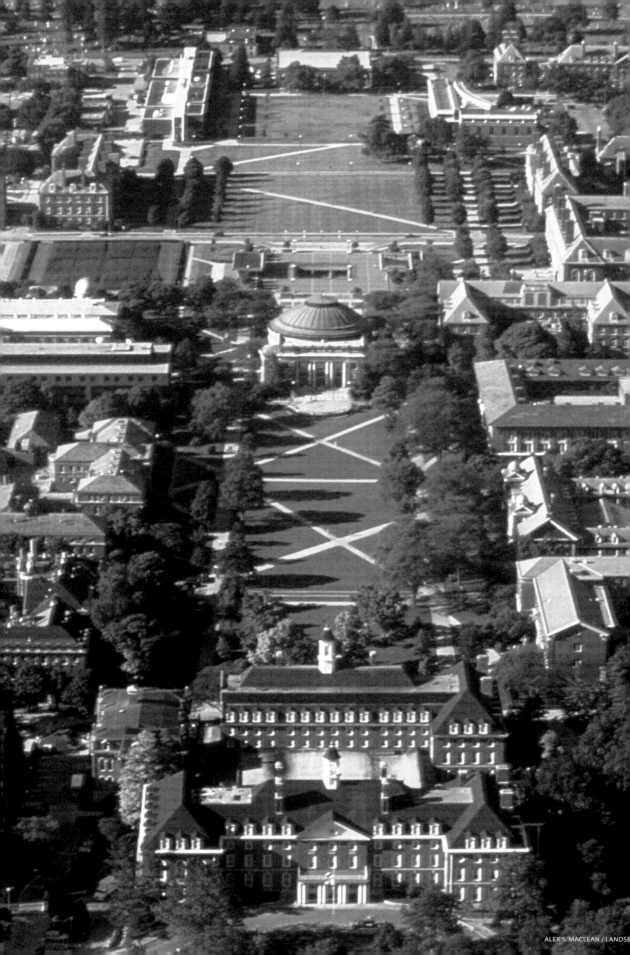

four

The Learning Campus –
Enhancing Student Learning and Engagement

Changing focus from teaching to learning

Forty-five percent of first-year students never discuss ideas from their classes or readings with a faculty member outside of class.[1] What can be done about it?

College students learn on the entire campus—not just in its classrooms and academic buildings. Instead of focusing most of their academic facilities resources on classroom additions and upgrades, institutions would do well to take into account the proven connection between academic performance, retention and graduation rates, and the qualities of the *entire* environment beyond the classroom.

Higher education began in the 1990s to evolve its focus from the act of teaching to the outcomes of student learning. Student learning styles differ in where, when, how, and with whom students learn. More and more students report going to class infrequently or not at all, going to the library only a few times before graduating or not at all, and engaging in study groups in non-academic settings. We have observed on many campuses that institutional physical environments have not kept pace with these students' learning patterns. In many cases, the physical settings may actually inhibit learning.

Educators today generally acknowledge that the didactic classroom-based teaching model common in American higher education is insufficient to instill in students the essential competencies of an educated person: effective communication, critical thinking, and a sense of social responsibility. At the same time, the division between academic and student-life elements on campus has relegated many important life skills—such as

The learning college places learning first and provides educational experiences for learners anyway, anyplace, anytime.[1]

- TERRY O'BANION

State University of West Georgia

teamwork and ethical decision-making—to the co-curriculum, exacerbating perceived problems with undergraduate academic learning. The rise in numbers of commuter students who do not participate extensively (if at all) in the co-curriculum makes these problems more critical.

The buzzword these days is *student engagement*. This includes and goes beyond just academic learning. Student engagement comprises the whole experience of education, broadening the mind, interacting, dialog, discourse—all the things higher education should be. Learning goes beyond just doing research in a library and submitting a term paper. Learning has multiple academic and social facets, all of which require student engagement.

To foster student learning, more and more institutions are creating "learning communities." While learning communities can take many forms, they generally link structured learning with environments that create opportunities for more interaction between students and faculty and among students. Many of these programs involve co-curricular and residential living experiences. Research indicates that, "learning communities and first-year programs can be effective in promoting and improving student academic achievement, academic and social integration, involvement, satisfaction, sense of community, and retention."[3] Critical to these programs are physical environments outside the normal academic classroom context, sometimes off campus, which encourage and support collaborative and active learning activities and social interaction.

Already, most learning takes place outside the classroom. Studies of learning communities and methods for improving student engagement reinforce the importance of the connection between out-of-class experiences and all elements of student learning. The definition of the learning environment must be broadened. When an institution looks at how resources could be allocated to improve the learning environment, it must include *all places* where learning takes place.

Enhancing student engagement

One new and promising study into the elements of institutional quality and learning effectiveness is the National Survey of Student Engagement (NSSE).[4] NSSE research assesses factors that are associated with high levels of student learning and personal development, for every type and size of college and university. Based on research studies, five key indicators are linked to desired outcomes in college:

· Level of academic challenge
· Active and collaborative learning
· Student-faculty interaction
· Enriching educational experiences
· Supportive campus environment

These activities generally fall under the concept of student engagement and are features of institutional quality that heretofore have gone under-recognized in their importance, partially because they are harder to measure than the quantifiable measures found in the "best colleges" rankings in national magazines.

Many activities that contribute to these indicators of student learning—collaborative learning, student-faculty interaction, enriching educational experiences, supportive campus environment—occur largely outside the classroom, and therefore may be partially invisible to faculty members, administrators, and board members. Yet these student-engagement activities are essential to effective student development and learning. They include:

· Preparing for class (including studying, reading, writing, rehearsing and so on)
· Working with classmates outside of class
· Tutoring or teaching other students
· Participating in a community-based project
· Discussing ideas from reading or classes with other people (faculty, other students, members of family) outside of class
· Talking about career plans with a faculty member or advisor
· Working with faculty members on activities other than coursework

- Working with a faculty member on a research project
- Talking with students with different religious beliefs, political opinions, or values
- Talking with students with different race or ethnicity or economic or social background
- Participating in various other non-classroom activities, including internships or field experiences, community service or volunteer work, independent study, and co-curricular activities

All of these activities require social interaction and dialog, most of which occurs outside the traditional "learning environments" (classrooms and laboratories).

Research in many disciplines has provided evidence of the value of active engagement and social interaction in enhancing learning. Even activities that seem to be solitary in nature, such as reading or preparing for class, people often enjoy doing in one another's company, leading one expert to state that learning is a social process.[5] This social out-of-the-classroom activity should be encouraged anywhere and everywhere on campus.

If the entire campus environment is critical to enhancing student engagement, development, and learning, then institutions need to focus on how they can leverage their resources to create an entire campus environment that supports student learning. Beyond academic buildings, other building types and the entire campus environment, if planned properly, can provide enhanced opportunities for students to engage in those activities that research has shown will enhance learning.

The learning campus

More than 50 percent of student learning in college occurs outside the classroom. Even for academic coursework alone, although students may spend forty-four to forty-eight hours per week on academic pursuits, they attend classes only twelve to sixteen hours per week.[6] Studying for those classes is done alone or in groups in every conceivable setting—in dormitories or libraries, on lawns under trees or in the sun, on benches or stairways, at cafes and dining halls—wherever a quiet space to think or read alone, or a public place to meet a friend, can be found.

Moreover, most institutions agree that their educational mission is more than just academic. They also have a mission to teach civic and leadership skills and to help mold the characters of their students, so that the students will achieve their best in every phase of their lives. Students spend on average seventy hours per week on non-academic activities other than sleeping, such as socializing over meals and participating in athletics or other co-curricular activities. All of this time is potentially usable in fulfilling this nonacademic part of an institution's mission, and almost all of it takes place in venues other than the classroom.

Add to these hours those in which engaged students pursue the kinds of non-classroom learning activities measured by the NSSE, and a picture of the *learning campus* begins to emerge.

Ways the physical campus can enhance engagement

How does the entire campus contribute to student engagement and learning during those critical hours outside the classroom? What is the character of a learning campus?

The stairways at Ithaca College are a crossroad of student activity

Clearly, the learning campus is one that maximizes the probability of chance encounters, and encourages lingering once an encounter—whether by chance or by plan—takes place. This means that it is an exciting place where students and faculty alike enjoy "hanging out," whether alone or in groups, where activities are available, or where pleasant places encourage lingering. Think about the places on the campuses you know. Does the parking lot contribute more to student engagement—or does the green at the historic core? Are students more likely to meet by chance while driving across campus looking for a parking space—or by walking? Is the quiet library the place where they get together to study—or the nearby Starbucks? Examples of engaging places on campus abound. A few are described here.

· The "Starbucks phenomenon" is a clear demonstration of the social influence on learning behavior. "Here in Augusta this afternoon, for instance," observes a writer for *The Chronicle of Higher Education*, "there are more Medical College of Georgia students packed into the tiny cafés of the local Borders and Barnes & Noble than there are in the college's sprawling library." Augusta State University in Augusta, Georgia noted a marked drop-off in the use of its libraries as students find new study spaces. Many institutional libraries are "fighting back" by adding to their traditional services coffee and food, as well as comfortable and attractive lounge and café spaces to enjoy them in. After Texas Christian University added a café and soft couches to the library, they observed a doubling of library traffic. And the café is profitable.[7]

Much-used courtyard
at Rollins College

- At Ithaca College, except in the most inclement weather, the stairways to and from the residence halls—designed with small seating alcoves to rest during the long climb—are always full of students hanging out. They meet there because the circulation system funnels people into this area and then provides a little seating area off to the side of the path where people can step aside and sit and talk.

- The University of North Dakota put a bank of computer terminals in the wide, glassed-in hallway that joined the library and the student center. Despite a noisy environment and large windows with potential glare, these terminals are constantly in use. By plan and by chance, students use the computer area as a meeting place.

Certain principles emerge. Places set aside for automobiles are almost never a part of the learning campus. But beautiful outdoor spaces framed by buildings often are. So are noisy, bustling, crowded public places—cafés, coffee shops, public computer terminals, perhaps even the mail room. Campus design principles that enhance student engagement—many of them discussed in more detail later in this book—include:

- A pedestrian campus environment reinforced by appropriate closeness of buildings (density) and by juxtaposition of activities that complement one another (mixed use).

- Indoor and outdoor social spaces scattered throughout the overall framework of the campus (not just in the campus center), such as lounges in the residence halls, meeting spaces in the lobbies of buildings, and outdoor sitting areas.

- Informal settings that provide opportunities for interaction, including adding cafés, coffee shops, and bistros in various places on campus. Providing food in multiple locations is clearly a draw both for faculty and for students.

- Integration into the wider community to take advantage of community-based learning resources, and to contribute to (and learn to be a responsible part of) the larger community.

- Access to technology and digital communication, including opportunities to socialize online and in person while online.

- Places and opportunities to participate in co-curricular activities.

In their book *Education by Design,* C. Carney Strange and James H. Banning emphasize the connection between learning and student involvement. "The key to successful learning and, indeed, to developing students' talents, can be simply stated: Students learn from becoming involved." [8] They elucidate how the design, layout, availability, and flexibility of all kinds of campus settings encourage involvement. Spaces for public interaction, for personal quiet, and for hanging out are all important. Indoor and outdoor public spaces that encourage interaction among members of the college community include alcoves and chairs in classroom building hallways, lounges with comfortable furniture in residence halls, and even wide stairways. Personal spaces where students can relax and think range from their own rooms to outdoor foothills, ponds, and hiking trails. Spaces to hang out and relax are also important to student involvement. Cafés, bookstores, and the student union can all play this role. [9] Every part of the campus must be thought of as part of the student learning experience.

Ways in which residences can contribute to student engagement

Many colleges and universities find that for competitive reasons they must provide ever more luxurious rooms and apartments in the residence halls. They also experience an increasing need to get students out of those rooms. Anecdotes are legion. One student-life director at the University of Rhode Island reports that in response to student requests, the university instituted room service in the residence halls. But shortly afterward, they noticed that attendance was down at the dining halls and in other areas where students used to meet. It turned out that room service was not, after all, a good idea.

Loyola Marymount University:
studying outdoors

But many other ideas are good ones to improve collegiality and student engagement in the residence halls. One is the trend toward creating more common spaces—small areas that students can use to study quietly together, or larger areas where they can engage in more organized activities.

Residential learning communities can enhance interaction, particularly at large schools. Some institutions are now adding classrooms, other teaching facilities, and faculty housing directly in the dormitory buildings. The president of Loyola Marymount University in Los Angeles, California lives in an apartment in an upper-division residence hall.

Virginia Woolf, in *A Room of One's Own,* offers a wonderful description of a dinner at the university in "Oxbridge." A lovely dining hall and a rich meal provide a fertile context for rich intellectual discussion.[10] The British university tradition of professors living and dining with the students has also continued in some American institutions such as Yale and Princeton, and is gaining in popularity.

Conversely, the trends to move student housing off campus or to remote locations and to provide parking at the front door of every student residence, and policies that don't encourage faculty to live near campus inhibit learning and engagement on campus.

Optimizing the campus environment for academic performance

Several recent studies have shown a significant correlation between specific environmental features and academic performance (grades and test scores).[11] Many of these features extend beyond the classroom to the entire campus.

Research conducted by the School Design and Planning Laboratory at the University of Georgia has shown that a number of design patterns directly influence student academic achievement in elementary and secondary schools. Holding all other factors constant, students learn more, get better grades, and do better on standardized tests when these design patterns are present in their schools. Many of these factors seem to reflect basic human needs and may therefore hold true for a university population as well. They also apply as well to an entire campus of learning as to a single building.

Numerous studies[12] have shown specific classroom design factors, such as natural daylight and operable windows, to be correlated with learning achievement. Less well known, perhaps, are factors related to the design of the entire campus. Significantly, many of these are also factors that encourage student (and faculty) engagement:

Harvard University
Business School

· The entire campus—not just the classrooms—provides a positive impression of a teacher- and student-oriented learning environment. A friendly and well-defined entrance space connects the school to the outside world and evokes a welcome feeling. Students and teachers feel safe throughout the campus. Walking paths provide an easy and pleasant way of getting from building to building, perhaps also providing shelter from the elements.

· A variety of different learning spaces is needed. The university offers a mix of public and quiet areas. Public areas foster a sense of community—a feeling of unity and belonging with one's fellows at the university. Quiet areas provide a setting "where students may go to pause and refresh themselves." In addition, spaces are designed for versatility. The same setting—whether a classroom, building lobby, or green quad—can host a variety of different activities.

· The buildings and the grounds are in harmony with both their natural context and with the surrounding neighborhood, reflecting the character of the region in which they are located.

· The outdoors is incorporated as part of the learning environment. Integration of the actual learning environment with the outdoors, where possible, is highly desirable. Educationally sound design of a learning environment includes outside places, close to academic buildings, that contain lawns and trees and do not contain cars, parking, or roads. Views of nature improve performance within classrooms. Partly enclosed or defined spaces may be used for reading, lectures, or performances. Outdoor learning environments may also include nature trails or ecological study areas.

These design factors create in aggregate the kind of setting that help achieve the learning results that all institutions hope to achieve.

Meeting new academic requirements

Since the majority of students live off campus at most institutions, special attention should be paid to planning and designing learning environments that support learning and engagement for this population. The Johnson Center at George Mason University broke new ground by combining the social aspects of a campus center with the learning and study environment and resources of a library. Institutions and designers are just beginning to explore possible hybrid building types such as this to support learning and engagement for nontraditional students.

Increasingly, institutional strategic planning goals include increasing interdisciplinary learning and research activity. The old model of individual buildings dedicated to individual departments must be looked at closely. The physical arrangement of facilities on campus can meet the growing need for faculty members as well as students to have exposure to one another across disciplines.

More class work is now done in group projects, with students learning from one another. This peer-to-peer interaction typically does not occur in the classroom or the library. How can the campus best support this learning mode? Informally, the authors have seen such activities in cafés and student lounges. More formally, the program for the new University of Missouri Kansas City Learning Center provides over a hundred group-study spaces to respond to the growing need for peer-to-peer learning areas.

Many colleges and universities are finding ways to integrate real-world learning experiences into campus life. Research laboratories may include partnerships with businesses. Many business schools have a room that simulates a trading room, where students can buy and sell stocks using real money. At Eckerd College, an art major can apply for a small studio of his or her own to complete a major project.

The entire campus can—and must—be designed to support a variety of student learning opportunities.

five

Community on Campus

Creating and fostering community has long been a core value for American colleges and universities. It is also a necessary foundation for a healthy and successful institution. Leaders in higher education consider a strong sense of community essential to maintaining a vital and open dialogue among students, faculty, and staff. Despite the widely acknowledged importance of this fundamental value, a 1990 Carnegie Foundation report identified the "crisis in community" as a significant problem plaguing the nation's colleges and universities. This crisis contributes to rising campus crime rates, sexual harassment, ethnic and racial hostilities, dormitory and other property damage, substance abuse, apathy, and a general decline in civility.[1]

La gente hablando se entiend. (People understand each other by talking.)

- MEXICAN PROVERB

What is community

On campus, the word "community" is frequently used among faculty, students, and administrators, as well as among planners, architects, and designers, but it can mean many things. We speak of the "student community" or the "faculty community," and by this we are usually referring simply to those groups of people in similar roles—regardless of how they feel about one another or how much they may interact with one another. But when we speak of "creating a sense of community" at the university, we are striving for more than an understanding of roles. We are striving for a warm feeling in the heart about one's fellows and a sense of identity with the institution and with one another that persists long after a person's immediate physical relationship with the institution has ended. Caring for one another and interacting in ways that matter are essential parts of community.

St John's College in Annapolis, Maryland and Santa Fe, New Mexico reflects a single academic community in two different environments

The need to create a sense of community also traces back to a fundamental component of higher education—the free exchange of ideas. Faculty members are given tenure in order to promote this unfettered exchange, and a sense of community is cultivated in order to nurture it.

A vital college creates the spaces where people can meet in a friendly way, where free interchange and discussion of ideas are fostered.

"Alumni," says the governing document of St. John's College, its Polity, "shall be life-long members of the College, since St. John's College is a community not limited by geographical location or fixed periods of time." What on earth can this mean, referring to a group of people spread over the entire globe, many of whom have not set foot on the campus in decades? In fact, how can this self-styled "one college on two campuses" manage to maintain a feeling of community that spans the two thousand miles between its Annapolis, Maryland and Santa Fe, New Mexico locations, much less the decades between its oldest alumni and its current first-year students? The unique educational program at St. John's College bonds its students, faculty, and alumni together. A recent survey revealed that the program is what alumni value most—more even than friendships—from their years at St. John's. Seminars, small tutorials, and informal discussion revolving around study of the "great books" are common experiences that the alumni share regardless of when (or if) they graduated, or which campus they attended. Places where conversation can continue before and after class—the main quadrangles, coffee shops, and other spaces on both campuses—provide a setting to extend this vital dialog that is essential to the St. John's experience.

Community for students

For students, meeting and interacting with one's fellows—students and teachers alike—in and out of the classroom is a vital part of the educational experience. In addition, contact with faculty outside of the classroom or office contributes to student satisfaction, learning, and a sense of fully participating in the college experience.

In *Millennials Go to College,* Neil Howe and William Strauss found that students entering college around the year 2000, and their parents, "place enormous emphasis on the quality of campus life."[2] Based on their research, Howe and Strauss predict that today's new collegiate generation will want to engage in campus activities that reinforce a collective sense of destiny. Therefore, an institution would do well to emphasize that its campus offers a place where students can meet and work, and develop lifelong friendships with other capable students.[3]

Most young people today have worked in cooperative activities in high school. When they enter college, they continue to look for participation in group activities. As teenagers have become more relationship-dependent, they are at more risk of dissatisfaction and depression if they can't find a social niche or identity on campus.

Student retention is also an issue. Twenty-nine percent of beginning students transfer to a different institution from the one where they first enrolled. Whether they transfer or not, more than one-third of beginning students drop out of college without completing a degree within five years.[4] Student involvement in campus life (a sense of community and engagement) is one of the top five conditions known to promote student retention. Students are more likely to stay at the institution and graduate if their institution involves them as valued members of the campus community. An article in *Strategic Enrollment Management Monthly* notes, "The frequency and quality of contact with faculty, staff, and other students is an important independent predictor of student persistence. This is true for large and small, rural and urban, and private and 2- and 4-year colleges and universities. It is true for women as well as men, students of color and Anglo students, and part-time and full-time students."[5] Student engagement is particularly important for first-year students because their connection to the institution and friendships with other students are tenuous.

To serve this growing requirement for community, colleges need to provide a vibrant and exciting campus life and increase the opportunities for students to meet one another.

Faculty community

For faculty, the uniqueness of university life lies, in part, in the richness of a multitude of perspectives within a compact face-to-face community of learners and scholars. Personal and social relationships can enhance interaction across professional and disciplinary boundaries. Members of the faculty need the opportunity and the places to interact informally outside of the classroom both with students and with one another.

Why we are losing a sense of community

Across the country on campuses of all kinds, universities and colleges have similar concerns about the loss of community on campus and feel strongly that creating and sustaining a strong sense of community is essential to their success and the success of their students. Starting in the 1970s, the feeling of community on college campuses has declined, as the growth of individualism has increased.[6] Current research[7] documents this continuing trend.

A sense of community is harder and harder to achieve. Why? Salient among the reasons are:

· The loner lifestyle
· Busy lives
· Suburbanization of the physical campus layout
· Residential trends away from dormitory-style living
· Faculty and student commuting
· Erosion of community dining
· Increasing diversity of constituencies on campus

Then

Now

JONATHAN AUSTIN

The loner lifestyle

With the growing rate and acceptability of single-parenthood and decreasing experience of extended families in America, more students on campus are living a lifestyle as loners. Requests for single rooms have skyrocketed.

People in general—especially, perhaps, students—are spending more time on the computer than ever before. They frequently use the computer for activities (such as buying books) that once required errands and in-person interactions.

Group activities that once connected students on campus don't work as well any more; for example, television watching, once a shared activity in common rooms, has now moved to individual residence-hall rooms, where many students have their own TV sets. A dean of students at one residential university, referring to a typical student's room, said, "Everything is right here. I can't imagine a reason for students to leave their rooms." At many schools, we hear from the deans of student life how hard it is to get students to attend organized group events.

Suburban sprawl on campus

Busy lives

People experience more demands on their time than ever. Students are not exempt from this trend. More and more students these days work as well as attend school. Work demands often extend beyond the "forty-hour week." In addition, many students are also married. Their spouses also work and may attend school. They may have young children. With all the demands on their time, something has to give—and usually it's the social life that is sacrificed.

Suburbanization of the physical campus layout

Regrettably, in many places the physical campus itself discourages community. Older colleges and universities with residential roots often have an historical "core" area of the campus with beautiful, human-scale spaces where students enjoy spending time. But with the trend toward larger buildings and isolated building complexes, as well as the demands of the automobile, many places on many campuses have become vast, unfriendly wastelands comprising acres of parking lots surrounding fortress-like, large buildings. These are not places in which to linger.

Residential trends

Current trends in student housing do not favor the development of a sense of community among students. Most students express a preference for single bedrooms, either as a single room in a traditional residence hall or in a suite or apartment with single bedrooms clustered around common areas shared by a few students. Some residences, built in the 1970s, lack even these few common areas. Five or six bedrooms on a narrow hallway share only a single bathroom. The trend toward single rooms shouldn't be surprising. "One college survey found that three-quarters of incoming freshmen have never shared a room with anyone (even a sibling)."[8]

Only 30 percent of all college students live on campus. This proportion has dropped by one-third since the late 1960s, while the proportion living off campus has tripled.[9] More students than ever live off campus. While off-campus living offers more privacy, it unfortunately affords less opportunity for participation in campus activities. Many student-oriented off-campus apartment complexes are not within walking distance of campus; once they have returned there from their classes, only the most highly motivated students will go back to campus to participate in student-life activities.

Furthermore (and worst, from the perspective of community on campus), an increasing number of students are engaged in distance learning that requires little presence on campus at all.

Faculty and student commuting

Contact with faculty outside of the classroom or office is an important component of overall student satisfaction on campus. Yet at many institutions, significant barriers stand in the way of this contact. Both in commuter colleges and in residential colleges where the majority of the faculty do not live on campus or nearby, the need to commute to and from classes sets a limit to the amount of time on campus, and therefore the availability, of both students and faculty. So how do we get faculty and students together?

Before Annapolis, Maryland became a pricey Washington D.C. suburb, most professors at St. John's College, a small, independent liberal-arts school, lived within walking distance of the college. The non-classroom interaction between students and faculty so vital to the college's program of education by discussion seemed to happen naturally. Before and after classes, students and professors would often meet—by chance or on purpose—in the coffee shop. However, these days, most young professors cannot afford to live close to the college. As commuters, they don't spend as much time on campus as they used to. St. John's has therefore adopted an innovative policy of reimbursing students who take faculty to lunch.

George Mason University addresses this issue by giving faculty a stipend to take students to lunch.

Erosion of community dining

Residential-based colleges, where students and perhaps also faculty living in a residence hall eat together in a common dining area in the same building, was, and in some places still is, a foundation of the social and community experience of an undergraduate education.[10] In the last several decades, however, with financial pressure to make food service more efficient, dining has typically been consolidated into one or a few (perhaps inconveniently located) large dining halls serving the whole campus.

Even this venue for social interaction and community building is eroding, because today's students have largely abandoned the practice of formal sit-down meals, opting instead for grabbing a quick bite to eat on the run. Perhaps the root of this behavioral change is in the decline of the tradition of the family sit-down dinner, made difficult by two-earner households and stressed schedules of active families. Whatever its cause, this recent trend toward fast-food take-out and vending machines in college settings is destructive to good conversation.

Food courts substitute for traditional sit-down dining

Increasingly diverse constituencies on campus

Fifty years ago, the college population was mainly white, almost entirely upper and upper-middle class, and disproportionately male. Homogeneity of the students made community on campus appear to be a natural phenomenon, so easily obtained that one hardly had to think of it as a goal. Nobody would want to return to those days. Diversity among the student body is a great resource and strength to an institution, as well as to the society the institution serves.

The increasing diversity of the student body, however, does make the need for community on campus more urgent. Students of each minority or cultural constituency can provide a resource and support network for one another, building a close community within that constituency. But the institution also needs to foster community across different groups, helping students to understand and interrelate with others outside their normal patterns.

Physical facilities must make people from a range of backgrounds and cultures feel "at home," providing a safe and comfortable place for all.

University of Colorado at Boulder

Nurturing community through the physical environment

Impact of physical environment on behavior

The physical environment has a major impact on human feelings, behavior, interaction, engagement, and community. This rather obvious fact has been confirmed in many research studies, including, for example, studies showing that environmental cues influence the energy level and positive attitude of people in a space as well as how much time they're willing to spend there.[11] Another study has shown that the behaviors of children could be predicted more accurately from knowing the physical setting the children were in than the actual individual characteristics of the children.[12] While these studies may not specifically refer to campus settings in particular, "common sense and experience suggest that when the physical environment of a campus, building, or classroom, supports the desired behavior, better outcomes result. From the behavioral setting point of view, campus designs and spaces do not merely create a functional space, mood, or atmosphere; they facilitate certain behaviors."[13]

Physical design that fosters community

Conversation is the backbone of community and personal growth; and the campus environment should be designed to nurture it. In their study of institutions that provide undergraduate students with an exceptional variety of opportunities to complement their in-class learning with enriching out-of-class activities and experiences, George Kuh and his

54 | *Community on Campus*

colleagues noted that "…interaction among community members is fostered by the availability of indoor and outdoor spaces where people can come together without much effort. Institutions should consider whether their campuses have adequate places that encourage spontaneous, informal interaction among students."[14]

Design that fosters community includes the organization of the overall campus framework as well as the creation of vital public spaces, both indoors and out.

Campus framework and organization

A number of the fundamental elements of campus structure, including the organization of uses, the arrangement of pedestrian pathways connecting those uses, the density and mixture of buildings, and the arrangement of open spaces, have a significant impact on vitality, interaction, and community on campus. We have learned a lot about how to be successful at this by applying to campuses many of the principles that we've learned about creating vital, lively neighborhoods and street life in cities.

What makes a neighborhood with a close community work? Everyone's out on the street. People don't need an appointment to see their neighbors; whether they are working in the community garden, walking the dog, or just sitting on their front stoop, people see other people around all the time. Just as its streets and public spaces are the venue of a neighborhood's community life, a college can build a strong sense of community on a rich network of public spaces.

The urban sociologist William Whyte spent over sixteen years studying how to create vibrant city spaces. One of his first insights was the importance of density of people and activities. "One of the first findings was that the 'overcrowded city' is a myth. Most of the spaces observed were not overused: They were underused. Conversely, the spaces that people most enjoyed and found most restful were the most intensely used. The street is a surprisingly sociable place, and high density is a condition of its vitality. A successful street has a critical mass of activity and of people."[15] This observation applies equally well to campuses.

Public spaces

Most institutions agree that college life outside the classroom is a vital part of the college experience and a significant factor in creating a sense of community. One sociologist of community life suggests a big step toward addressing the community crisis on campus can be taken "if higher education's leaders and faculty would pay more attention to promoting better talk among students, and if architects and planners would provide better places for students to 'hang out.'"[16]

Community cannot exist in the absence of public space that supports communication. Institutions need to understand the characteristics of the physical environment that foster community, and to recognize the role that many parts of the physical environment play in enhancing the richness of community on campus. The places that can play vital roles vary greatly; they include places like the mail room, library steps, residence hall common rooms, student lounges and game rooms, dining halls, snack bars and coffee shops, bookstores, local hang outs, outdoor cafés, conversation nooks, gardens, student centers, generous lobbies, benches in hallways, and outdoor walkways. A few of these are discussed here by way of example.

The mailroom. The mailroom today is one of the few places on some campuses where impromptu meetings occur. If institutions have a choice, they should try to have a single mailroom, not two or three, so that students can see each other and be seen.

Faculty club or coffee lounge. Faculty members usually feel a strong need for a place to meet. However, at one institution after another, we hear faculty members say they have nowhere to go to share their ideas informally with one another. Where an institution has no faculty club or faculty meeting area, faculty members typically see creating one as an important way to enhance collegiality.

Spaces for hanging out. Young people are feeling pressured to perform in every way—academically, in sports, and even in leisure activities. To ameliorate this pressure on campus, some researchers suggest, "Look for ways to create stress-free zones on campus—quiet, out-of-way places where students can gather to play high-tech games, or low-tech ping pong or pinball, or just sit on cushy couches and watch videos in small groups—and make such zones available as close to 24/7 as possible."[17] Campus hangouts should be conveniently located—easy to get to without needing an automobile. To make them more welcoming, they should offer food and beverages on site.

Institutions with a large population of distance learners might consider creating online virtual "hangout" spaces for distant as well as residential students who share classes or interests. In some cases, students who lacked such online spaces have created them for themselves.

Computer areas. Students are spending more time on the computer than ever before. To the extent that students are holed up alone engaged in individual activities on their computers instead of interacting with one another, institutions are rightly concerned about this trend. However, institutions should recognize and encourage the use of computers for social interaction—whether instant-messaging a classmate in a distant residence hall about meeting for lunch the next day, keeping in touch with friends in distant states, or emailing parents.

Often the social aspect of computer use is physical as well. On many campuses, it's not unusual to see students chatting amiably in line while waiting to check their email on a public computer, or to see groups of students working together or side-by-side on a project with an on-line component. The organization of campus facilities should encourage community around this growing campus activity. Public computers should be located in areas where people are likely to go, rather than in remote basements, and group projects should be encouraged.

Computer café at Pepperdine University

Places to eat. Food attracts people and is a marvelous stimulant for conversation. Universities should look at food neither as a profit center nor as a necessary service they must provide. It is one of the biggest single tools for creating community. Meals are a time when people can meet by prearrangement or chance and sit and have a conversation. More and more campuses now offer a library café to draw people in. When people are there, they have conversations over a meal or coffee.

The trend toward institutionalizing food service through large, corporate outside vendors makes it difficult to respond to opportunities for using food to create community. Food service vendors tend to want to consolidate food venues into fewer larger dining rooms oriented toward scheduled meals rather than casual food service. Georgetown University, for example, wanted to have a light coffee service in the lobby of the engineering building, creating an opportunity for students and faculty to linger and chat. But the food vendor refused because of concerns about profitability. Hollins College considered moving the bistro out of the basement of the student union building and into a more central location on the main quadrangle, but, not wanting to open an additional venue, the food service provider wanted the college to guarantee them an income in order to do it. We see this time and again. Worse, the contract with the large food service provider frequently prevents the institution from finding a smaller, local vendor who might be able to make a go of it.

On-campus housing. If implemented properly, on-campus housing can also be an important community builder. Institutions that are primarily residential adhere, either implicitly or explicitly, to this principle. Many such institutions require that all students through a certain year (freshmen or sophomores at many institutions, juniors and even seniors at many private, residential colleges) live on campus.

Even if they don't see themselves as residential colleges, most of the schools Sasaki Associates works with want to add more on-campus housing. Despite its roots as a commuter college, George Mason University,

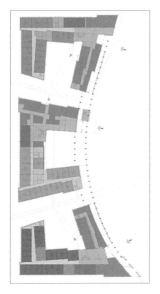
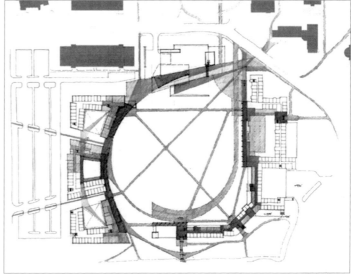

for example, established in 2001 a goal to add five thousand beds—going up from 10 percent to 20 percent of its total enrollment. Experiencing a lack of a sense of community, the administration hopes that the additional on-campus housing will make the campus a more vital place during the evenings and weekends. The University of Central Florida, also primarily a commuter institution, wants to put housing for all freshmen on campus. They see it as a bonding experience, an important aspect of university and college life that helps to build a sense of responsibility and teach how to interact with other people.

To encourage interaction among residential students, institutions should design residence halls in ways that maximize interaction, drawing out single-room occupants through attractive, shared common spaces and activities in or near the residence halls, such as dining or exercise.

Characteristics of spaces that facilitate interaction

Human-scale design. Just as most institutions would agree that smaller classes are more conducive to learning than lecture classes with hundreds of students, so also they should not be surprised that human-scale environments encourage interactions that can contribute to social cohesion and a greater sense of community. For example, research studies have shown that "a greater sense of community and increased incidents of helping behavior are exhibited by residents of low-rise units when compared with counterparts in high-rise units. In addition, cohesion and social interaction characteristic of small living units seem to mediate tensions and stress common to academic communities."[18] "Settings characterized as human-scale in design tend to encourage greater participation and involvement...."[19]

New freshman village at the University of Iowa has deep, traditional residential college roots

Flexibility. Flexible spaces increase the opportunity for engagement because they can be used for multiple activities and arranged for individual or small or large group interaction. When people have some control over their space, they're more likely to want to be there and to make the space suit their needs. Flexibility encourages use, and does so in a way that allows interaction. The work of William Whyte shows this in the use of outdoor space. Through the use of time-lapse photography, Whyte discovered that people used outdoor space and interacted with one another much more if the space had movable chairs than if it had fixed benches.

Like a town or small city, the campus is a community that is defined, in part, by geography. Within this geographical area, students (and sometimes faculty and staff) sleep, eat, work, study, play, and socialize. Unlike many new parts of our cities—suburban communities that are often gated or without sidewalks—the American campus has the potential to nurture the elements of active community life—places for conversation, discourse, and social engagement.

six

Neighborhood and Urban Community

Unlike the cloistered European campuses from which they sprang, American universities look outward as well as inward. They always have. American campuses were built to reflect this value. Harvard University, founded in 1636, began as a single building on nine acres of land and expanded to a number of separate buildings facing the roadways and opening outward to the community of Cambridge, Massachusetts in which it was rooted. In laying out the campus this way, Harvard's founders were making a statement concerning their connectedness to the community. "Harvard knows nothing either of jealousy or the dignity of high walls and guarded gateways," wrote Henry James as late as 1886.[2] Not until the end of the nineteenth century was Harvard Yard turned inward with construction of buildings along its perimeter and a fence to enclose it.

Commitment to education, to development of students as whole people, to community on campus is strong in American colleges and universities, but outward moral obligations to the community and to society are just as profound. American universities overwhelmingly continue to emphasize in their statements of mission and values their ongoing commitment to the outside world. Educating students to be responsible participants in society is inextricably linked to an institution's own activities in that society. These activities are often most strongly expressed in the institution's relationship with its neighboring community.

The only way to achieve true success is to express yourself completely in service to society.[1]

- ARISTOTLE

The town-gown relationship

Cities and towns may experience a kind of "love/hate" relationship with their institutions. They are aware, at least in part, of the benefits the institution brings them, but they are also frustrated by the day-to-day problems that they sometimes blame, at least in part, on those same institutions. Sometimes the relationship is uncomfortably adversarial. Immediate, day-to-day goals may be opposed. But with a longer-term perspective, institutions find that promoting the welfare of the neighborhood and town is not only consistent with their missions—it is also in their own best interest, and it is the right thing to do.

As a first step, institutions and their neighbors need to understand each other's point of view. Every situation is different, but the outcomes that most institutions and communities desire are similar—though they sometimes seem distressingly hard to achieve.

Services, parking, and transit

Faculty, staff, and commuting students require good vehicular access through the neighboring streets on their way to and from the school. They don't want to be held up by traffic, finding and using alternative routes, sometimes through formerly quiet residential streets, if they don't have to. When parking is difficult or inconvenient on campus, they may look for parking in the neighborhood as well.

Some institutions take for granted and expect that the network of neighborhood streets and parking facilities will serve them, unaware that automobile traffic and parking generated by the university can be a significant issue for their neighbors. Institutions, especially large ones, can be a major source of traffic in surrounding areas. University-related traffic and parking congest the city streets. Even when the many benefits an institution provides to its neighbors are well appreciated, the concomitant traffic is resented. When institutional parking lots encroach where houses once stood, resentment can deepen.

In these situations, institutions must take great care that they do not worsen the neighborhood as they work to solve their own traffic and parking problems.

Money

Tax-exempt status of institutions, provision of services

Many towns resent the tax-exempt status of their neighboring institutions. This feeling is exacerbated when the town considers that it must provide services, such as increased policing of student activities (on or off campus), toward which the institution does not contribute. The property taxes that are not collected each year are often the most visible issue that neighboring cities and towns experience.

The property tax issue flared up for Harvard University in 2001 when it purchased a thirty-acre, 765,000-square-foot office complex in Watertown, Massachusetts from a private developer. With over a decade of planning and more than $100 million in federal toxic-waste cleanup and infrastructure improvements, the city of Watertown counted on the money that this private development would bring onto the tax rolls to account for about a third of its tax revenue. Harvard initially offered about $3 million per year, generous by standards of most agreements for payments in lieu of taxes, but far less than the amount that the town was expecting. The resulting controversy, as reported in the *Boston Business Journal,* "caused something of a backlash, focusing resentment against wealthy institutions like Harvard and the Massachusetts Institute of Technology."[3] Harvard owns 18.6 million square feet of property in the region, 11.8 million of it on 215 acres in Cambridge, where it pays about $6 million per year in lieu of taxes—an amount that Cambridge officials have called "laughable."[4]

Institutions defend strongly their tax-exempt status and therefore must strive to reach out in other ways to their neighbors. The sizes of Harvard's and MIT's endowments may worsen their neighbors' resentment, compared to the experience of most other institutions. However, Harvard, MIT, and six other Boston-area institutions are counteracting the issue in part in the effective way that many other institutions have also done—by collecting and publishing information on their overall economic impact on the area. A draft report described in the *Boston Globe* on March 8, 2003, shows that eight local universities contribute about $7.4 billion annually to the local economy, with Harvard itself contributing over $2 billion.[5]

Harvard University and MIT
have significant presence in
the Boston area

Fiscal benefits

The economies of towns, cities, and in some cases, entire regions are supported by the presence of colleges and universities. For every full-time student, a complement of professors, administrative staff, and people who run and maintain the facilities is required. Most of the spending of the institution stays within the local economy. Salaries are distributed; rents are paid to local landowners; goods are purchased in local retail districts. Students themselves spend their money locally—on housing (sometimes), food, movies and entertainment, and consumer goods. In addition, many visitors to institutions spend money locally. Many colleges and universities engage in a certain amount of construction and other capital projects each year, hiring contractors, many of whom are local.

Even where colleges and universities do not formally pursue such a policy, they typically do contribute substantially to the local economy:

· The University System of Georgia calculates that in 2001 – 02 it directly and indirectly infused $8 billion into local economies—about $5 billion in direct spending by the institutions and their students, and the remaining $3 billion in the re-spending of these dollars within the communities.[6]

· According to an independent study, "for every dollar Brown [University] collects from Rhode Island sources, it spends more than 9 dollars in the Ocean State."[7] Brown is also one of the state's leading employers, with over 3,000 regular employees, over 80 percent of whom live in the state.

· A similar report for Columbia University shows that "the combined value of economic activity directly and indirectly generated in New York City by the University, by various affiliated institutions, and by students and visitors to Columbia was nearly $2 billion in 1994 – 95."[8]

· Silicon Valley in California is inextricably linked with Stanford University. According to Richard M. Rosan, president of the Urban Land Institute, "In 1996, half of $100 billion in GDP of Silicon Valley economy came from Stanford-related firms."[9]

Cities that have not experienced knowledge-industry growth are beginning to understand that their colleges and universities represent an opportunity. "When it comes to attracting the best and the brightest," states a *USA Today* Life section cover story, "colleges and universities aren't the only stakeholders. Civic, business and government leaders here also want prospective students to fall in love with their college experience—so much so that they'll stay in the area after they graduate…It's all part of a push, primarily in large metro areas, to become more competitive in a rapidly changing economy fueled increasingly by the ideas, knowledge and talent produced inside the ivory tower."[10]

Safety and security

One major concern that the authors frequently hear on campuses of colleges and universities, especially those in larger cities, is a feeling that the neighborhood is not safe. On many campuses, students worry about when and how far they can go out into the city. In some cases, as with Lehigh University and South Bethlehem, Pennsylvania, this is more of a perception than a fact. In other cases, the neighborhood may be so unsafe that violent crime, including toward students and faculty, occurs.

Where security issues exist, the university faces a dilemma of how best to deal with them. If the crime is motivated by hostility toward the institution, what can they do to gain the understanding and cooperation of community residents, thereby reducing the risk of hostile incidents? If crime threatens the neighborhood as well as the institution, will it be possible to work in a broader community context to deal with it?

Where students live in the neighborhood in large numbers, institutions must also sometimes address student misdeeds in the community, including rowdiness and vandalism.

Institutional encroachment

Land owned by institutions is constantly increasing, taking money off the tax rolls. Many academic institutions, especially in confined cities and towns, are on a continual quest for space and land, a threatening reality to many neighboring communities. If not done carefully, institutional expansion can damage the fabric of the neighborhood. The likelihood that an expanding institution may buy a property at a good price encourages both real estate speculation and neglect of properties that may be purchased by the institution. Also, if the institution uses the land it buys in ways that are not constructive in the neighborhood, e.g., for parking lots, property values may go down. The pattern of a deteriorating neighborhood, institutional encroachment, and lower property values can turn into a downward spiral that is unwittingly abetted by institutional actions.

Even without actual purchase of land, institutions may encroach on their neighborhoods. Lehigh University, for example, discovered in planning workshops with the community that too much rental student housing relative to owner-occupied housing caused at least the perception that a block or neighborhood is deteriorating.

Reasonably priced, attractive housing close to the institution

Nonresident students who don't commute from home hope to find reasonably priced housing close to the institution. So do many members of faculty and staff, provided that the housing stock is good, the streets are clean and safe, and the local K – 12 schools are good ones. When they have a choice, no one prefers a long commute to a short one (much less a short walk!). Unfortunately, in some places this can be a large proviso. West Philadelphia in the early 1990s is an example. Like many urban neighborhoods, it had fallen on hard times. Much of the housing stock in this once-stately neighborhood had become rundown, and some of it abandoned. The local elementary schools were poor. A significant turnaround on many fronts would be needed to make this neighborhood—and others like it—an attractive place for faculty, staff, and students to live. The University of Pennsylvania was willing to make just such a commitment, and the results have been extremely positive.

Government and neighborhood support

Cultivating good communication and a mutually beneficial relationship with the neighboring communities and local government is one way to ensure that the neighborhood and local government understand and support the university's needs and new projects. They do so both because they experience the university as an ally rather than an adversary, and because, with open channels of communication, the university can develop better solutions to its problems—ones that are acceptable, even beneficial, to the community.

The University of Washington in Seattle proactively works with its neighborhood organizations and with the city of Seattle. An organization called the City/University Community Advisory Committee (CUCAC) provides input to the university's master plans, in accordance with a formal agreement drawn up with the city in 1977 and revised in 1983. In addition, the agreement facilitates participation by the university in neighborhood planning in its area.

Attracting and retaining the best students, faculty, and staff

The neighboring community establishes the backdrop against which prospective students and their parents, as well as current students, faculty, and staff, experience and judge an institution. A good quality of life in the neighborhood, town, and region is an important asset for the institution. Students, professors, and staff desire to be involved in institutions and communities that provide and promote an urban environment. Cities, towns, and districts adjacent to an institution, if they are vibrant and lively, can offer an enormous lure against which other, less fortunate institutions compete only with difficulty.

Conversely, some colleges and universities find themselves in a neighborhood so unappealing that they experience an impact on their ability to recruit new students and faculty. "Almost every major city has a major university that started out in a neighborhood and ended up not being in the kind of neighborhood they thought they wanted to live in,"[11] stated Ron Mason, former director of the Center for the Urban Community in New Orleans and now president of Jackson State University. Everyone knows of cases where a neighborhood appears run-down enough that some prospective students and their parents won't even get out of their cars as they drive by.

Quality of life

One of the strongest demographic trends today is the growth of college towns and districts across the country. One aspect of this growth is that many members of the empty-nester (over 55) age group are returning to towns and cities with collegiate environments. This regeneration comes at a time when most small towns and cities are facing loss of population, especially the young, and with it, local economy and most destructively, local vitality.

Perhaps the largest social benefit that a college or university can offer its community is its youthful energy and idealism. Most institutions provide cultural resources and activities that their communities can take advantage of. These may be the cultural mainstay of smaller communities. Institutions also often offer their communities an enhanced identity, including being rated as "best places to live."

Ranked first among *Money* magazine's "Best Places to Retire" in 2002, Providence, Rhode Island is home to a number of colleges and universities. In its description of Providence's attractions for retirees, *Money* magazine noted, "Both Brown University and RISD offer continuing education classes. And Johnson & Wales University not only offers vocational education classes to all ages but has also left its mark on the food scene...Plus, Brown's medical school is affiliated with seven hospitals, providing them with a steady stream of Ivy League-caliber doctors."[12]

While Providence may have benefited indirectly from its collegiate environment, some institutions are becoming more proactive in trying to attract retirees. In 2000, the *Orlando Sentinel* reported that the University of Florida at Gainesville "has joined forces with developers on a retirement community that revolves around university life."[13] The development, which is aimed at retired alumni and faculty, offers university classes, concerts, games, and other activities as well as more traditional retirement amenities. Some 100 retirement communities are already located near colleges and universities, and as more affluent, well-educated people reach retirement age, the number is expected to grow.

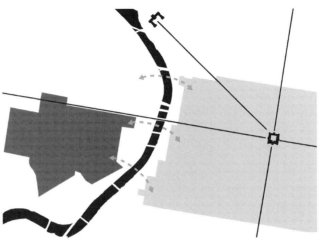

The University of Pennsylvania has made a significant commitment to the city of Philadelphia

Furthering the institutional mission

"If you really are going to support the mission of the university, you have to have that type of vibrant city life that goes along with an institution such as Penn in a city such as Philadelphia,"[14] observed Jack Shannon, when he was Managing Directory of Economic Development at the University of Pennsylvania. Most institutions have some kind of neighborhood outreach or community service in their mission statements. For some, service is mentioned equally with teaching and research. Yet, how to actively engage the students, much less the institution as a whole, in service to its community is less than clear. Ira Harkavy, director of the Center for Community Partnerships at the University of Pennsylvania, notes, "Universities teach far, far more by what they do than by what they say." University action in support of its neighborhood does not go unremarked by students. This is especially true when an institution can integrate its efforts in the community with academic courses. Judith Rodin, president of the University of Pennsylvania, evaluated Penn's extensive interaction with its community as follows:

> Penn's investments over the past several years have produced a safer, more vibrant neighborhood and a flourishing academic environment on campus. Our rankings have soared. Research dollars are flowing in at record levels. Our students are thriving in their surroundings. Just as important, our engagement with the community has renewed Penn's spirit of activism and purpose among faculty, students, and staff, while strengthening town-gown bonds.[15]

By not losing sight of their most important goals—creating a vibrant neighborhood, taking action in accordance with their basic mission, and doing the right thing for their neighbors—Penn can serve as a model for many institutions in creating a neighborhood relationship that works.

Part III.
Principles

seven

Meaningful Places

The significance of place

Working hard to raise funds for more research and classroom space, some institutional leaders don't want to spend money on anything they see as a low priority. While institutional leaders and governing boards generally want their campuses to be beautiful, some think that spending money on creating a more beautiful and memorable campus is not an important priority, and they think that it would cost them more money. Both these assumptions are frequently in error.

The physical campus sends a message about the institution. The meaning of the physical campus and the message it sends to students, faculty, staff, and visitors is fundamental to achieving every part of the institutional mission. Further, money already committed to campus maintenance and improvement may well be adequate to the task of furthering this message—but it must be spent in the right way.

Even with the best intentions, governing boards still sometimes make decisions (or allow decisions to be made) about the message they want the campus to send, about the meaning of the institution's places, while unintentionally creating the opposite effect. These fundamental decisions are too important to be left to routine operations. Institutional leaders must take charge of the message they deliver through their campus.

Sometimes an institution needs an internal champion—or a good planning consultant—to help articulate the value of the special places on campus. For example, a board member of a community college told one of the authors that parking at the front door of the classroom building was "exactly who we are—a box and a parking lot." Students coming in at the end of a busy day wanted to park right by the door of the building, get in, go to class, and then go home. This might have been the end of the story, but the college had a planning consultant who acted as its champion.

Places, like people, touch our lives more than we know…Whether grand or humble, the best architecture defines a place that holds deep emotion for those whose lives the place has touched.[1]

- J. SCOTT ODOM

He listened to the faculty and president complain that they needed more of a place. "We don't feel like a campus." Their image of the campus affected their sense of self-worth. They needed a place where they could interact with one another and with the students, and the parking lot wasn't it. The campus needed a heart. When the consultant articulated the need to replace close-in parking with a green quadrangle, students, faculty, and board members alike were willing to trade a five-minute-farther walk to get it. The value was clear.

The significance of the places on campus is different from one institution to another, even from one place to another. But the meaning of the campus and all of its component places should always express the mission, values, and vision of the institution itself.

Placemaking—why do it

A memorable campus with unique, inviting spaces strengthens the institution by deepening the ways in which people experience it. The meaningful places on campus enhance a student's college experience from everyday experiences to once-in-a-lifetime events.

Quality and strength of everyday experiences

Institutions of higher education care about the quality of the experience of being on campus. Institutional leaders talk frequently and passionately about creating and strengthening learning and community on campus—endeavors, as we have seen, that are intimately tied to the quality of the places the campus provides. Students may not worry as much about these issues, but they do care about the quality of their lives. For them, as for everyone, this quality is bound to the places where they live, work (study), play, and travel through while moving from one activity to another.

Think for a moment about a scene that typifies your everyday undergraduate experience. This could be an experience of *coming or going* somewhere. One person's memorable experience, for example, was of walking through a wooded park on the way to class. Another person recalls walking across the campus green when all the trees were flowering, with the petals covering the ground and falling through the air. Yet another person walked a block down a college town's commercial street that was just opening up for the morning. These moments of transition and arrival are special. We remember them forever.

Alternatively, your typical undergraduate experience may involve *being somewhere*—in a seminar held around a polished wood table in a classroom in a building from the early 1800s; studying on the lawn in the springtime or in the library as a commuter student; meeting friends as you cross the quad or at your favorite hangout; or endless hours of football practice as the weather turns colder.

Whatever memories you have of those special years, you will notice that they are always set in a place. And most likely, it is a place that you cherish because of the experiences you had there.

Traditions and special experiences

Traditions also provide important memories of the college experience. Traditions build loyalty, connect to the history of the institution, and help students bond with their class and college. Most college traditions are tied to a place: freshmen and graduating seniors pass through the Van Wickle Gates at Brown University; seniors jump into the fountain upon graduation at Ithaca College; birthday celebrants are thrown into the fountain on the main quadrangle at Stetson University; freshmen dormitory residents steal the thirteenth plank from the Rustic Bridge at Allegheny College.

The memories of everyday experiences, traditions, and special events in their lives—usually tied to special places on campus—that most students retain long after they have graduated affect their relationship to the school as alumni. We wonder, for example, whether meeting his future wife by the fountain in the quadrangle at Southwestern University played a small role in an alumnus's eventually becoming the school's chairman of the board. At the very least, that fountain provides a backdrop to a story he enjoys retelling.

The fountain at Ithaca College
supports tradition and placemaking

Memorable and sacred places

Everyday memories as well as special experiences are often tied to special open spaces on campus, such as the Oval at Ohio State University. They can also be tied to iconic and symbolic buildings that make the campus unique. Many land-grant institutions, for example, have a building called "Old Main," generally one of the first buildings on campus. Old Main was typically built in the late 1800s, often on high ground with a tower. Centrally located, Old Main houses the president's office and other administrative functions of the institution. For these campuses, Old Main is the icon building.

Memorable places on campus can help create a sense of belonging, and sharing these places helps to create a feeling of community. Memorable places may be indoors or outdoors. The student center might be such a place, or it could be a central quadrangle on campus. A sensitively designed building lobby, with little nooks where people can hang out, might be such a place, or it might be the student hangout in town. Typically, students remember the open spaces of the campus more vividly than they remember the buildings.

Frequently, memorable places are at a crossroads, such as a mailroom, stairway, or plaza, where many paths intersect. A crossroads is not a comfortable place to hang out and stay for an interchange. When people meet a friend there, they probably don't find a place to sit down, or to hang out and review notes if they're fifteen minutes early for class. Crossroads are vibrant, active places that bring people together, but they are not places to linger.

Memorable events happen in memorable places.

Competitive advantage—creating a good first impression

Whether created by walking through the college town, by sitting on the campus library steps overlooking the quad for the first time, or by touring a campus on the web, the power of the first impression cannot be overstated. Institutions are well aware of this power.

Admissions directors have stated that prospective students form an opinion of a campus in the first ten minutes of their visit, and in the next thirty minutes they make a decision whether to rule the college out or to continue the application process.

Old Main at Auburn University

More than luxurious residences and signature facilities, the vitality and the beauty of the campus and the feeling of collegiality in personal interactions are among the most important decision criteria for prospective students. Clear signage and wayfinding, a well-maintained campus, and attractive landscaping may be much more effective per dollar spent than expensive new non-academic facilities, such as student centers and fieldhouses, in attracting new students.

Symbols of institutional identity

Some institutions have places on campus that immediately identify them. These places can be open spaces, such as Harvard Yard or the Oval at Ohio State University. They could be buildings, such as Old Main or the Moorish main building at the University of Tampa. Often, the identifying item is another type of campus element, such as the fountain at Ithaca College and the tower at the University of Texas. It can also be a gate or even a system of signage.

These places and campus elements can be used in branding by tying the idea and reputation of the institution to the image of the place, thereby making the idea of the institution more concrete and meaningful.

LINDA A. CICERO, STANFORD NEWS SERVICE

Palm Drive at Stanford University

Making meaningful places

Different campuses present themselves differently, and different people perceive even the same campus in different ways. For some, the focus is on the setting, for example, the view of Cayuga Lake at Ithaca College; at other campuses, such as Princeton University, the architecture is the main focus. Some campuses organize themselves around a defining big idea, such as the Oval at Ohio State University; others, around the landscape, as at Vassar College.

Whatever the organizing principle, creating good first impressions and ongoing feelings of warmth and belonging on the campus and its institution involves every aspect of the campus from the first glimpse to the smallest spaces.

The first action institutions must take is to make sure that they identify the sacred places (places that have special meaning) that already exist on campus, and preserve them. These unique spaces are critical to institutional identity. They can be outdoor landscape elements, such as Stanford's great entryway at Palm Drive, or they can be architectural features, such as MIT's two great domed spaces: Building 7 (facing Massachusetts Avenue) and Building 10 (facing the river).

Preserving sacred places does not mean that nothing can change. As the campus grows and changes, these sacred places can be enhanced, emphasizing their uniqueness.

In addition to preserving and enhancing the old, institutions should look for opportunities to build additional, new special places by building remarkable buildings and creating enjoyable open spaces. A campus or district can foster more than one space or building that carries special significance. As the campus grows and the institution changes, its leaders need constantly to be looking for new opportunities—new spaces, buildings, or features—to create meaningful places and enhance institutional identity.

For a new campus or district, an institution might even think about creating a new "Old Main." In this case, the institution might want to consider designing a signature building, as it would become a special place on campus that carries symbolic meaning.

The campus entrance is a particularly significant space. Creating distinctiveness and impact in the architectural and landscape composition of the campus entrance may be the single most effective way to add a sense of identity to the institution as a whole. Iona College, for example, commissioned a new entry gate that expressed the institution's roots and religious heritage, as well as its vision for the future.

Institutions should also think about creating significance and symbols of institutional identity at a smaller scale than that of buildings and open spaces. Elements of identity can include the institution's system of signage, certain walls, banners, and signature features such as a clock tower or a kiosk.

Top: Main gate at Iona College
Bottom: Albritton Bell Tower at Texas A&M University

The principles of placemaking

Place comprises a combination of physical elements. How much of a role each element plays varies by the character of the institution and the place—but all play some role.

The chapters that follow in this section of the book describe the major elements that contribute to making great campuses that help a college or university achieve its mission and strategic goals. Many of these principles contribute to more than one of the elements of institutional missions, and many of them work harmoniously together in ways more powerful than they could alone.

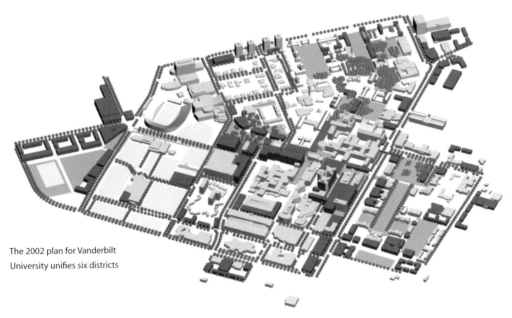

The 2002 plan for Vanderbilt
University unifies six districts

The role of a plan or overarching physical vision in unifying the campus

A campus plan does not simply show the layout of the campus like a stylized aerial photograph. The plan embodies institutional values, giving the institution's vision tangible form. In specifying the numbers, location, and arrangement of classrooms and of informal spaces that can be used for conversation and study, it provides the setting in which students and faculty can learn both formally and informally. The plan promotes community on campus and sets a social agenda by the proximity and placement of buildings and their inhabitants. It supports the institution's relationship with its neighbors, its physical and cultural surroundings, and the community at large. The plan dictates the arrangement and proportion of campus uses, reflecting the phasing and priorities of overall institutional strategy.

Density or compactness of uses and spaces for interaction

Density works together with enclosure, green space, mixed use, and a pedestrian scale to create vital spaces on campus. In a densely built and lively community, people are more likely to run into one another than in a spread-out one. Creating the right kind of density is all about creating human intersections—and intersections and the collegiality they generate are at the heart of community on campus.

Synergism provided by intermixing various campus uses

The more that people's paths cross and intersect, the more a campus—or a town—feels like a community and a place to be cherished. Collegiate places where seeing colleagues—fellow students and professors alike—is a common event promote the exchange of ideas vital to the educational mission. This was accomplished at early colleges and universities in part by mixing the many campus uses together in one compact area. As institutions have grown, the uses have often been separated. But more and more institutions are coming to understand the need to mix campus uses again.

Landscape

American institutions have always had a unique relationship to the landscape. People are attracted to unique places—places that resonate with the personality of the region they inhabit, that are dynamic yet enduring. More than just a collection of lawns and trees, a properly designed and implemented campus landscape establishes the campus's overall character and beauty. It shapes and solidifies the campus plan and provides the campus with a sense of unity. The landscape embodies the essence of the place the institution strives to be.

Stewardship of the campus and its environment as a contributing factor to, and as an outcome of, campus placemaking

Educating students to be thoughtful citizens of their community and their world is a fundamental value that in one form or another relates to the mission statements of most colleges and universities. Most institutions therefore want to teach and to find a way to model environmentally responsible behavior. Just as care for the environment is inextricably related to an institution's mission, many of the actions recommended in this book to foster community and learning on campus also, at no additional cost and often with cost savings, significantly promote environmental stewardship. This means that, as the institution takes action to improve community, collegiality, and learning on campus, it can also reap the tangible and intangible benefits of environmental stewardship.

Mastering the need for automotive access on campus

Next to sports and recreation, the automobile is the single largest user of land on campus. On some campuses, roadways and parking consume up to 40 percent of the developed campus land. No matter how much parking is available, most colleges and universities find themselves under a barrage of pressure to build more. Through its destruction of the campus environment as a pleasant place to spend time and interact with people, and through the very door-to-door convenience that it promises, the automobile is a major factor in the erosion of community and collegiality on campus. When the full costs and impacts of letting the automobile dominate campus environments and patterns of interaction are identified, the communities on many campuses are motivated to take back their campuses from the automobile in favor of environments and life styles for human interaction.

Architecture

Buildings provide the space in which necessary institutional functions—such as classroom learning, administrative work, residential life, and indoor recreation—take place. They are also a major component of the framework of the campus as a whole; they shape space; they contribute to the overall life and vitality of the campus; and they are a key element of institutional identity. Buildings reinforce the vision and identity of the campus by establishing character and providing focal points.

The impact of computers and technology on campus, and the potential of a campus inside the computer

Often seen as a significant detriment to community on campus, computers, when integrated properly into the fabric of the campus, can also enhance community. The impact of technology on campus community is still unfolding. Will wireless networks, by allowing opportunities for instant messaging, email, and other Internet uses without the need to find a public terminal or even talk with a friend, subvert it? Or are we looking at new opportunities, yet unforeseen, for social experiences of the future?

The richness of the Internet allows online users to create, inhabit, and explore virtual places as vividly realistic as any described in books. Can these be used to enhance the experience of community among residential, commuter, and especially distance learners? However, even beautifully and realistically designed virtual spaces may not be enough. Many distance learners benefit from integrating some degree of physical presence into their learning experience. Most institutions that offer remote learning also provide, in one way or another, the intimate contact of a real physical place.

Being in a neighborhood, city, or town.

Whether an institution is located in a small town, a suburb, or an inner city, a relationship that is mutually beneficial to both the institution and its neighbors can be hard to achieve. An unattractive or hostile neighborhood environment can have an impact on recruiting top students and faculty. And when the college community experiences a lack of safety in the neighborhood, the university faces the dilemma of how much to emphasize campus security and how much to join in the larger urban community in order to gain the understanding and cooperation of community residents, thereby reducing the risk of hostile incidents.

Many institutional leaders have found that they need to take the lead in building a healthy community. Those institutions that have achieved enduring symbiotic relationships with their neighboring communities or city districts are conscious of, and cultivate, the many benefits that both the institution and the city or neighborhood can realize from this relationship. As with institutional community, physical places play a pivotal role in engendering a sense of community with the neighborhood and city.

eight

The Plan Expresses the Big Idea

The campus plan expresses the mission of the institution by illustrating the institution's academic, social, and environmental values. A well-crafted and well-implemented plan can inspire students to attend, professors to come, and alumni to give generously for generations. As the manifestation of the institutional idea, the plan is the starting block from which great campuses, large or small, begin their history and guide their future.

...the future becomes the present, the present becomes the past, and the past turns into everlasting regret if you don't plan for it.[1]

- TENNESSEE WILLIAMS

Why plan?

High expectations should be standard for a planning process and the resulting plan. A comprehensive and sensitive plan (and planning process) can guide growth of a lively campus so that its vitality and sense of identity are retained as it grows, and it continues to support the academic mission of the institution. Or it can resurrect a campus in trouble, transforming a campus without a vision or a sense of place into a vibrant and memorable place.

Despite this potential, institutions frequently lack good campus plans. The reasons are legion, and mostly mistaken. Often, the reason given for not creating or maintaining a good, current plan are actually the very reasons such a plan may be needed.

An historic vision too sacred to change

The original historic vision and campus may be so sacred in the minds of board members, alumni, and current students that institutional leadership finds great difficulty in moving toward a new, updated, or expanded vision. An insightful analysis and story about the original plan and how the idea can guide the future of the institution once again can inspire the board and the entire campus community when they see how the new plan respects the old plan and grows out of it.

No growth

Institutions with flat or receding enrollments often think that they do not have to plan. Historically, however, campus facility needs grow an average of 1 percent to 1½ percent per year regardless of enrollment growth. Programs change; buildings go out of date and need replacement; changing demographics of students, faculty, and staff require parking and circulation increases. Changing neighborhoods off campus may require a response from the institution. The reasons to plan even without enrollment growth are numerous.

Planning when growth is declining may be an *absolute necessity.* Examining the reasons for the decline in enrollment may be the key to solving the problem. The reasons for enrollment decline can be tougher competition, outdated academic facilities, perception of unstable surrounding neighborhood, or perception of poor campus conditions. An integrated campus plan can perhaps contribute to reversing all these conditions.

Tight financial constraints

Institutions may not want to spend money on planning when fiscal constraints are tight. In addition, the lack of strategic planning capacity internally can lead to a disconnection between institutional financial planning and physical planning. However, financial concerns may be precisely the reason to plan. An integrated plan can reduce operational cost through recommendations for efficient building systems or through reducing grounds maintenance. Institutions fortunate to have land or building resources beyond their need may be able to devise strategies for sale, lease, or development that either generate revenue or put unneeded resources and deferred maintenance of those resources in someone else's hands.

Organizational structure and poor communication

Planning that does not recognize the many overlapping intricacies of a well-functioning campus or that plans a single aspect of the campus without realizing the effect on everything else is poor planning. The lack of a coordinated and unified administrative system can cause poor planning when administrative units do not communicate. Facilities administration may be unaware of academic departments' new building needs, or academic departments may be unaware of new planned construction that they might be able to utilize. This situation can be exacerbated when the planning staff is too low in the organizational structure to have effective input in campus-wide planning decisions. Some institutions have found they must remove recently completed parking or open space because a new need has arisen, or because no one investigated the expansion needs of an adjacent academic department. A comprehensive campus plan can eliminate unnecessary moves and attain full value with every dollar spent.

Focus on architecture

Administrators, board members, and donors sometimes think that individual or multiple building projects can be built successfully without an overall guiding plan—or that a plan might in some way inhibit the creative talents of the architects. Sometimes they think that architecture projects can solve campus issues beyond their own scope. Rarely can an isolated new building project achieve the full potential *for the whole campus* that it could if informed by a plan. Conceiving a single- or multiple-building project without a comprehensive plan leaves too little guidance for the architect and can damage the institution as well. A campus plan can aid the architect, providing the context and framework in which to design and allowing him or her to focus on how the building can contribute to the overall campus. Great, enduring, contributing architecture needs the focus that a visionary and comprehensive campus plan can give.

History of unrealized plans

Some institutions have a history of creating plans that, for the most part, go unfulfilled, leaving the institution reluctant to invest in planning again. This lack of follow-through may be due to a plan that is developed with too little involvement by the campus community or to a vision that is ungrounded in thorough analysis. Some plans are unrealized because they call for removal of entire precincts of the campus, or they fail to address the magnitude of difficulties such as topography, river corridors, and town-gown relationships. Recently, for example, a firm doing campus master planning for Harvard University suggested moving the Charles River to best unite that institution's landholdings. This solution was challenging from an engineering and financial perspective, but more important, the antagonism it would arouse in the community politically made it impossible to consider.

Desire to maximize flexibility

Cash-strapped institutions that look increasingly to donors to fund campus facilities may focus mainly on securing the gift at any price rather than on institutional imperatives. They fear that a plan could inhibit flexibility. How to accept well-meant donor contributions yet preserve the institution's right to implement that project or utilize that contribution to the institution's full advantage is a serious issue on today's campuses. In response to this issue, an institution may be able to utilize the planning process to illuminate the strategic principles behind the plan and secure vested interest by board, alumni, and contributors. When contributors know that there is a larger idea behind the project, a visionary plan can excite and promote involvement. People are often more ready to give to ideas such as enhancing learning and community on campus than to a single building project.

New leadership

The arena of campus leadership today is markedly different than that of the previous generation. Leaders, presidents, and chancellors, once stalwarts of the institutional memory, move from one institution to another on average every five to seven years and are judged primarily on their specific, tangible accomplishments within the short period of their tenure. To deal with this new pattern of leadership, the planning process and the resulting plan should be far-reaching in their horizon, envisioning a campus future beyond five- and ten-year cycles of leadership change. This long-term view must be described in short increments of achievable goals that move the institution toward the longer vision with or without the leader who has initiated them. In this way, both the institution and its leaders can achieve the results they want.

Fear of expectations

A plan establishes a vision, directs growth and change, and marks the course to achieve that vision. Having a plan establishes expectations to raise the necessary financial resources and to achieve that plan—and thereby provides a gauge of success. Setting marks of "quantifiable" achievement for institutional leadership and boards can be daunting. On the other hand, a plan that inspires involvement and a visible, engaging process of implementation can enable leadership to be successful because the entire community is vested in the ideas embodied in the plan; the well-done plan represents their aspirations and has marked a clear course to achieve fruition.

What the plan should do

Great campuses adapt well to change and growth. They preserve their most cherished characteristics while undergoing growth, change, and renewal, however subtle or bold. From their inception through their growth to their great leaps of reinvention, these campuses have a plan to chart their individual course.

The plan provides all the details needed to manifest the central idea of the campus. Even if an institution lacks a cohesive vision, idea, or strategic plan for itself, a campus plan can at least guide the most fundamental aspects of a campus' needs, such as placing a building, parking, or recreation facility based on a thorough and logical review of existing conditions.

A comprehensive campus plan should:

- Express the idea or vision of the institution
- Guide growth and change
- Reinforce the strategic plan

Expresses idea or vision

Academic and civic vision, history, tradition, culture, and context are the foundations of great campus plans. They give meaning and purpose to all who pass through the institution. The plan should always be far reaching in its horizon, knowing that each move furthers the *idea* of the institution and will contribute to its long-term success.

Many of the great campuses of the world started as an idea. From the medieval cloistered universities of Europe to the over 4,100 institutions of this country, many institutions had at their beginning a vision for the campus. These visions had social roots, such as the land grant schools established after passage of the Morrill Act in 1862; had academic ideals, such as the University of Virginia; or expressed a relationship with a dramatic physical place, such as Carnegie Mellon University. Whether the instigation of the idea was social, academic, or physical, the plan was the instrument of the vision.

Social ideals

Access to education for all is an American ideal. The Morrill Act, which established the land-grant mission and provided the foundation for a number of state institutions nationwide, manifested this desire for open higher education. "The land-grant university," states Iowa State University president Martin Jishcke, "is a uniquely American idea, defined by a commitment to the land-grant values of access and opportunity, combining practical and liberal education, conducting basic and applied research, and reaching out to extend the university to serve the people of the state."[2] The establishment of community college systems in the mid-1900s extended the concept of accessible education for all by offering affordability and local proximity.

Historic image of main quadrangle at Utah State University

Early plans for land-grant institutions set out a plan that was generally visible and accessible, reflecting their charter for educational accessibility. The central building, Old Main, was typically set on a hilltop, the highest point on the campus, so that it was a visible landmark. The grid of the surrounding city was extended into the campus, to connect the campus to the city.

Academic ideals

Perhaps because its founder, Thomas Jefferson, was also its designer, the core campus of the University of Virginia is one of the finest examples of how the physical form of the campus can be designed to reflect its academic vision. "We fondly hope," Jefferson stated to the Virginia Board of Visitors in 1821, "that the instruction which may flow from this institution…may ensure to our country the reputation, the safety and prosperity, and all the other blessings which experience proves to result from the

The "academical village" at the
University of Virginia

The "academical village" at the
University of Virginia

cultivation and improvement of the general mind."[3] Jefferson believed
that the college experience should extend beyond attendance in classes.
He envisioned an "academical village" inhabited by professors and their
families along with students, in which the shared life experience formed
the foundation of the learning community. The education thus obtained
would be one suitable for responsible citizens of a republic.

The original plan of the university, as laid out by Jefferson, reflects this
vision. Ten "pavilions" faced each other across a gracious lawn, each
housing a professor and his family upstairs, with classrooms on the
ground floor. Joined by colonnaded walkways and student rooms, the
pavilions are flanked by working gardens and, behind the gardens, by
two additional rows of student rooms connected by arcaded walkways.
Although each pavilion is unique, all are joined by a unifying colonnade
strongly suggesting classical Greek or Roman culture. At the head of the
central, shared lawn is not a church (as might have been the case in colleges and universities in Europe at the time) but the university's library, a
strong statement about the importance of education and enlightenment.
The library's domed and columned architecture, reminiscent of Rome's
Pantheon, recalls the virtues of the republican form of government. Altogether, in its plan and design, the original campus of the University of
Virginia speaks to the importance Jefferson placed on an educated citizenry in a democratic republic.

Response to physical place

In many cases, the form of the campus responds strongly to its physical setting. Cambridge University responds both to the river and to its interwoven relationship with the city of Cambridge. The river and university are so intimately intertwined that it seems impossible that they could exist apart. Much the same can be said physically about the university's relationship with the city.

Several campuses in the United States are as much a response to their stunning physical settings as they are to their institutional ideals. Carnegie Mellon sits atop a natural plinth in Pittsburgh, Pennsylvania, on the edge of the hill commanding its district setting. The formal early building groupings of the campus seem to grow out of the tree-covered slopes of the hill. They frame a central open space where today art, science, and engineering come together. Form, function, and place are united in a complete and enduring composition.

The University of Colorado responds directly to the background of the Rockies with its bold building groupings and roof forms.

Ithaca College, which is located on a scenic hilltop just outside of Ithaca, New York, developed a master plan that creates "three-sided quadrangles"—areas enclosed on three sides by buildings—to generate pedestrian traffic and increase community, with the fourth side left open to the splendid views overlooking Ithaca and Cayuga Lake in the valley below.

University of Colorado at Boulder

| 1900 | 1950 |

Guides growth and change

The plan should guide institutional facilities growth, which averages 1 percent to 1½ percent per year regardless of growth in enrollment—but every new building, every dormitory renovation, every parking lot can also challenge the original vision. Perhaps an opportunity arises for a dormitory on the edge of the campus when the plan called for creating more residential space near the campus core. Should the institution take advantage of this opportunity, or let it pass? If the institution decides in favor of the new dormitory, what other modifications must be accommodated in the plan so that the overarching goals of the institution are not weakened?

Over time, the vision itself of the institution may change. New visions call for new plans. But the institution now has a campus—a campus that has reflected the original vision and changed over time in planned and perhaps unplanned ways; a campus that has the patina and character that reflects—and also influences—the essence of the institution. It probably has some "sacred" spaces, and it may also have some features that the institution would like to change. A new plan for an existing campus must strike a balance between the institution's current assets and its new aspirations. History, tradition, and culture *must* color some portion of the new campus vision.

2001 Master Plan

Links to the strategic plan

A major motive for creating a new campus plan is the institutional strategic-planning process. Institutions generally conduct strategic planning about once every five years. They ask whether they are performing at their best academically. Do they have the right technology and enough of it? Should courses take new directions? Are new initiatives needed in recruiting or student life? Often, the answers to these questions have implications for the physical campus.

· The strategic planning process instituted by president Kermit Hall at Utah State University proposed bold academic initiatives in research, arts, and residential life in the quest for an excellent cross-disciplinary living-learning and environmental community. It also instituted new initiatives—unprecedented at this public university—to raise needed capital from private and government sources. The strategic plan was then translated into a series of district plans for compact, sustainable campus growth. These plans have succeeded in harnessing individual donor, government, and private-sector capital for implementation, partly because of the strong link between the strategic objectives and the plan for facilities to support these objectives.

· After allowing its once-strong astronomy program to languish, Wesleyan University in Connecticut decided to reinvest in this core discipline. New faculty members were brought in. But in the meantime, safety concerns had led the school to add lighting throughout the campus—lighting that obscured the view of the nighttime sky at the campus observatory. The new astronomy faculty led the way in setting new standards for campus lighting, making it safer than the existing lighting as well as glare-free and night-sky-friendly.

· The strategic planning efforts at Lehigh University led to an initiative to improve interdisciplinary communications among academic disciplines. This idea was the impetus for a master-plan recommendation to move the Graduate School of Education, then in a remote district of the campus, to a new site in the historic core campus near a number of related academic disciplines. The proposed location was also adjacent to the existing Southside neighborhood schools. This placed the graduate school at the crossroads of both interdisciplinary work within the institution and application of that knowledge in the neighborhood.

An institution's strategic plan and its physical plan go hand in hand. The physical plan lays out the priorities and time phasing for changes to be made to the campus. This plan should connect these changes with the financial realities and the academic and social priorities of the institution. Each project, no matter how large or small, should fulfill a strategic purpose. Campus plan changes must respond to changing strategic emphasis on academic priorities, on recruiting, on campus social life, and other factors. Every facilities investment should be made to improve the quality of the whole campus environment—academic, civic, and physical. The more the institution can tie its strategic and physical plans together through a defined process, the more the campus will continue to support and enhance the institution's strategic directions.

Plan elements

The plan integrates and orchestrates the three fundamental physical form-giving components of the campus: the landscape framework; the use of roadways, parking, and paths for circulation; and the buildings and architecture of the institution. The plan creates a balance among these components, causing them to interact and collaborate gracefully with one another in a manner that is supportive of the fundamental idea of the institution. The amount of land area devoted to buildings should have the right proportion to the amount of land area given to circulation and parking and to the amount of open space.

The uses of the buildings and open spaces are also balanced. No one element should be allowed to overwhelm a campus or campus district, but the proportions of elements vary based on organization of functions, position from the centers, and other characteristics of the overall plan. By identifying the principles for location of uses on the campus, now and into the future, the campus plan is a road map of the intent and purpose of the physical campus.

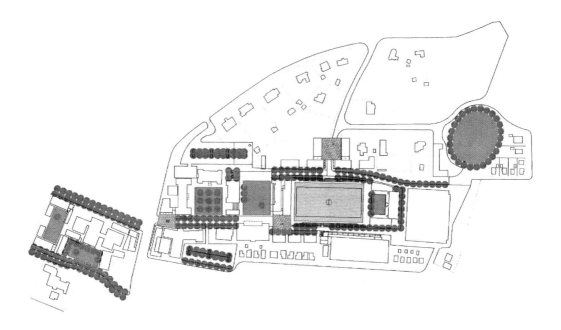

Landscape framework

The plan focuses first on the campus open spaces, not on its buildings. In this, campus planning remarkably resembles urban planning. Towns and cities have always grown around their public spaces—from the *agora* of ancient Greece or the forum of Rome, to the town commons of New England. The *Laws of the Indies*—the dictum of colonization principles laid out by King Phillip II of Spain in 1573 to govern (among other things) the development of settlements in the new world—specifies first the town plaza, which "is to be the starting point for the town." In order, after the main plaza, the king specifies the principle streets, which begin at the main plaza, then smaller plazas, and finally the town's buildings, main buildings first.[4]

Plan and model of landscape vision for Iona College

The main quadrangle, green, square, street or avenue is the starting point of the campus just as the town plaza is the starting point of the town. The plan dictates the character of this and other important open spaces of the campus. These are the "outdoor rooms" where the community of the university sees itself and interacts with itself both in formal gatherings, such as the annual convocation and graduation ceremonies, and in informal situations, such as the intervals between classes. The plan surrounds and frames these spaces with buildings—not the other way around.

The plan also lays out other campus open spaces—its formal quadrangles and informal residential courtyards as well as its athletic fields and nature preserves.

The plan can manifest vernacular landforms and architecture of the region to create a style of expression and instill the campus with a memorable sense of place. Does the institution want to express itself formally or informally? With its virgin site on rolling California hills, Stanford University could have done either. Frederick Law Olmsted's vision for the campus preferred a site in the foothills and, likely, a concomitant informality in the overall plan "probably with winding roads, and buildings nestled asymmetrically in the irregular topography, precisely as in Olmsted's earlier designs."[5] But Leland Stanford's desire for a monumental and formal plan prevailed, and the university was located on the flatter portion of the site.

The plan can also encourage collaboration with the city or town that the institution resides within. The cloistered institutions of Europe and elsewhere controlled their involvement with their neighbors; some institutions in America emulate this precedent, but many others prefer to blur the boundary between the campus and the community.

Circulation

Circulation comprises all of the aspects of a campus required to move people, goods, and services from place to place, and to move and store cars on campus. Students walk from residence halls to classes; faculty and staff bicycle or drive to the campus and park near their offices; food and supplies are delivered; garbage is removed. In the nineteenth century and earlier, circulation was a relatively minor consideration whose primary function was a pictorial approach to the campus; with the advent of the automobile, circulation has become a dominant factor in campus organization. Today, circulation (including parking) is the second largest user of land on campus, after sports and recreation.

The plan provides a logical infrastructure system. Efficient paths and corridors to deliver energy, services, goods, and technology can reduce both initial cost and long-term operating cost for the institution. They are also critical elements of a sustainability plan for the campus.

At the historic core of older campuses typically sits a central quadrangle that was once, or has always been, a pedestrian space. Its simple diagonal pathways are a focus of interaction and community on campus. Outside of this quadrangle, the struggle to reach a reasonable balance with the demands of circulation begins. The campus master plan addresses circulation issues such as:

· The extent to which pedestrian and bicycle activity is encouraged or automobile use is accommodated
· How close vehicles are allowed to which buildings or functions for convenience or for maintenance

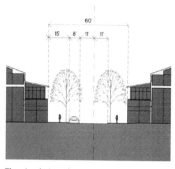

· Whether access for servicing is centralized or decentralized
· What considerations are required for safety

The plan must deal with issues around the integration or separation of vehicular, service, pedestrian, and sometimes bicycle traffic. In many places, these can be combined, much like in a vibrant city street, often in ways that preserve and enhance the vitality of the campus spaces.

Almost every plan wrestles with the problem of storing automobiles. Creating a rim of parking around the campus can have a disastrous impact on the image of the campus, the surrounding neighborhood, and the institution's relations with its neighbors. Large parking lots in the center of the campus spread out the functions, desired academic adjacencies, and buildings, increasing the amount of driving that must be done and creating places where no one wants to linger. Distant parking lots do not adequately serve faculty and staff who drive; parking must be in relatively close proximity to their destinations. Each precinct of a larger campus must accommodate some parking, with the remaining parking (as large a percentage as reasonably possible) in satellite areas served by a shuttle system of some kind. Structured parking is generally preferable to land-consuming lots, particularly in core areas of the campus, near neighborhoods, and in areas with an ecological impact. Given the cost of parking in general and garages in particular, and the value of land resources, the plan must provide a well managed circulation and parking system that collaborates with mixed land use to dampen parking demand, increase safety, and contribute to a positive campus image.

The circulation plan at Heartland Community College extends the street grid of the city and provides sheltered parking in courtyards

Housing at Colorado College

Buildings and architecture

From a planning perspective, the buildings of a campus are tools to define campus outdoor spaces. They provide the walls to the outdoor spaces that they border, and the character of these walls defines in large measure the character of the spaces they define.

Buildings also provide internal spaces to serve program needs, provide needed academic and social adjacencies, accommodating uses that must be integrated into the campus as a whole and adequately served by circulation.

Collectively, buildings also contribute to the character of the campus as a whole. Restrictions promulgated in the plan specify height limits, massing and allowable materials, as well as possibly specific architectural styles or forms. The plan identifies how each new building is to relate to or depart from the buildings around it. Even on campuses where many different building styles and materials are allowed, a good plan should describe the building's contribution to the overall pattern of campus buildings—how its campus presence and placement collaborates with other buildings and enlivens the outdoor spaces it neighbors; and whether it also serves an iconic or landmark function on campus.

In addition, through its integration of the architecture, the landscape, and circulation, the plan can manifest the institution's commitment to a sustainable world. Commitment to stormwater quality, alternative transportation, and reduction of energy usage can all be incorporated into the campus plan.

Bringing it all together

A well-crafted campus plan expresses a long-term vision or idea of the campus that is simple, powerful, and memorable. It organizes the campus around a clearly identifiable big idea. A successful plan promotes the desired institutional identity, which should in turn differentiate the institution and ground it to its place. The examples in this section show how campus plans can meet the objectives of providing vision, guiding growth, and supporting an institution's mission and strategic plan.

University of South Florida

The University of South Florida in Tampa in 1995 developed a new master plan[6] to create a strong physical institutional identity while accommodating significant growth. The single form-giving big idea of the plan was the creation of a "greenway" that traverses the campus diagonally, connecting two large natural areas with the central lawn at the heart of the campus and providing a counterpoint to the more urban building densities that campus growth would require. The plan combined strategic growth, visionary, academic, place-making, and community-oriented goals:

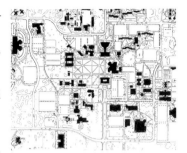

- Accommodate a ten-year program of academic research, residential and support facilities expansion of nearly 80 percent on the 815-acre suburban Tampa campus.

- Create a sense of place by providing a more urban spatial order and identity and a more pedestrian-oriented environment on what had become a sprawling, automobile-dominated campus.

- Strengthen the functional and collegial connections among the campus's various academic, research, residential, and recreational districts.

- Restore the indigenous landscape of the university by creating a natural system of open spaces for amenity, recreation, and stormwater management.

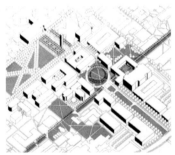

- Enhance the university's presence as an educational, cultural, and economic resource in the Tampa Bay region.

To meet these goals, the plan established a hierarchy of connected pedestrian open spaces framed by the substantial building program to create a series of unique places where none had existed before. Building infill was used to shape the open spaces of the campus in a variety of settings such as quadrangles, courtyards, and plazas. Arcades and breezeways were used to connect buildings in a response to the long, hot summer seasons with afternoon downpours characteristic of the regional climate. Most significantly, the plan recommended the creation of a "greenway" that traverses the campus in a diagonal to connect the central lawn at the heart of the campus with a botanical garden on the southwest and a vast, regional ecological preserve to the northeast. Combining an indigenous, semitropical landscape with a series of informal ponds and basins also used for stormwater management, this greenway provided a counterpoint to the higher-density urban structure of the campus built environment that would be needed to meet the growth program.

Using a phased implementation based on institutional strategic objectives, the plan coupled implementation of architectural projects with the creation of new public spaces to fill in gaps in the pedestrian fabric of the campus with active uses and animated spaces. It also simplified the vehicular circulation and replaced surface lots needed for new buildings and open spaces with structured parking.

University of South Florida
From Top: Existing conditions (1994), proposed plan (1995), design guideline, and the new greenway

Since adoption of the plan, the university has constructed nearly two million square feet of new building facilities, strengthening program linkages among its academic and research precincts. New residential space has enlivened the campus by bringing twenty-four-hour life into the academic core. Creation of animated, open spaces in conjunction with building development has had a profound effect on the quality and clarity of place on the campus. In particular, the new Martin Luther King Plaza, a gracious ensemble of shade trees, trellises, fountains, and seating areas on the university's central lawn, has provided an iconic space that has enhanced the identity of the institution. The greenway system has been substantially implemented and brings a natural, indigenous environment to the campus to act as a foil to the increased density of development; in addition, it provides a system of ponds that provide stormwater management capacity for the campus as it develops. A new landscaped gateway has been created at the main vehicular entry into the campus, and pedestrian concourses have been created by the conversion of roads and parking areas in the academic core to tree- and building-lined walkways connecting major districts of the campus.

University of California, Berkeley

In its first comprehensive master plan in one hundred years, the University of California, Berkeley[7] addresses the need for major physical change. "The New Century Plan is a national model to renew a campus by linking academic mission, investment, and design through vision." The campus plan responded directly to the university's strategic academic plan, its growing enrollment, and its need to functionally upgrade its facilities, while leveraging each investment in the campus to enhance campus life and to build on the campus's extraordinary legacy of landscape and architecture.

Since space was at a premium on the Berkeley campus, institutional leaders and planners focused on ensuring that each new capital investment be designed to maximize its contribution to intellectual community by creating dynamic, interactive places. The plan "reinforces the distinctions between the Beaux Arts features of the classical core, with its axial vistas toward the Golden Gate, and the ambling frame of riparian glades and picturesque buildings that line its edges and weave through it." These distinctions became, in fact, the unique, organizing principle of the plan. The ravine and stream that cut through the center of the campus had been preserved, but over time the campus had turned its back to them. Parts had been covered up, and they were perceived more as an obstacle than a feature. The new plan for the campus restored the Central Glades

as a natural amenity and primary organizing element, and oriented new campus development toward it. The plan proposed removal of a "ten-story concrete monolith" building, which would be replaced by two smaller pavilions that would frame a cascade of steps from a public plaza to the Glades.

To enhance social and intellectual interaction and generate activity in outdoor public spaces, the plan places active uses, such as library reading rooms, classrooms, and food services, at the entry level of buildings. It relocates nonessential uses off campus to increase the university's on-campus inventory of academic and research space, placing administrative and public functions (including a new hotel and conference facility and university museums) at the edge of the campus near downtown Berkeley where they can contribute to the quality of the neighborhood and be served by public transit. New housing is planned in concert with local community plans as infill high-density housing within a twenty-minute walk, bike, or public-transit ride of the campus. The plan also establishes a hierarchy of gateways and movement systems that preserve and enhance the pedestrian orientation of the core campus. Sustainability is addressed through policies and initiatives to conserve energy and enhance the natural environment, such as retention of stormwater and removal of impervious surfaces.

University of California at Berkeley
Top Left: Rendering of restored entry drive
Top Right: Central Glades
Bottom: New Century Plan

Project guidelines that support the university's strategic goals and policies provided more detailed criteria for location, space utilization, and design of buildings and open spaces. Capital-approval processes were amended to ensure that project scale, form, and character were taken into account so that project decisions could be made in the overall context of the plan and strategic goals rather than on an ad-hoc basis.

Hollins University
Top: Central campus
Bottom: 2004 campus plan

Hollins University

The 2004 campus master plan at Hollins University[8] addresses land management, campus structure and organization, landscape, circulation and parking, space use, deferred maintenance, flood protection, phasing, and implementation funding. It organizes the structure of the campus around the traditional, iconic, and much-loved central quadrangle around which the earliest buildings stand, and which forms a substantial part of the institution's identity, restoring the historic buildings and revitalizing them and the central quadrangle with student-oriented activities. The goals of the plan were to:

- *Invest in existing facilities.* The plan gives priority to capital investments that renovate existing facilities to meet program needs, attend to deferred maintenance, and address accessibility. It also looks at opportunities to use improved facilities to generate additional revenue.

- *Enhance campus vitality.* Addressing a generally acknowledged lack of vitality on campus, the plan provides expanded, visible space for student activities.

- *Reinforce academic mission.* The organization of academic uses is strengthened, encouraging opportunities for interdisciplinary interaction.

- *Build on the beauty of the campus.* The campus contains an impressive collection of historic buildings sited within a stunning natural landscape. The plan preserves these features, defining a strong landscape framework and providing for adaptive reuse of historic buildings that is sensitive to their historic character.

- *Improve circulation functionality.* The plan defines major entry points to the campus core and provides clear access to public destinations and sufficient convenient parking.

As a central organizing idea, the plan revitalizes the campus's main quadrangle, making it a new focus for campus life. It provides for the restoration and renovation of the surrounding buildings, completely replanning the use of their ground floors with active, student-oriented uses, including student services, clubs, and a café. The plan establishes two "academic axes" extending from the main quad as the principal locations for academic uses on the campus, relocating some academic programs from other parts of the campus. It also defines three residential districts—one utilizing the upper stories of buildings right on the main quad and the other two at the ends of the academic axes. Each district provides support amenities for residential students.

The plan provides a long-term vision and physical design for the campus intended to guide decision-making for ten years and beyond, and it establishes a phased structure for investment in campus land and facilities that reflects the university's academic mission, history, and traditions. It has been adopted by the university's board and is in the process of implementation, with enthusiastic support by the university community.

Recommended initiatives

Creating a good campus plan requires both discipline and vision. Plans are not born in isolation—and they cannot be put together piecemeal. The following initiatives support effective campus planning.

Integrate the campus plan with the strategic plan. A great campus supports its institution's strategic objectives when the institution's campus plan manifests and supports its strategic plan. When the campus plan is grounded in the strategic imperatives of the university or college, its goals are clear and achievable, and everyone involved in the planning process understands their importance.

Capitalize on unique campus attributes. An institution should capitalize on opportunities to create uniqueness in its campus plan. These opportunities may come in the form of the character and personality of the region or the site or the traditions and culture of the institution itself. Sacred or special places should be celebrated in the plan.

Plan comprehensively. Institutions should plan primarily for the whole campus and for the long term. The clarity of that entire vision will illuminate achievable short-term objectives.

Organize clearly. A campus should be legible to all who come. A good plan unites the campus behind a single vision. It is simple, comprehensible, and unified.

Challenge traditional ideas respectfully. New plans for existing campuses must honor traditions—but also reinterpret them as needed to meet today's needs and tomorrow's challenges.

Build consensus. Institutional leadership can use the master planning process to create unity among the campus constituencies. A unified vision is a product of open process and the informed constituency behind it. Because the process builds consensus, unified visions move forward.

Never stop planning. A dynamic institution must stay in front of its growth needs with continual review to ensure that development takes place within the context of the larger plan framework.

nine

Creating Interaction through Density

Density of interaction

Density. No other planning idea provokes such controversy. The idea of a dense or compact campus (the terms are used interchangeably to describe a close adjacency of buildings and functions) can seem unpleasant to some institutions, conjuring visions of the tenements that in the late 1800s threatened public health, safety, and welfare. On the other hand, in America and elsewhere, the tightly built small town centers and city districts that are often cherished have relatively high densities, as measured by building site coverage. Indeed, many of the core areas and older centers of great American university and college campuses have densities that equal or exceed the densities of many of the negative stereotypes that the word density evokes. This physical compactness allows students and faculty to walk more easily from one place to another, encouraging interaction and community, and reinforcing a sense of place and institutional identity.

Within certain limits, a town or a college can be a vibrant community whether it is compact or spread out. The perceptions of compactness and vibrancy are functions of many things, including the visual context and the landscape, architecture, and topography. The way the space is designed, as well as the physical and cultural context in which it is located, are much more important in determining its vitality than its measure of density alone.

The most useful way to consider the compactness necessary for community and vitality is to look at the human qualities of the place—the intensity of its use and the opportunities for intersections that this intensity creates. When a place promotes interaction through compactness appropriate to its size, location, and culture, then the benefits of density may be realized even in a small, rural setting.

Density has a far-reaching effect on the site plan and the quality of life within it.[1]

- KEVIN LYNCH

Density issues in campus development

Institutions need to find a way to balance the human desire for enduring, symbolic places with the dynamic growth and change emblematic of great campuses—without creating a sprawling, centerless campus. One of several issues related to density may upset this balance.

Large expanses of surface parking force apart campus uses

COURTESY OF MICHIGAN STATE UNIVERSITY

Suburbanization

To accommodate growth, many campuses over the last forty years have followed the general American model of suburbanization. In particular, many of the American land-grant institutions, with their generous land resources, have fallen into this pattern. As these campuses grew over the last several decades, the creation of vital, lively places was not a prime consideration. Colleges and universities were facing other issues. Even today, many institutions do not understand the link between their sprawling campuses and the lack of community they experience.

Many American institutions still resist building densely. The choice to spread out is often based on the feeling that spreading out preserves open space between buildings and is more beautiful than building compactly. The choice to spread out has also been made in conjunction with several other campus trends:

Proliferation of the automobile on campus

The automobile has made sprawl both feasible and, to some degree, inevitable. As many as 75 percent of on-campus residential students have cars on some campuses. Students can drive a considerable distance from their dormitories at one end of the campus to their classes at the other. But cars also require roadways and parking lots at all major destinations, pushing new buildings farther apart.

Development of large building types

Buildings such as recreation centers, athletic centers, large laboratory buildings, and student centers have a different scale from older campus buildings. More massive, they also tend to have less façade articulation. Each of these building types occupies much more land than the older buildings. Creating vibrant spaces around these building types can be a challenge. Some institutions solve this problem by avoiding it—by locating the newer, larger buildings far from the campus center. This dispersal of campus functions requires ever more use of the automobile.

Memorializing the center

Interestingly, the original centers of some campuses have become static spaces, no longer changing or evolving. Respect for the historic center is merited. Not touching it is better than some of the changes on campuses where later infill buildings have destroyed the original character of the center. But if the center is not allowed to change at all, then as the institution's needs grow and change, the center becomes secondary to the emerging growth areas of the campus. Campuses may develop centers of activity apart from or in addition to their historic centers. Vanderbilt University, for example, didn't want to build or add to its historic center, while its Medical Center (and associated research) grew increasingly demanding in its need for space, becoming the dominant area of the campus. Over time, the geographic "center" of the campus moved to the parking area between the Medical Center and the traditional campus center. Vanderbilt is now making the emerging medical area into one of several new, vital district centers, as well as addressing the revitalization of the historic core.

The shopping mall syndrome

Just as development can be too spread out, it can also be too unevenly distributed, so that it is too compact in some areas and too sparse in others. When functions are densely grouped together and surrounded by seas of parking, a sense of human scale is lost, and the land area as a whole is not well utilized. Interior retail shopping malls, for example, are much denser than retail on even the most vibrant Main Street. But to achieve the density of shopping that mall-developers desire, most of the land is used as a paved and inhospitable parking area. The mall sits like a fortress in the middle of this asphalt. Many large campus venues such as campus centers and recreation complexes share this problem.

Some colleges and universities have created a barrier of lifeless surface parking between the campus and its adjacent neighborhood. Where a sea of parking surrounding a mall might be acceptable, a sea of parking surrounding a campus makes—perhaps unintentionally—a hostile statement to its neighbors. Indeed, the parking may create a neighborhood environment that is not desirable from the point of view of the institution itself. No building or campus exists in isolation. The desirable density in the campus center must transition smoothly to neighboring uses.

Capacity limits

Every place has limits on how dense it can become. Too much density, like too much sprawl, can cause problems. "There is no ideal density. For any given activity, there is a range of densities outside of which conditions are likely to be substandard and within which there are a number of thresholds marking a shift from one character with its particular advantages to another with other advantages."[2]

Usually, the solution to a capacity problem is unique to a particular situation. Vanderbilt's Medical Center is a case in point. Growing rapidly, the area was reaching a limit in the amount of parking that could be handled within a reasonable walking distance of the hospital. Uses such as office space did not need to be in the core hospital area and were using a large share of the available parking. The core hospital uses alone were growing and required location in close proximity to one another. They would soon also require all the available parking capacity. An obvious, but expensive, solution might have been to add structured parking capacity to the infrastructure of the area and to then deal with traffic capacity limits. Instead, Vanderbilt saw an opportunity in the situation. A plan was developed to move clinical and other offices out of the core to much less expensive space where they would in turn stimulate activity in areas that the university and the city wanted to revitalize.

In addition to traffic and parking, capacity limits can also arise along a number of other dimensions. Some overbuilt areas can use up too much open space, leaving too little or poor quality spaces that are too shaded by adjacent buildings. The utility infrastructure may also reach a limit, requiring expensive upgrading.

Reaching a capacity limit may be a sign to direct additional needed development in new directions.

An elusive concept

Few planning concepts are as difficult to define meaningfully and make use of as *density*. How can we achieve the kind of density that leads to interaction, vitality, and community?

Campus Comparisons

	Building Footprint (sf)	Total Area (sf)	Total Area (acres)	Total Build- ing Area	Total # of Buildings	Floor Area Ratio (far)	% Building Coverage
Ithaca	695,325	5,052,960	116.0	2,000,000	48	0.40	14%
Lehigh-Parker	646,880	3,898,620	89.5	2,624,080	53	0.58	17%
Lehigh-Mountaintop	289,974	3,012,669	69.2	1,014,909	9	0.34	10%
Brown	736,880	3,332,340	76.5	2,579,080	83	0.77	22%
Carnegie-Mellon	866,560	3,441,240	79.0	3,032,960	44	0.88	25%
Dartmouth	393,810	2,183,200	50.1	1,378,335	33	0.63	18%
Harvard Business School	704,176	2,571,474	59.0	2,464,616	33	0.96	27%
Harvard Yard	251,375	1,046.062	24.0	879,813	31	0.84	24%
Rice	856,245	3,778,830	86.8	2,996,858	40	0.79	23%

Traditional density metrics

In the planning field, the concept of *density* was initially applied to urban areas, not to campuses. Metrics were created in the late 1800s to provide standards for new development or renovated areas that would avoid the unsavory slum conditions, with their concomitant disease, filth, and crime, which had sprung up in industrialized cities. These metrics include the ratio of built space to land area known as Floor Area Ratio (FAR), building coverage, and people per unit of land area (typically, per square mile).[3] Although the conditions that gave rise to the need for these measurements mostly no longer exist, the concepts have become embodied in zoning and building codes in communities across America.

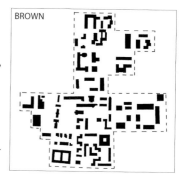

BROWN

The use of density metrics on campus is a relatively new phenomenon. Within the last ten years or so, some institutions have begun to look at FAR and other metrics mostly as a way of comparing their own campuses to others.

Metrics are not enough

Planners today generally recognize that while these metrics can be used to make comparisons and to record facts about places, by themselves they do little to predict whether one community will be more livable or vibrant than another. A high-rise laboratory building in a sea of parking may have the same density measurements as Harvard Yard, but there is no doubt which is the more collegial space.

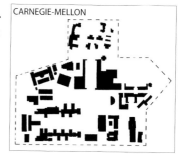

CARNEGIE-MELLON

Building coverage, floor area and plan are typical density comparison metrics

Sweet Briar College:
Aerial view of existing campus and
model of proposed redefined core

In fact, using density metrics in institutional planning may have unanticipated and undesirable consequences. A cap on the building coverage ratio at Sacred Heart University in Connecticut, for example, forced the institution to build residential towers to accommodate its growth needs. These towers limited activity at ground level and therefore reduced the interaction and community that the university was seeking to create through its residential-life program.

Concepts of density should not be applied uniformly across a campus. Density measurements are only meaningful as the selection of the area over which they are measured. When looking at density with an eye toward creating an active campus center, institutions should include only the core areas, excluding any surface parking, playing fields, and undeveloped land that might be at the edges or outside of the core area. Stanford University, for example, defines an "Academic Growth Boundary" within which it allows new infill construction under certain guidelines, while leaving other land undeveloped.[4] Sweet Briar College, likewise, has a densely developed fifty-acre core campus surrounded by three thousand acres of undeveloped land. Although the density of the entire campus would be so low as to resemble farmland, the core campus is walkable, vital, and surprisingly dense.

Density redefined

The measures that are generally used to quantify density, while providing ranges that may serve as guidelines, do not allow us to predict which campuses will be lively and vital places, reaping the benefits that a compact community provides. The essential aspects of density that constitute a barometer for success are proximity, centers of activity, and character of space.[5]

Proximity

Putting buildings and uses in close proximity is a key factor for a thriving community. This proximity improves the chances that people will cross paths with other people, thus increasing the likelihood for spontaneous interaction and exchange of ideas, which are fundamental to collegiality and to interdisciplinary communication. To the extent that learning is a social activity occurring as much outside the classroom as within it, an environment that maximizes collegial encounters and exchange of ideas also maximizes learning on campus.

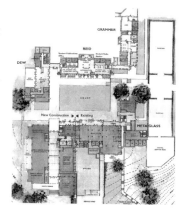

Different environments affect people's perception of proximity. How active or visually interesting a journey is can greatly affect our comfort with distance. The planner Christopher Alexander describes the choice of route for walking from one place to another as a subtle interaction of the shortest distance, intermediate attractions, and the destination itself.[6] Walking nine hundred feet (three typical city blocks) from a remote parking lot to a classroom can be tedious and feel unsafe, while the same distance past connected buildings, multiple entries, and visually diverse ground-level uses can seem pleasurable—and brief.

Centers

A district, even a densely developed one, should have a special place that is clearly identifiable as its center. The center may be an area that is even more densely developed than the surrounding district; it may provide important functions that draw people to it; or it may be a space of iconic significance readily identifiable as the district's heart. Under the right conditions, people begin to conduct more and more of their activities in the center, adding vitality. On campuses just as in urban centers, people are drawn to these vital areas to see and be seen, or just to enjoy the sense of activity.

Sweet Briar College: Buildings and uses in close proximity create a center with special character

The center may not be physically denser than its surrounding areas by traditional metrics, but it is the place with the maximum density of interaction of the university or district community with itself. As distance from the center increases, the density of these interactions decreases—whether the university is gradually giving way to an equally dense surrounding city or to unpopulated rolling countryside.

Character of space

Character of space describes the way in which the various attributes of a place harmonize with one another and with the physical qualities and the culture of the environment. The attributes of a place that affect the feeling of density include its degree of enclosure or openness, the distances between buildings, the quality and opaqueness of building facades, the size of the open space compared to the heights of buildings around it, the amount of land covered by buildings or left open, and the amount of sunlight and vegetation in the space. The character of a place responds to the sensitivities of the people in the community. This response includes preserving important views and movement corridors and providing location-appropriate height limits or ratios of building height to width of open space. Every place is unique, and thus, every place has—or should have—a unique character, a quality that lets its inhabitants feel at home.

Designing the right density

Is there an objectively optimum density to ensure that an area will be beautiful, vibrant, or livable? On the surface, it would seem not. An acceptable density must be designed to take into account a number of considerations: context and of culture; the arrangement and structure of the campus's spaces; and walking distance.

Context and culture

What feels like just the right density in one place may feel too spread out or too dense in another. Buildings on campuses in rural or remote sub-urban areas may feel comfortably close to one another at distances that in urban settings would feel distressingly undeveloped. The University of Colorado at Boulder, for example, has created a master plan that allows a maximum density in its most dense area that is about half the density of Brown University in Providence. In Iona College in New Rochelle, New York, adding infill buildings was not the issue it might have been in a more rural location. New Rochelle itself is quite dense and proximate to New York City, so the infill development didn't violate the people's sense of openness and space, and the added density seemed reasonable.

For colleges and universities located far from an urban center without the benefit of an adjacent college-town neighborhood, urban density may be inappropriate. But, in the context of the setting, planners and administrators must still take care to create on campus a level of density that maximizes meetings of students, faculty, and staff. Sweet Briar College and Hollins University are both located in rural settings but have created vitality in a compact core campus.

Where no neighboring town provides community, vitality, and activities for the students, the institution itself must create an environment that fosters them. The University of South Florida at Tampa, located in a suburban setting, has deliberately allowed a higher density on its campus to create the needed feeling of a city center on campus.

Arrangement and structure

Density works together with enclosure, green space, mixed use, and a pedestrian scale to create vital spaces on campus. The structure and pattern with which these elements are assembled over the core campus area and extend toward the neighboring functions is important. A large recreation center surrounded by a vast parking lot does not create the kind of density of use and interaction that is conducive to a rich community life. Neither does a high-rise dormitory surrounded by open parkland. All of these elements are necessary, but they work best when the parking is in human-scaled courtyards or on the street, when the green space is sheltered and surrounded by interesting functions, when the buildings relate to people's movement at ground-level, and when the functions blend one into the next over a short walking distance.

Walking distance

None of the metrics of physical campus density predicts the density of interaction that is conducive to collegiality, community, and learning on a particular campus, but there is an optimum size for a densely developed community. Planners increasingly rely on the idea of the ten-minute walking circle for academic uses, reflecting the time limit for changing classes. When they are not faced with a short time limit, and when the walk is pleasant, people will walk up to fifteen to twenty minutes. Urban studies have shown that beyond this point, people will tend to drive rather than walk, with concomitant need for more parking, deterioration of the environment, and reduction of the number of chance interactions while en route. On campus, some faculty members may demand two dedicated parking spaces—one near their office or lab and another by the classroom building where they teach. Students will feel the need for parking near the classrooms as well as at the residence hall. Increasing parking may start a vicious cycle that spreads even more of the campus beyond a reasonable walking distance.

As institutions increase the number of their students, faculty, and other people on campus, they need more space. The amount of space needed per hundred or thousand new students varies from one campus to another, but eventually, some growing campuses become so developed that it is no longer possible to go from one location to another in a ten-minute's walk between classes. This ten-minute class-change time equates to about 2,400 feet from desk to desk (*not* doorway to doorway). This, in turn, depending upon the characteristics of the campus, limits the core campus area to a maximum size of about fifty-five to seventy acres. Each core campus area, again depending on the building density of the institution, will serve a limited number of students, faculty, and staff. The planner

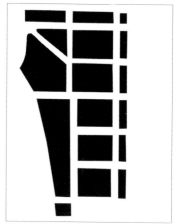

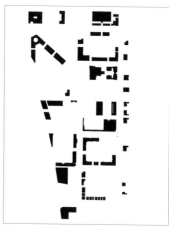

University of Scranton
Top: Master plan model
Middle: Street blocks framework
Bottom: Building framework

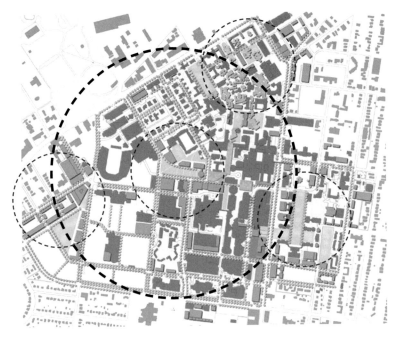

The larger circle indicates the approximate ten-minute class-change distance overlayed on the four districts at Vanderbilt University

Christopher Alexander[7] suggests that the optimum city or town community size is about 7,000 people. Many universities are larger than this. Beyond this approximate limit, institutions should consider the creation of additional core centers rather than increasing the amount of sprawl.

One major university that has about 15,000 students and a total community size of about 35,000 long ago grew from its original historic core campus area to two core areas. But it has now outgrown even two centers. The master-planning process allowed the university to balance its desire to be one community against the constraints that size imposed, and to strengthen each of its component communities to achieve a more human scale. The university has decided to move some of the functions in its overcrowded centers to new campus centers now being created. Each center will be more physically self-sustaining, providing all its community's necessary functions within a ten-minute walk.

Benefits of density

Although the density measurements may vary widely depending on culture, context, and the area under consideration, compact campus development is clearly important.

More conducive to learning

The student at Boston University burst into his Latin classroom two minutes late—as usual. The other students could set their clocks by his arrival amid a flurry of books, papers, and apologies. Red-faced and out of breath, he had run several blocks from his music class, but he could never run fast enough to make it in just the ten-minute period between classes. He would have the same problem again when Latin ended because his next class was back in the music building. Although located in an urban, lively environment that is the envy of many schools, Boston University's campus, spread out a mile or more along Boston's Commonwealth Avenue, is itself not very compact. Resignedly, students and professors adjusted themselves to the student's habitual lateness.

This student was lucky. He had the self-confidence to show up late and a professor and classmates who tolerated his disruptive arrival with good-natured resignation. A recent study at the University of Maryland[8] showed that close to 30 percent of all students who had scheduled back-to-back classes could not get from their first class to the second within the allotted ten-minute class-change time. More than three fourths (77 percent) of the students in the survey reported a number of significant adverse impacts of this insufficiently compact campus on their ability to learn:

- Classroom disruptions as some students are forced to leave class early or arrive late
- Insufficient time for some students (39 percent) to finish exams in class
- Inability or unwillingness of a significant percentage (11 percent) of students to attend class at all
- Limitation of student contact with faculty (and each other) before or after class
- Disproportionate impact on freshmen, probably affecting the university's retention rate

The problem, once identified, was troublingly hard to fix. The obvious solution—modifying the class-change time from ten to fifteen minutes—was (according to university sources) too costly, requiring reprogramming of the university's course registration system. Other changes in schedule or building location were either difficult or controversial. In the end, all the university could do was to issue a warning to students who attempted to schedule back-to-back classes with too-long walk times and to plan to study the effect of this change again. With a more dense campus, the issue might never have arisen in the first place.

Given the changing nature of academic teaching and learning styles and the softening of disciplinary boundaries, flexibility in the academic core is becoming a requirement on more and more campuses. Greater density, by improving the closeness of buildings and departments, helps to provide that needed flexibility.

Community

A compact environment increases the number of unique moments when one person crosses paths with another and has a possibility of interaction. They may smile and say hello; they may stop for a chat; or they may just be aware of each other's presence. These intersections allow people the opportunity to communicate, to exchange goods, services, and ideas, or just to see and be seen. This simple contact generates vitality in the space and encourages people to spend time, making more intersections possible, leading to more contact, generating more vitality and more desire to be there, and so on. In a densely built and lively community, people are more likely to run into one another than in a spread-out one. Creating the right kind of density is all about creating human intersections—and intersections and the collegiality they generate are at the heart of community on campus.

A sense of place and a place for everyone

Suburban-style campuses are the ones where the authors hear the most complaints about isolation and lack of community, about a need for more interdisciplinary communication and more interaction among students and faculty. There is no sense of the whole. A common complaint from students on large, sprawling campuses is, "I feel like a tiny ant here. I can't connect to this place."

Small sprawling campuses in rural settings can be unattractive to prospective students precisely because of this feeling of isolation. "There was nothing there," said one prospective student who visited Hampshire College in rural Massachusetts. "It was too spread out for how small it was."

Our colleges and universities have dense roots—many of our oldest campuses started in one building (e.g., Brown, Princeton, and Harvard Universities) or in one small cluster of buildings. Densely built campuses still tend to be oriented around one or more recognizable centers full of people and activities. There is definitely *something* there.

Freedom from the automobile

Given an equal (and not too great) distance, people are more willing to walk when the way to their destination is full of interesting sights and other people they might meet. They are also more willing to walk if the pedestrian way is clearly laid out. Walking promotes health as well as neighborly interaction. In less dense settings, with nothing of interest between the trip's origin and destination, people are more likely to drive. One person recalls with pleasure his walks to the store to get milk when he lived in a teeming urban neighborhood. Now a suburbanite, he drives to the nearest store—and is surprised to discover that the distance is the same as it was in his old neighborhood.

Safety

The more spread out a campus is, the less safe people feel. Roadways, paths, and parking lots that are not bordered by buildings are harder for people to keep an eye on. Conversely, areas surrounded by occupied buildings and areas where people are out and about feel much safer. People also feel safer when they can see the path leading to where they are going, when it is not isolated, and when other people are visible along the way.

Efficiency

The close proximity of buildings in a dense environment increases operating efficiency. Buildings placed close together can create microclimates that positively affect energy usage. They can afford protection from the hot summer sun by creating adjacent shade, thus cooling both interior and exterior environments. In the winter, the same buildings can store and capture warmth or shield from winter wind.

Initial sketch for the University of Scranton residential quadrangle envisioned a tight and efficient grouping of buildings

The initial infrastructure cost of bringing utilities (including heating, water, electricity, telephone, and computer cabling) to support a new building can be well over $1000 per linear foot. This initial cost is minimized by proximity, as is the long-term efficiency of operating and maintaining these utility systems.

Dispersal forces people to drive, either through distance or through preference, thereby increasing construction and maintenance costs of additional roadways, parking, and other transportation infrastructure. Grouping buildings together can minimize street and walkway length to serve those buildings. On a more dense campus area, a smaller percentage of the land is required for roadways and parking. The average initial construction cost of a two-lane street, including street surface, pedestrian walkways, curb, and lighting can be $550 to $625 per linear foot, and this additional roadway must be maintained. In addition, buildings placed too far apart require additional parking, which can run from $2,000 to over $14,000 per space. Additional maintenance costs incurred when buildings are built far apart includes installation and maintenance of lawn and other landscaped areas, and perhaps the need to provide additional security.

Better land utilization, preserving options for the future

Infill buildings can often serve multiple functions. They provide more than just dormitory beds or space for classes. Properly situated and designed, they can also help frame and structure the spaces of the campus.

On campuses with sufficient land, densely building the core area can preserve the natural environment much more effectively than spreading out the buildings over all the available land.

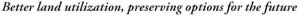

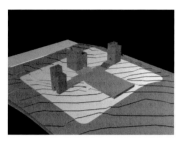

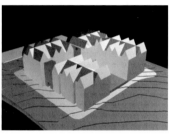

Infill along primary pedestrian paths at the University of Scranton provides an opportunity to create a rich residential environment

Although some facilities administrators feel that they are preserving options for the future by spreading out campus development, the opposite is true. More options are available—at less cost—for unbuilt land than for land already occupied by scattered buildings, parking, and roadways.

Actions for optimizing density on campus

We need to stop shying away from density on our campuses. It offers far too many advantages for enhancing learning, community, and collegiality. The right degree of compactness for a particular campus or part of a campus depends on many factors, including environmental context, topography, climate, and culture. For its unique situation, each institution should strive to develop an appropriate *degree* and *quality* of density to foster contact, community, and interaction on campus. To meet this challenge, institutions must use a process involving guidelines, careful design, and campus community input.

· *Establish campus guidelines and principles for appropriate density.* Visualizing in three dimensions, using tools such as models and renderings, is crucial; plans alone are not enough. Traditional measures, such as Floor Area Ratios, by themselves are not enough. In response to a commitment to a walking range, together with the "feel" of a place appropriate to the location, region, and character of the campus, institutions can begin to establish their own metrics for FAR, building coverage, height, massing, and other qualities that can guide future development.

· *Ensure vitality in the heart of the campus.* Institutions should find ways to capitalize and expand upon the often-stunning assets of the iconic campus core. Buildings and open spaces in the core should be restored and well maintained. New buildings may be added—respectfully. Uses should be selected for these areas that bring people to them during a large portion of the day.

· *Look for opportunities to infill within the existing built campus framework to enhance proximity, intensity of use, sense of place, and vitality.* Infill development should capitalize on existing major pedestrian corridors and open space.

· *Repair existing undefined districts.* Poor planning of the past can be repaired. Institutions should identify the strong features of existing favored districts and emulate them in the weaker districts, avoiding copying style but instead replicating density, open space definition, and mixture of uses.

· *Create new campus districts when needed.* Campuses occupying an area that is more than a ten- or fifteen-minute walk across may require division into two or more individual campus districts. Each district should have a compact plan with a clear identity and an iconic space. Its center should enhance vitality and provide intensity of use all day long.

· *Envision large campus programs such as recreation, performance, and student centers as groups of buildings rather than as single, massive buildings.* By planning these large uses as if they were small districts of independent but linked buildings, institutions can weave them into the existing fabric of the campus around usable courtyards and other spaces.

· *Respect community density values.* Every campus is unique. Those developing and approving long-range campus plans must sense and respect their own comfort levels about density, but they should also be open to change. They should study local densities carefully and should understand the densities of some of the college and university districts and college towns that they cherish.

· *Balance density issues carefully.* The planning process must reach an equilibrium between the community's desire for proximate parking, for preserving green space, beloved vistas, and a sense of openness, and for respecting site conditions on the one hand; and on the other, its need for better academic adjacencies, greater community and vitality, and cost-effective use of resources.

Top: The main quadrangle at Iowa State University offers tremendous potential to add vitality through infill
Middle and bottom: The campus center at the University of Scranton is designed as a grouping of smaller buildings

Many American college and university campuses have become distinctly un-collegiate places. To become more collegiate and vital places, most of these campuses must develop centers that are more compact and dense with human interactions. The campus can serve as a model of the collegiate excellence, cultural richness, physical benefits, and fiscal common sense that density can provide.

ten

A Mixture of Campus Uses

One main goal for creating or updating a campus master plan is to address a perceived lack of collegiality and community on the campus. Campuses lacking a sense of community are often zoned with discreet areas for academic, residential, recreational, and other uses—a separation that can have serious adverse effects on campus collegiality and community.

What is mixed use?

A vital and diverse campus. This fundamental aspiration of today's institutional leaders was also the aspiration of the early campus founders who espoused the ideal of the living and learning campus. The founders envisioned a collegiate place where seeing colleagues—fellow student and professor alike—was a common event. Because of this, the university promoted the exchange of ideas vital to the educational mission. It made possible the meeting of individuals from diverse backgrounds, and created some of the students' most enduring personal relationships. This was accomplished at early colleges and universities in part by mixing many campus uses together in one compact district or even in a single building. Sadly, many of today's campuses have—perhaps inadvertently—moved far from the living and learning ideal of our earliest campus environments.

A college or university requires multiple activities to accomplish its mission. These activities collectively comprise the uses of the campus's various buildings and facilities. On campuses, the major categories of uses are academic; research; residential; offices and support services (such as the physical plant, storage, and printing facilities); sports and recreation; student services (including coffee shops, dining, bookstores, movies, and extracurricular organizations); and parking. Physically mingling these uses within a single building or in a group of buildings arranged in such a way that they utilize common spaces collectively over an extended period of time is known as *mixed use*.

> The district...must serve more than one primary function; preferably more than two. These must insure the presence of people who go outdoors on different schedules and are in the place for different purposes, but who are able to use many facilities in common.[1]
>
> - JANE JACOBS

The mall at Texas State University
Top: A quiet time between classes
Bottom: Class change time

Use patterns

To achieve the community interaction that institutions want, the various uses have to be close enough together so that people can move easily from one to another. Jane Jacobs's observation about cities is also true of campuses: They fail when they do not respond appropriately to the hour-by-hour patterns of individual activities. When the uses are separated, some parts of the campus are intensely active at some times of the day—and decidedly inactive the rest.

The academic district

If academic use is exclusive to a district, then institutions will tend to have a pattern of use that is active only during the hours when classes are scheduled. At traditional residential institutions, the academic district is particularly busy during the heavily scheduled times from 10 A.M. to 2 P.M. By late afternoon, the district can be dead because students have moved on to other activities such as clubs, sports, homework and lab work, and dinner. Some of the more lively campus academic districts are the ones that have expanded to encompass residential or community-oriented uses, or where the academic district is also used for evening classes or community education during non-peak hours. Housing that is adjacent to the campus core, or that over time has become surrounded by academic buildings, is usually among the most desirable housing on campus, and on nights and weekends it brings to the academic district activity that is valued by the entire campus community.

Changes in academic pedagogy, including more group work and student-directed learning, and changes in student study patterns demand a new look at learning environments. The access that students need to computers, to group study areas, and to informal study spaces can be provided most effectively by an environment that combines these uses in buildings and spaces with easy access to food service. The study patterns of today's students almost demand a mixed-use environment. This mixture of uses can also benefit the institution, enlivening the academic district during off-peak hours.

Increased emphasis on involving undergraduates in research and on mixed graduate/undergraduate programs also suggests new building use patterns, as classrooms and research labs may have to be located closer together. In addition, institutions may want to consider other changes that create opportunities for these two populations to interact. For example, in its new master plan, Hollins University relocated the graduate studies program from a facility outside the academic core into a renovated and expanded space in the core of the campus to make it more visible and accessible to undergraduate students.

Research laboratories

Because the often-intense nature of the work requires ideally almost twenty-four-hour access to these facilities, mixing research and teaching laboratories in with classrooms activates the academic part of the campus during hours outside normal class time. Also, professors typically prefer to have their research laboratories next to their offices, in the academic center of the campus. Today, however, these laboratories are often moved to the campus perimeter because of the need to build more classrooms within the ten-minute class time change of the academic core. Research investment by government and large private corporations, with concomitant security requirements, also tends to isolate the research function. Removing research from the core areas of the campus, however, has had the unfortunate result of removing graduate students and some of the star teachers themselves from the campus core, to the detriment of the entire community.

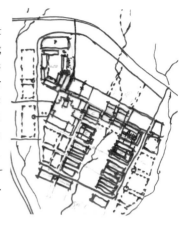

The scale of the required architecture also separates research from other campus functions, even when it is located near them. Research laboratory buildings are typically much larger than traditional academic campus buildings. Many times, students and professors are not the only workers in these facilities. A private work force demanding its own parking and facilities creates an environment much like a suburban office park—automobile-dominated, single-use districts. Examples of this phenomenon are Princeton Forrestal Center, the Research Triangle of North Carolina, and the University of Utah Research Campus.

Research laboratories are tightly linked with offices and administration on the new Mayo Clinic campus in Phoenix, Arizona

Ironically, this sort of isolation inhibits the very nature of research. Many of the greatest breakthroughs in science occur in the interstices between disciplines. Bringing researchers from different departments together is increasingly important. One way to do this, even if the research campus

Mixed-use village center at Princeton Forrestal research campus

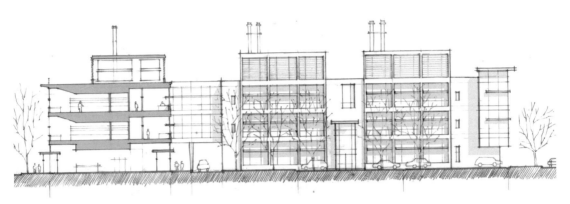

The new research campus at Utah State University envisions a mixed-use environment to complement the research facilities

is separated from the rest of the university, is to mix the departments (respecting the requirements for specific types of labs and facilities). If for proprietary reasons this is not possible, another method is to provide common campus functions that can be shared by all research departments. A number of research facilities can be organized around a common courtyard, sharing a cafeteria or café, administration facilities, and so on, as planned in the new campus for the Mayo Clinic in Phoenix, Arizona and the Innovation Campus at Utah State University in Logan, Utah. As populations in these research areas rise, the need for support facilities, such as copy centers and cafés, increases so that the researchers don't have to leave the campus to find a meal or run an errand. Further adding to the vitality of the area would be a conference center, inn, or hotel (with associated restaurants) to support visiting researchers and visitors from private corporations.

But why remove these facilities from the main campus at all? In many cases, research facilities might be built at the edges of the original campus, where access by outside workers is convenient, the required parking can be provided, and administrative support can be shared. In addition, faculty, graduate students, and others using the research laboratories can have access to the many facilities available on campus. Graduate housing is generally not in the core campus, but in peripheral areas. Graduate research laboratories at the edge of the campus can be located conveniently close to this housing, which might in turn blend into a residential neighborhood beyond.

Residence halls

After World War II, new residential districts, separate from the academic functions, were created on most campuses. This change paralleled the creation of residential suburbs and "bedroom communities" in American cities. Urban planners have re-learned since then that residential life closely intertwined with other activities (offices, retail, and entertainment) ensures not only the vitality but also the economic success of cities and towns. The same is true on campus.

Many institutions not only separate the residential use from other uses, but they also separate student class years from one another. First-year students in particular are often segregated into separate residence halls to ensure that they meet one another, establishing class unity and class recognition. Administrators in university development departments often cite these factors as key in fostering a long-term relationship beyond graduation and in alumni giving to the institution. While acknowledging the reasons for class segregation, how can institutions encourage interaction and learning from older peers, graduate students, and professors? In addition to mixing residential and academic uses, institutions can also mix student class years and professors in the same residence hall. This is the hallmark of the residential-college system, where professors and students of all ages live, eat, and study together, forming lasting friendships with one another and intense bonds with the institution.

The residential-college approach is gaining adherents among many leading institutions. Vanderbilt University, which historically created residence halls segregated by year and housing type, is in 2003 in the process of restructuring its residential-life program into a number of small residential colleges. The university is retooling existing facilities to accommodate professors and their families as well as undergraduate first-year and upper-division students. At Loyola Marymount University in Los Angeles, even the president lives in an apartment in one of the student residence halls.

Living/learning communities are also gaining institutional interest. By locating classrooms and other study areas within a residence hall, an institution can provide facilities for educational programs of particular relevance to the students who live there. It can also use these facilities to draw others in. The University of North Texas, for example, plans to use classrooms in one of its residence halls for class meetings of distance- and hybrid-education students who do not live on campus.

Many suburban residential communities are essentially segregated by wealth. The same segregation also occurs in campus residential life when more money is charged for more desirable housing. Utah State University is mixing highly desirable singles as well as doubles and triples on one floor, so that the different costs of these room types does not segregate the students from one another, either by wealth or by their year at the university.

Offices and support services

Professors generally like to have their offices near a majority of their classrooms. But cross-disciplinary contact requires that the offices and classrooms of one department not be isolated. To improve interdepartmental communication, the offices of several departments should be mixed together or adjacent. Common functions, such as a coffee lounge, administrative assistant and graduate offices, library, and copying area, should be provided in areas shared among departments to efficiently use services and space and—more importantly—to facilitate the exchange of ideas among individuals and departments.

In many institutions, administrative offices are the first use removed from the center of the campus when space is short. This approach is reasonable but may not always be the best. Often, when this is done, administrators feel isolated from the students they serve. The camaraderie of being part of one place is lost, and the student perception of a faceless bureaucracy is increased. In addition, when the institutional offices are isolated from the core campus, the administrative part of the campus (whole groups of buildings in large universities) tends to go dead after 5 P.M. and on weekends, when the administrative staff is not there. This issue is shared by downtowns that are dominated by office use. The solution is the same as well. Mixing offices in with other uses benefits all.

Sports and recreation use

Sports and recreation are typically isolated from the main part of the campus, in part because of the large amount of land needed. Historically, however, many schools have had sports and recreation integrated into the hearts of their campuses. The central green of Wesleyan University in Connecticut, for example, is a playing field. Lehigh University once had—and Rensselaer Polytechnic Institute still does have—the football field in the heart of the campus. Utah State University's stunning main quadrangle also serves as a primary intramural field, creating a place of great vitality after the academic day winds down—from about 3 P.M. until nightfall.

The main quadrangle at Utah State University provides fields for intramural sports programs

Sacred Heart University, historically a commuter school with limited land resources, is adding intramural activities to the main quadrangle of the campus, surrounded by academic, library, and chapel, to encourage students to stay on campus after class. This change will benefit the center district of the campus as well as the intramural program itself with increased attendance and participation.

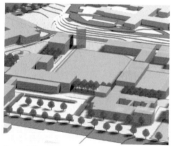

Sacred Heart University:
Proposed new quadrangle

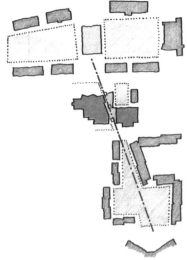

Merrimack College has mixed
the uses of a campus center
and a student recreation
center in a single building

Merrimack College has mixed the uses of a campus center and a student recreation center in a single building. The building was designed to allow these activities to be seen either while walking the central street of the building interior or when participating in either activity. Students can sip coffee at a café and watch their peers playing basketball or exercising. Even more dramatically, large areas of glass on the building perimeter allow these activities to be seen from outside the building, acting as a great beacon for the center of campus.

Student services

The student or campus center is a modern manifestation. It provides a number of functions needed for student life and shares a number of attributes with commercial shopping malls. The functions within the student center are conveniently close to one another and protected against the weather. The center also provides an important venue in which students can see and be seen. It also shares some of the mall's weaknesses. By isolating its functions from others on the campus, a student center can, ironically, contribute to lack of community on the campus as a whole. The inwardly oriented student center at George Mason University was so successful that community and activity suffered on the rest of the campus. Like a shopping mall, it provides many functions that students want—library, café, bookstore, mailroom, bank machine, and so on—all within one building. And like a mall, the functions face inward. Large, inactive walls and undefined grass strips face the neighboring parts of the campus; the intensity and activity within the building does not spill outward to invigorate the rest of the campus.

Other alternatives exist. Today's mixed-use market centers, like public squares and business streets, provide people with the shopping benefits of proximity and variety. Market centers also provide a wealth of activities that people seek in addition to shopping, such as restaurants and cafés, post offices, printing services, and banking. This model has been applied successfully on several campuses. Sweet Briar College combined several separated campus functions such as student organizations, dining, café, financial offices, and bookstore, and arranged these uses in "storefronts" surrounding an exterior square. Above most of these uses are residence halls, which ensure activity in and around the square eighteen hours a day. In addition to creating a lively campus center, this idea highlighted sustainable building practices and reduced cost by combining new construction with reuse of underutilized existing space.

Institutions embedded in lively campus neighborhoods can take advantage of their proximity to the neighborhood, and in fact can strengthen this connection, by moving many of the campus student-service uses to the public street. For example, Brown University's bookstore is located

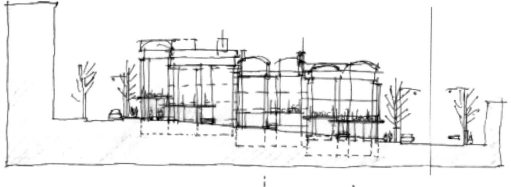

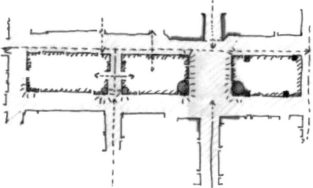

Lehigh University created a student service district when re-thinking its student center

on Thayer Street, a lively adjacent commercial street. In fact, some dormitories are built with shops facing Thayer Street on the first floor. The bookstore for Wesleyan University is on Main Street in Middletown, Connecticut. Lehigh University has moved its bookstore, as well as several other services and shops from the center of campus, to the campus perimeter with the adjacent South Bethlehem retail district. Above and adjacent to these uses, they have added residential uses in order to strengthen this new neighborhood edge—to the benefit both of campus life and the adjacent retail district.

Parking use

Everyone wants to park at the front door of his or her destination. Creating large parking lots in the center of the campus, however, can overwhelm other uses, creating a barren and hostile-feeling space. To retain a mixture of uses in the campus center, structured parking can be provided. Although it is generally seen as a desirable solution, structured parking is four times more expensive than surface parking. Further, structured parking alone does not fully address the need for mixed uses in the campus core because parking garages typically lack active uses at the ground floor. Both the cost of the garage structure and the lack of activity at its edge can be addressed at the same time. Ohio State University and other institutions have activated the ground floor of parking structures by adding uses such as cafés, book stores, print shops, and so on. These uses generate revenue

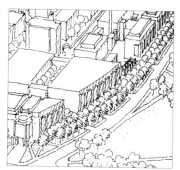

The Ohio State University parking structures with café and bookstore at street level

to augment the fees from parking. By placing the parking structure in a location convenient to facilities that attract the general public, such as sports, arts, entertainment, or conference facilities, an institution can both generate additional revenue from the parking structure and enhance the activity in nearby spaces. Building residences around the perimeter of the garage, as Lehigh University has done, generates revenue, activates the garage perimeter with twenty-four-hour residential use, and provides residences that are highly desirable to students, who will often pay more to have their cars close to where they live.

Factors working against mixed use

In most eighteenth- and nineteenth-century colleges, all the uses occurred in close proximity, if not in the same building. Few American campuses today still use this model. Instead, paralleling the general urban-development trends since World War II, we have drifted to a model where the functions are spread out. Research stands in isolated enclaves. Academic buildings are located in one area and residence halls in another. Where private developers have built campus housing, these residential buildings may in fact be located off campus, often not even within walking distance.

Several factors have undermined the ideal of the living and learning campus and have led to our present condition:

· Desire for organizational clarity
· Academic competition and the drive for program identity
· Separate ownership of facilities

Desire for organizational clarity

Many people on campuses where functions are dispersed and separated from one another find this model of development clear, organized, and attractive. From the perspective of a facilities manager, the costs and revenues of each use can be clearly understood and managed. Ironically, dispersing these uses usually creates physical inefficiencies with concomitant increased cost of construction, operation and maintenance.

Academic competition and the drive for program identity

The desire for a separate program identity can sometimes drive one department or school to establish its location apart from the mixed districts of the central campus. These separate enclaves of individual programs stifle interaction among academic peers. They tend to be marked by underutilized teaching space while other campus programs scramble for such space; and they promote the use of cars to travel back and forth from the core campus.

Academic competition, too, has contributed to the isolation of campus uses from one another. A competitive spirit can encourage innovation and new ideas. But when competition arises not only among peer institutions but among academic units of the *same* institution, it can go too far. Seeking to differentiate themselves from their peers at other schools and to attract the best students, academic departments feel they must offer the best facilities. To afford those facilities, departments compete for donor gifts. Gifts given to one school become the property of that school rather than of the institution as a whole; and the school uses the money to further its own priorities rather than institutional priorities, perhaps building new academic facilities without the vital mix of campus uses and departments common to the original campus districts or buildings. The need for proximate housing on campus, for recreation, for food, for places to "hang out" is seen as someone else's problem—a problem that often seems to lack money to create a solution. What is best for the institution becomes second to the goals of the individual school or administrative unit.

The Darden School for Business at the University of Virginia received a large gift, which it used to move its academic functions from the main area of the campus to a remote area accessible mainly by automobile or shuttle bus. No housing was created in this new district, which is, not surprisingly, quiet outside of classroom hours. If it wants to enliven this district, the university will need to add residential housing and other uses, in effect creating another campus center for the business school.

Separate ownership of facilities

On many campuses, an individual department may "own" a building or facility, taking it out of the pool for university-wide use. When classrooms, labs, and common spaces become the property of a particular department rather than a common asset shared by the entire institution, the excellent facilities within one school may have extremely low utilization while other academic units of the same institution deal with overcrowding or physically inadequate space. This inefficiency not only leads to building and maintaining excessive academic space, but also creates barriers to interdepartmental study and cross-fertilization. At Ithaca College, the constituencies that felt most deprived by the School of Music's singular ownership of its building were the students and younger professors of the school itself. They would have enjoyed opportunities to run into more of their peers from other schools more of the time. In this case, mixing academic uses among a variety of departments in the one building would have been an improvement for all departments.

Active pedestrian paths of
Texas A&M University

Benefits of mixed use

The social, academic, and fiscal benefits of mixing campus uses include:

· Increased collegiality and community
· Enhanced learning
· Safety
· Competitive admissions
· Flexibility for growth

Each of these is discussed below.

Increased collegiality and community

Perhaps the most positive aspect of mixed use is an increase in the potential for greater interaction on campus and the feeling of community that this interaction engenders. Bringing diverse uses in close proximity increases the number of people present in an area as well as the amount of time they are likely to be there. This, in turn, improves the probability that their paths will cross. The more that people's paths cross and intersect, the more a campus—or a town—feels like a community and a place to be cherished.

Enhanced learning

Numerous sources[2] cite studies showing that academic performance is improved when students live near their classes. Some institutions have had success in putting classrooms into the student residence halls, creating living-learning communities. Residential college systems mixing undergraduates, graduate students, and professors of an institution stimulate students and professors alike and provide the opportunity for continuous learning and discussion of ideas outside the classroom.

Safety

Single-use districts, whether academic, residential, or recreational, are unoccupied for large portions of the day or night. Vacant and deserted, they contribute to the perception, if not the reality, of a lack of campus safety.

Mixing uses improves both the reality and perception of campus safety by activating campus districts around the schedules and patterns of campus activities throughout the entire day. It capitalizes on these normal patterns of activity to put people in contact with one another because they have reason to be there—whether working, teaching, studying, or relaxing.

Competitive admissions

A less obvious benefit to the ongoing activity of a mixed-use environment is its attractiveness to prospective students and parents. The campus that looks lively, collegial, and safe makes a powerful first impression on a campus tour.

Flexibility for growth

Some institutions resist mixing uses on their campuses because they fear that doing so would rob them of needed flexibility for the future. This apprehension typically arises when discussing putting residential uses among the academic ones. These institutions are concerned that mixing these uses would leave less room for the academic facilities they will need in the future. Though the core of academic facilities should be within walking distance of one another during the ten-minute class change time, ample room is often available to insert appropriately sized enclaves of residential use among academic and administrative uses. Many times this proximity has the added advantage of overcoming students' perceived need to have their automobiles on campus.

Housing near the academic and administrative areas of the older core campus, unlike housing developed on the campus periphery, often has the added benefit of also being near the most beautiful and sacred areas on campus. This location is frequently the most treasured by the students who have a chance to live there. An extreme example of this—though far from the only one—is the University of Virginia, where students vie for a chance to live in Jefferson's "academical village" even though they suffer a long outdoor trek to the bathrooms.

Where larger campuses encompass multiple districts beyond the core academic area, like Ohio State University and Vanderbilt University, these campuses should have a balance of uses and identifiable centers in *each district*. Research districts for example, should have a complement of housing, open space, food service, convenience, and other uses, thus choreographing the various usage patterns into an attractive liveliness in the district for the entire day.

Initiatives to promote the mixed-use campus

Even institutions with highly dispersed, use-separated campuses can take steps, both immediately and over time, to attain the vibrant feel of a mixed-use campus. Every campus planning or building-programming project provides an opportunity. Individual institutions may find many other opportunities as well when considering space allocation, departmental priorities, capital allocations, or other topics.

When the situation arises, institutions should seek opportunities to mix uses within *individual buildings* whenever possible. This can include:

· Intermingling similar functions, such as offices or classrooms, of different departments and schools of the institution

· Incorporating residential use above social uses such as student organizations and cafés

· Placing synergistic uses, such as recreation and a campus center, or a library and a campus center, near one another

In addition to uses within single buildings, institutions should search for opportunities for *fine-grain mixing* of uses among buildings within the campus district. Academic, residential, administration, support, cafés, open space, and parking uses should be mixed in the appropriate proportion to one another. The goal is to orchestrate the patterns of usage so that it will enliven the district, create opportunities for the intersection of people and their ideas, and create a self-sufficient and efficient use of land and building resources.

Instead of dispersing functions, larger universities should create *multiple campus districts* with the attributes described above when the campus population is too large for a single district. Campus districts, like neighborhoods in cities and towns, should be no larger than two thousand feet across, the distance one can walk in approximately ten to fifteen minutes. Open space or streets should form strong connections between these districts. Each district should have an identifiable anchor or center of common activity and support, which would ideally draw not only district residents and users but also users from other districts.

Colleges and universities that are located within a city or town should create edges or other campus areas where campus constituents and outside community residents can mix. Either on the campus edge or within a district, institutions should consider incorporating residential, commercial, market, food and entertainment uses that draw a diversity of constituents and enliven the area for the greater part of the day.

Penn State University commercial district is adjacent to main entrance to campus

eleven

Landscape

If the plan orders the ideas and aspirations of the institution, the landscape expresses its soul and personality. One of the fundamental ways an institution can distinguish itself is through the development of a coherent and consistent landscape. People are attracted to unique places—places that resonate with the personality of the region they inhabit, that are dynamic and enduring. An inspired and well-implemented landscape establishes the campus's overall character and beauty, shapes the campus plan, and provides the campus with a sense of unity. It expresses how the institution belongs to a location, and at its best can also be a provocative and artful expression of its culture.

The transformative potential of a powerful landscape idea is rarely identified and utilized. Many of our campus landscapes today lack boldness, unity, and clarity. Solutions more often than not occur as a series of independent, unrelated measures taken on a project-by-project basis, damaging or destroying the unity of the campus. Numbers of well-meant unrelated donor gifts add pressure on some institutions to undertake various unrelated projects on their campuses. When Sasaki Associates first started working with Ohio State University, for example, the facilities staff had undertaken a large number of small, unrelated projects in different parts of the campus. While each project was pleasant, the overall effect was to diminish the unity of the campus. As one landscape architect put it, the campus as a whole "was dying of a thousand little paper cuts." When thinking about the landscape of the campus, it is critical to think holistically.

The occasional contemplation of natural scenes of an impressive character…is favorable to the health and vigor of men and especially to the health and vigor of their intellect beyond any other conditions which can be offered them….[1]

- FREDERICK LAW OLMSTED

The landscape master plan for Sweet Briar College utilizes a prominent campus dell as an ampitheater

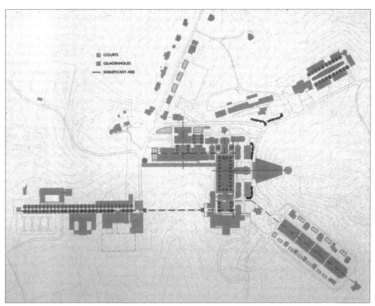

Role of the landscape

A well-ordered landscape structures and reinforces the big idea in the campus plan; defines the campus's outdoor spaces; provides, through pedestrian and vehicular circulation, effective means for movement of people, automobiles, and goods; expresses the institution's roots in its site and region; and expresses the institution's unique culture and identity.

Structuring and reinforcing the big idea in the plan

The landscape structures and reinforces the overall campus plan, making it tangible. Important places should be recognizable as unique and singularly important. On some campuses, such as Sweet Briar College, the landscape reinforces the plan, whose main idea is established by the organization of the campus uses and the architecture of the buildings. On others, the landscape is the defining element that structures the campus plan and gives the campus its unique identity. The 1910 Cram, Goodhue, and Ferguson General Plan for Rice University is a good example of this. As the architectural historian Stephen Fox explains, "Trees and hedgerows were specified in the General Plan as the components defining lines of view and movement volumetrically. More so than buildings, hedgerows and trees planted in allées reshape the vast, immeasurable, and monotonous space of the flat coastal plain, imposing rhythm, measure, direction, sequentiality, and hierarchy—what might in literary terms be called a narrative structure."[2]

STU DAWSON

The great spaces of Rice University are defined by both the landscape and the buildings

Defining space

The campus landscape defines the campus's spaces, providing the great outdoor "rooms" and places in which the campus community interacts. The importance of the campus open spaces for meeting, for education, for contemplation, and for communal activities cannot be overstated. These open spaces range from well-defined streets and room-like quadrangles and courtyards, to orderly, well-tended athletic fields, and to the natural forest preserves and agricultural fields of land-grant institutions. The primary landscape elements used to define many of these spaces are walls, hedges, lighting, topography, and trees.

The principal outdoor spaces at Connecticut College are a series of athletic fields with clearly defined borders of rows of trees framed by a consistent edge of buildings beyond. In contrast, the entire campus of Vassar College is an arboretum that provides an informal landscape setting for its buildings. Each of these landscapes is an appropriate response to the environment and culture of its institution. The composition, proportion, and material palettes of these spaces are crucial to campus beauty, efficiency, and vitality.

Left: The character of walks at Middlebury College was drastically altered with the demise of their stately elms
Right: Live oaks border the drive at Rice University

Providing circulation

Providing connections among the campus's outdoor spaces, its buildings, campus entries, and the areas beyond the campus perimeter requires a well-conceived system of circulation. Students and professors must move from building to building between classes; campus commuters arrive, depart, and search for proximate parking; goods must be brought to campus and refuse brought out. The orderly function of this system is critical to the institution.

The system of circulation provides the main connections between campus districts and features. Well designed, it is paramount to achieving and supporting campus community with patterns of movement that bring people into contact and connect campus activities. An example is the plan for the River of Trees at the Ohio State University. This plan creates a new and dramatic open space linking Mirror Lake Hollow to the Olentangy River in one direction and the river to the Oval at the core of the campus in the other. The design of the corridor integrates adjacent new buildings and site development into an overall concept that emphasizes continuity of pedestrian movement, diversity of landscape plantings, and framing of views to important campus destinations and landmarks.

Streets, walks, stairways, and arcades provide the campus with connective elements. Streets, whether part of a network of the surrounding urban community or internal to the university, should be defined by landscape elements that establish a hierarchy and clarity to the vehicular and pedestrian circulation of the campus. This definition can be accomplished through the consistent treatment of tree plantings that provide structure, walks that create a positive pedestrian experience, both vehicular- and pedestrian-scale lighting, and wayfinding signage. Within the campus, pedestrian walks and bikeways should connect destinations in a hierarchical way, focusing major pedestrian activity on primary desire lines, increasing opportunity for interaction while enhancing security through the volume of pedestrian activity. Stairs, where the topography requires them along major pedestrian ways, can provide an opportunity for creating places for people to pause with friends.

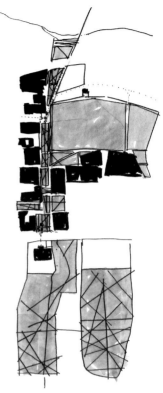

Connecting campus and region: understanding the context

When the campus expresses the nature of its site, its region, and the local culture, it also articulates the institution's commitment to regional distinctiveness. It does this through harmony with the regional landscape and the unique characteristics of the site itself, and through expression of the culture and history of the area. In an increasingly homogenous world, the uniqueness of place can be a powerful attraction to students and faculty. An understanding of the site and context can be the most potent driving force of form on campus.

The region

The campus landscape should reflect the essence and specific characteristics of the regional landscape. Wisely used, regional characteristics can instill a campus with a specific sense of place and sustainable, cost-effective operational efficiency. Regional characteristics include:

- *Ecology.* The local ecology comprises the interrelated natural systems of area.

- *Unique geology and topography.* Geology and topography might manifest in the flatness or hilliness of a campus, or its openness to views; or they might be indicated in an historical use of local building stone.

- *Hydrology.* Rivers and lakes and their respective waterfronts can add tremendous value and identity to a campus. Understanding more subtle hydrologic patterns such as groundwater conditions can dictate placement and function of building and campus exterior space such as athletic fields.

- *Vegetation.* Using local plant materials enhances the sense of campus identity through belonging to a specific place or region. Plant materials of the region can line campus streets and form hedgerows to define parking lots; the strong grids of trees can recall orchard country; and bold informal groves of trees can bind a campus to adjacent forests.

Top: Initial sketch for the "River of Trees" at the Ohio State University
Bottom: The gorge at Cornell University is a defining feature of the campus

· *Climate.* Adaptation to regional climate patterns is critical to creating efficient, comfortable, and enduring campus settings. Coordinated tree planting can substantially reduce summer and winter cost of building operation. Exterior spaces can be screened and shaded to promote comfort, use, and interaction.

At St. Edward's University in Austin, Texas, for example, one of the notable natural qualities is the climate, which is generally hot and dry. This has become a driving force in the form of the campus. Because of the oppressive heat, the university is planting hundreds of evergreen live oak trees, greatly increasing the number of this species on campus. This singular species, the largest shade tree native to the region, has become the dominant species on campus. The live oaks require little water, and they address the need for shade.

Built on a red rock plateau overlooking the Wyoming wilderness, Western Wyoming College participates in the beauty of its rugged natural surroundings. The buildings utilize the colors of their site, and the landscape reflects the beauty of the area. Because of its exposed, windy location, the campus landscape has been organized around small, sheltered courtyards where students can gather. Lawns are limited to these courtyard areas, while the natural rugged beauty of the site is retained in other parts of the campus.

The site of the campus

By working with the unique qualities of its site, the landscape design of a campus can express its institution's distinct identity. Vassar College is well aware of the role its campus plays in attracting and retaining students. "If you ask a Vassar student why she/he picked Vassar," states the college's Web site, "the answer almost always includes the campus."[3] The site of Vassar is a rolling landscape bisected by streams. The institution has capitalized on this site by developing an informal landscape composition in which trees are used to frame and enhance views of the buildings and the rolling hills beyond.

Preserving the integrity of the site does not mean that nothing can be touched or changed. However, where possible, campus projects should retain and enhance the natural features of the campus site and ecosystem.

Campus landscape should respond to the size of the site as well as its other unique characteristics. The unifying design of precious courtyard space on campuses with only a few acres is as important as the appropriate stewardship of campuses with thousands of acres of natural environment. Whether a campus is large or small, every square foot counts.

ANTON GRASSL

Vassar College

The courtyards at Stanford University express unique regional characteristics

Expressing the culture of the institution and region

In addition to the physical qualities of a campus's region and site, the landscape should express the social qualities of the institution's environment. The human influences on the landscape include:

· *Local history and culture.* From the symmetrical, formal layouts of some older, eastern campuses to the tight courtyards of the old south to the spaciousness of the west, many campuses have features that reflect the history, development, and culture of their regions.

· *Regulations and covenants.* Zoning encourages some types of development and discourages others. Regulations concerning building density, parking requirements, preservation of open space and trees, and other requirements all influence the overall composition and quality of the campus landscape.

· *Context of the existing built environment.* The landscape of institutions in urban areas is typically different from that in suburban or rural environments. The fabric of Boston University, for example, blends into the city blocks of the Commonwealth Avenue area of Boston so much that a visitor is sometimes hard pressed to distinguish a university facility from a private building. Off-street parking lots are mostly few and small, located unobtrusively behind buildings. Compare this to more rural Vassar College, whose landscape responds to its informal, forested setting.

· *Anticipated or observed behavior and use patterns on campus.* The needs and use patterns of the student population may influence the form of the campus landscape. Lack of residence halls and associated quadrangles and courtyards together with a greater need to park near academic buildings, for example, lend a different quality and functional imperative to commuter campuses than to residential campuses.

The campus of Stanford University strongly expresses its cultural history and values. The Richardsonian Romanesque style of its buildings and courtyards (developed by H. H. Richardson, one of the most famous architects of the late nineteenth century) reflects the European Romanesque style that evolved from the growth of abbeys and monasteries as cultural centers. The cultured European values of Stanford's founders, Leland and Jane Stanford, are also reflected in the formal Palm Drive main entrance to the campus. But the landscape architecture of the campus evokes as well the Romanesque Spanish mission style and the Laws of the Indies, which laid out in 1573 the principles for Spanish colonials to guide the construction of new settlements in the Americas.[4] These laws dictated that settlements be laid out around a colonnaded plaza faced by important buildings, with streets extended from the plaza to allow growth of the town with additional plazas over time. In fact, the growth of Stanford, with its new, additional quadrangles, is in complete harmony with this original vision and has come to epitomize the beauty of a Spanish-inspired American West campus.

Role of landscape in supporting institutional mission and objectives

Whether by specific design intent or not, the landscape of the campus makes a statement about the institution. The composition and definition of campus buildings, streets, entries, quadrangles, and courts should be arranged in an order that supports the institution's philosophies.

Sweet Briar College in Virginia was established at the turn of the past century in the rural foothills of Virginia's Shenandoah Mountains. The original purpose of the college was to establish a close-knit educational community for women. Collegiate architect Ralph Adams Cram translated this original premise into a stunning assemblage of buildings and spaces connected by porches and arcades, all of which surround intimately scaled courtyard classrooms that extend the classroom into the Virginia countryside beyond. By organizing the buildings into tight mixed-use groups—utilizing only fifty acres of the college's three-thousand-acre landholdings—the landscape composition responded strongly to the unique topography, views, and climate of the site. It also nurtured the community so desired by Sweet Briar's founders. The building-to-building and building-to-courtyard relationships promote the educational and communal imperatives of the institution as well as a connection to the land and regional climate. One hundred years later, that plan and philosophy were interpreted into a master plan for the college's next one hundred years. The new plan strengthened the physical and communal attributes of the original compact plan in existing campus districts and instituted them in new districts. These attributes are still stunningly relevant to the community and environment mission of the campus today.

The Cranbrook Schools in Bloomfield Hills, Michigan provide another excellent example of the evolution of the landscape to reflect both regional and cultural values. The schools were originally housed in a large country estate with extensive grounds surrounding the initial buildings. As the schools grew, new buildings were built around new courtyards, turning inward. Over time, the establishment of a number of exterior courtyards has integrated the original estate and the courtyard and building additions, to the enrichment of the campus as a whole. "What distinguishes Cranbrook from other educational complexes," the school proclaims on its Web site, "is not the types of institutions established—for there are great centers of learning the world over—but what was conceived and built on these grounds. At Cranbrook, institutions were conscientiously developed and designed to encourage individual growth and excellence by providing a built environment [integration of buildings with landscape] that promoted artistic, cultural, intellectual, and spiritual ideals. Here, students had only to look about them for proof that personal dreams and goals—no matter how grand—can be accomplished."[5]

Benefits of great campus landscapes

A well-designed campus landscape provides both human and environmental benefits. Institutions with beautiful campuses know this and emphasize their landscape on their Web sites and on campus visits. The University of Missouri, Columbia, for example, describes its campus as "…a garden; a place of beauty; a distinct community that creates an outstanding and lasting impression of the University."[6]

Human benefits

At least as much as the fine buildings of which many institutions are justifiably proud, the campus landscape creates an overall impression of beauty on the campus. "One of the University's most valuable resources is the beauty of the campus landscape," wrote Harold T. Shapiro, president of Princeton University. "The landscape is similar to a work of art in the powerful responses to beauty it is capable of eliciting from us, and the pleasure it gives us."[7] The sensory richness of color, texture, and scale in the landscape contribute to its beauty, and is also a deeply satisfying experience in itself.

Great landscapes enrich the human experience

People have an innate affinity for the natural environment. This affinity is reflected in the impact that natural environments have on people's ability to learn.

The campus landscape can provide a laboratory for classes in biology, ecology, and related work. But the learning connection goes even deeper. At times, the lawns, arcades, and courtyards of the campus become a natural setting in which both formal classes and informal studying can take place. Even when it is only observed through the windows of a classroom, the natural landscape contributes to the learning environment.[8]

Environmental benefits

Awareness about the environment is increasingly one of the criteria by which students judge whether they want to come to an institution. Many prospective students consult sustainability awards and lists such as the Top Ten Green Projects of the American Institute of Architects (AIA). The University Leaders for a Sustainable Future maintains a list of signatories of the Talloires Declaration—a ten-point commitment to sustainability that has now been signed by over three hundred college and university presidents and chancellors in more than forty countries (over one hundred in Canada and the United States). The environmental benefits of the campus landscape can be greatly improved by good planning and implementation. They include controlling erosion, thereby improving water quality in watersheds and aquifers; providing habitat for native animal and plant species; reducing energy costs through temperature amelioration; and reducing air pollution.

On the basis of beauty and tranquility alone, trees are valuable assets on campus. In addition, trees can provide great economic benefit through temperature amelioration. Deciduous trees in colder climates let sun in during the winter but shade buildings in the summer. Shade trees can cut air-conditioning bills in half when planted on the sunny side of the building. When used as windbreaks, trees and hedgerows can also cut heating bills in winter. Trees also provide stormwater control and wildlife shelter.

Existing Agricultural Features

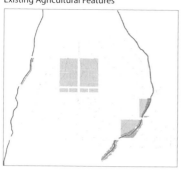

Urban Public Places

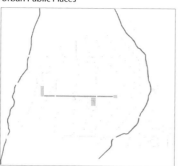

Green Public Spaces

Semi-private Gardens

Tree-lined Streets

Parking Canopies

Stormwater Strategy

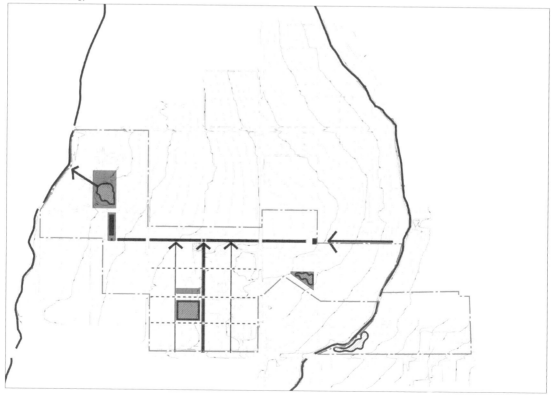

A quadrangle will replace a large parking lot at the research district of Michigan State University

Stewardship of landscape

The landscape is a living organism. A well conceived plan factors the growth and evolution of the landscape into their plans.

Duke University addressed this issue head-on. Ninety-five percent of the university's 1997 – 98 annual tree-maintenance budget was used to remove dead or dying trees and provide safety pruning. Little funding was available for preventive maintenance of larger, older trees. Therefore, Duke University's facilities department factored the campus's long-standing trees into its deferred-maintenance audit. Four hundred fifty trees were selected for this audit because of their size, age, and location near buildings and high-activity areas. The average worth of the trees in the sample, based on size, species, condition, and location, was established to be $15,600. Thus, the four hundred fifty trees—only 13 percent of Duke's major tree population—were worth about seven million dollars. The university's facilities department was able to use this valuation to justify a more proactive tree maintenance program.

Many institutions with a substantial amount of acreage and open space around the campus and buildings have developed the practice of maintaining much of it as turf. As an alternative in rural areas, institutions might look into reducing the acreage of high-maintenance lawns and manicured lands in favor of low-maintenance landscapes such as meadow and restored wildlife habitat. In accordance with its master plan, Northfield-Mt. Hermon School is keeping maintained land in the central campus spaces while converting the rest of the land at the campus perimeter to meadow that flows into the surrounding forests and agricultural lands. This strategy is visually appropriate for a school in a rural setting, as well as cost-effective.

Michigan State University has developed a landscape master plan that connects the diverse districts of the campus to the wooded historic core

Landscape master plan for
Vanderbilt University

through a series of expanded and boldly reforested campus avenues. This restored the native forest of the region to areas that had been removed during earlier campus expansion.

Initiatives to attain a distinctive, unified collegiate landscape

A beautiful, unified landscape doesn't just happen. It is achieved through vision and purpose. To create or enhance the campus landscape, institutions and their designers and planners should take initiatives:

Develop a landscape master plan. The landscape master plan should reinforce the ideas in the overall campus master plan. It establishes the hierarchy and vocabulary of the landscape elements on campus. Whether a project is undertaken based upon a study of an entire campus or district or upon a singular site plan, the understanding of the landscape vision for the entire campus provided by the landscape master plan can ensure that the project contributes to the overall unity of the campus.

Conduct a thorough analysis. A thorough understanding of the campus setting for all projects is critical. It is also the best way to ensure that landscape development activities are efficiently integrated with existing resources, taking advantage of an understanding of the campus as a whole. The analysis typically should include topography, vegetation, soils, geology, storm drainage, climate, and man-made features.

Make site selection decisions for buildings in the context of the campus plan and landscape framework. A poorly sited building can harm campus unity. Once the building is complete, the institution must live with the results for decades. Each building project should reflect the principles of the plan, positively contribute to the definition of all exterior space adjacent to it, and support the overall landscape framework.

Define civic space. The formation of exterior civic campus spaces, such as the Oval at the Ohio State University, the Lawn at the University of Illinois, and the main axis and parallel east-west axes at Rice University, is one of the hallmarks of great collegiate campuses. Well-defined streets, quadrangles, courtyards, and plazas offer places for the daily informal meetings and group activities that form the backbone of campus community.

Make bold, clear, unifying landscape initiatives. Attaining a unified campus takes great restraint and conviction. Trees should be planted in strong formal or informal groups. The grading of the earth can make a strong statement. It can be used to create spaces with an eye to strong architectonic forms such as useable terraces or simple, elegant, undulating forms either in sympathy with or in contrast to existing terrain. Grading can also unify building groupings and spaces. The selection of pavements and groundcovers should promote simplicity and unity. All decisions must allow easy, thorough, and long-term maintenance.

Respond appropriately to scale. Residential-scale plantings around large institutional-scale buildings have issues of appropriateness to scale, costliness of maintenance, and safety, and should be avoided. A small bed of daffodils that is so charming at the base of an Edwardian fraternity house on campus would be inappropriate at the foot of the thirteen-story science laboratory building—but an acre of daffodils in front could be stunning.

Establish a consistent palette and guide to materials. Guidelines for campus identity, expressed through signage, pavements, edges, lighting, furniture, stairways and railings, and planting, are essential to ensure unity. Clear guidelines foster and promote high-quality implementation in the field through repetition of craft and detail.

Parking at Weyerhaeuser World Headquarters

Make strong first impressions. The first impression is a great determinant in decision-making for potential students and faculty. The structure of the campus, the views of the surrounding area, the approach to the heart of a vibrant campus through a gateway or a tree-lined walk or street can make the first impression memorable, enduring, and decisive.

Enclose parking and service courts. Parking and service courts are necessary elements of the campus landscape. Even where it has minimized parking through demand management, shuttles, parking garages, and other methods, the institution will need some surface parking lots on the campus. These should be surrounded and screened with walls or hedges. Where the lots remain large, they should be divided into smaller enclosed "rooms." It helps to think of parking lots as "parking gardens."

Act sustainably in defining the institution's landscape agenda. Wise stewardship of campus natural and landscape assets can save money, enhance school reputation, and assist recruitment.

Coordinate to enhance unity. Planning, engineering, landscape architecture, architecture, parking, and athletics administrations must work as a team to support the institution's vision and plan for a cohesive landscape.

twelve

Environment and Sustainability

Educating students to be thoughtful citizens of their community and their world, and instilling in them a commitment to passing on to generations unborn a world at least no worse than they inherited are values that in one form or another relate to the mission statements of most colleges and universities. Habits of respect for the planet as well as for one another are solidified in college, and people take these habits with them all their lives. Most institutions acknowledge the need to be leaders—or at least not to be laggards—in teaching and modeling environmentally responsible behavior. Almost all colleges and universities in the United States offer some educational opportunities related to the environment. Fifty-seven percent of the 891 four-year colleges and universities participating in a recent survey offer a major or a minor in environmental studies.[2] Approximately one-third of them include or plan to include environmental responsibility as a written part of their mission statement, and more than four in ten schools have or plan to develop a written commitment to promote environmental responsibility. Almost two-thirds of the presidents surveyed felt that environmental programs fit in well with the culture and values of their institutions.[3] Still, clearly most institutions could be doing more.

The resoundingly good news of this chapter is that—just as care for the environment is inextricably part of an institution's mission—many of the actions recommended in previous chapters to foster community and learning on campus will, at no additional cost and often with cost savings, also significantly promote environmental stewardship. This means that, as the institution takes action to improve community, collegiality, and learning on campus, it can also reap the tangible and intangible benefits of environmental stewardship.

First, all education is environmental education. By what is included or excluded, students are taught that they are part of or apart from the natural world.[1]

- DAVID W. ORR

Environmental stewardship benefits the institution

Environmental stewardship in itself contributes to implementing the educational mission of most institutions. The ancillary good effects of environmental action in many cases actually reinforce community and learning on campus through the form of the environment that stewardship promotes—a campus that is not swimming in a sea of cars, that provides beautiful natural spaces encouraging people to walk around and spend time together. Further, the actions promoting stewardship that are described in this book may provide some direct financial benefits. In addition, stewardship can help make institutions more competitive.

Provides an exemplary education, furthering the institutional mission
The most central benefit that institutions can realize from programs of environmental responsibility is an extraordinary and relevant education. Students learn both through hands-on projects solving real-world problems as well as through the example of concern established by the institution.

Conservation initiatives, when made visible, can be used in conjunction with the educational program of the college or university. Brown University's "Brown is Green" program is well known for this, and many other universities now engage in such practices. Many colleges and universities are using campus land resources in environmental coursework.

Improves students' academic performance; increases productivity and overall well-being
Some of the most pleasing and healthy places for students, staff, and faculty to work and study are also the most environmentally sensitive. Other chapters have shown the measurable positive impact that fresh air, natural light, and a connection with outdoor green space have on academic performance and staff productivity, with some studies measuring improvements of up to 25 percent.

Helps attract students and faculty
A poll in 1999 showed that almost two-thirds of Americans identified themselves either as environmentalists or as sympathetic to environmental concerns.[4] And young people feel the need for environmental action more keenly than their elders.[5] Students have often been the leaders and visionaries in institutional programs to "reduce, reuse, and recycle," although many universities and colleges can rightly take credit for picking up on student initiatives and even organizing and leading them.

American corporations are aware of the appeal that positive environmental action has to consumers. Not only do companies whose identity is closely affiliated with wholesome environmental practices engage in "green marketing"—so do mainstream companies. Companies that have used the environment in their marketing efforts range from Stonyfield Farms (yogurt) and Patagonia (outdoor clothing) to Eastman Kodak, Heinz, and Rubbermaid.

Colleges and universities can benefit from green marketing as well. By addressing environmental issues on campus, colleges and universities can promote themselves as "green" to students and parents, aiding admissions and perhaps also student retention. For example, when the National Wildlife Federation commended the University of Oregon as among the best schools in developing and maintaining a sustainable campus, the university promoted this accomplishment to its students and others in its *Campus News*.[6] In its Environmental Commitment Statement, Warren Wilson College in Asheville, North Carolina states: "One of the major factors that encourages students, faculty, volunteers, and staff to come to Warren Wilson College is the perception that we are an active, participatory community that shares a deep commitment and a passionate concern for the health of our planet."[7] With intense competition for the best students, admissions officers of many institutions would do well to add this aspect of their institutions to their promotional efforts.

Warren Wilson College
Ecodorm

Environmental efforts can create or reinforce a positive impression of the institution among alumni and potential donors. Brown University provides a small example of this. The university uses the non-recyclable food waste from one of its main dining halls to support a pig farm with 170 pigs. Sending edible garbage to the pig farm rather than to a land-fill not only makes sense ecologically, but also saves the university about $10,000 per year. It's also good public relations: An article about the pig farm appeared in the November/December 2001 issue of the *Brown Alumni Magazine.*[8]

Provides financial benefits

Planning, designing, and building with sustainability in mind can significantly reduce operating costs, thereby saving money over the lifetime of a building's operation. Sometimes these projects can also save money in campus infrastructure costs; and in many cases, even the initial investment is not greater than less environmentally sensitive alternatives. Savings from sustainability initiatives on campuses such as parking demand reduction, recycling, and building energy conservation are well documented and can add up to millions of dollars per year—a benefit that no institutional business officer or facilities manager should overlook.

Creating a green campus

A campus that is planned well to provide memorable places that promote community, collegiality, vitality, and a learning environment is, in many important ways, a green campus. This chapter focuses on ways to further environmental sustainability that relate directly to the themes discussed throughout this book. Because of this focus, the chapter does not cover many other laudable and effective methods, such as recycling, reduction of pesticides, and use of water-saving fixtures and energy-saving light-bulbs. The lack of focus does not reflect a lack of interest. The authors heartily recommend that institutions pursue these activities, as they are good for the planet and often provide cost savings for the institution. Similarly, some institutions have chosen to demonstrate their commitment to leadership in sustainability by building landmark, signature buildings incorporating leading-edge technologies. These buildings provide positive visibility for the institutions and are used for educational purposes as well. But they are not necessary for a sustainable campus, and at costs of two to three times that of a normal building, they are not for everyone.

Any institution can carry out a sustainability program on its campus. By implementing initiatives discussed in this book, the institution can be green without additional expenditure while improving its campus as an environment where people like to be together and where they can learn. Institutions can promote environmental sustainability through the overall campus plan and layout, through the use of the campus site and landscape, and through individual building siting and design. As leaders and as educators of responsible world citizens, institutions need to take advantage of more of these opportunities.

Campus plan and layout

The single most important influence on achieving a sustainable campus is the overall organization of the campus and its facilities. This largely overlooked and undervalued element of sustainable planning comes at no cost, and often with cost savings. For example, something as simple as the orientation of a quadrangle to take advantage of exposure to breezes and sun can save substantially on operating costs. This section sets forth principles for energy conservation over the campus as a whole.

Use existing space thoroughly before building new

Since the cost advantage of not having to build and maintain a new building is compelling, the attractiveness of this principle—even without considering the reduced environmental impact—is clear. Yet many institutions do not use existing academic facilities as well or as intensively as they could. On many campuses, classroom buildings are used fully only from midmorning until midafternoon. The experience of the planning and design firm Sasaki Associates with some three hundred institutions has shown that all but a few institutions could achieve a 20 to 30 percent improvement in utilization of existing facilities by promoting use of classrooms and laboratories at earlier and later times. Although classes outside the core hours are not the most popular with students, the University of Oregon and a few other institutions have taken an innovative step to motivate students by offering a tuition discount for late-afternoon classes.[9]

Minimize impact by reusing sites and buildings in all ways possible

Environmental concerns as well as an institution's strategic and financial advantage are often aligned when it comes to building construction and siting. Better yet, following guidelines for environmentally sensitive siting can also promote the sense of place and overall building density that creates opportunities for enhancing community on campus.

Use of pervious materials on parking areas is becoming accepted practice

From an environmental perspective as well as a cost perspective, re-using existing buildings is preferable to new construction. In 1995, the United States consumed about one-third of the world's total non-food, non-fuel raw materials production, of which construction used about 60 percent.[10] A study conducted by the EPA determined that in 1996, building-related construction and demolition generated approximately 136 million tons of debris.[11] Reducing the amount of this debris can cut project expenses by reducing disposal costs; it also conserves landfill space and reduces the environmental impacts of producing new materials.

As with buildings themselves, sites for buildings or other campus projects should be considered from an environmental perspective. Generally, infill development is better from an environmental perspective than sprawl. Other chapters in this book lay out the benefits of dense development in promoting community and communication, and in creating lively campus spaces. Infill development by definition occurs in the context of an already developed area and therefore does less environmental damage than sprawl. In addition, infill development is more likely than low-density development to be able to connect to existing infrastructure. Requiring less new infrastructure is both an environmental and a cost advantage. Also, shorter utility runs save on long-term maintenance and ongoing operation and energy costs. If, for some reason, development on an undisturbed site is required, institutions should choose areas that minimize environmental damage or negative impact.

Reduce dependence on the automobile

The chapter on "Taming the Automobile" covered in depth the need to reduce dependence on the automobile, and the ways in which doing so promotes community on campus. Automobiles also play a major role in the pollution of our campuses as well as our cities. Therefore, reducing their use on campus also makes sense for environmental reasons.

The paved areas on campus are a source of pollution from the automotive oil that drips onto the pavement and then runs off into the soil and groundwater in the rain. In addition, paving with impervious materials affects the speed and amount of stormwater run-off, possibly creating flooding and erosion problems downstream. These two factors can significantly affect the ecology of the area. Parking areas should be built to minimize this impact through the use of pervious materials in parking areas, as well as through the use of water detention areas and natural vegetation filters.

Other ecological impacts of the automobile are less directly felt on campus but are of global significance. They include use of nonrenewable energy sources and generation of significant amounts of carbon dioxide that contribute to the greenhouse effect on the planet.

Reducing use of the automobile involves changing people's attitudes and behavior. This is far more difficult than the substitution of a new technology or process that other environmental initiatives may entail. Therefore, the successes achieved by some institutions in this area are all the more notable. The well-publicized Transportation Demand Management Program at Cornell University, for example, has saved the university an estimated thirteen million dollars over the six years from 1991 to 1997 by avoiding the construction of some 1,200 new parking-ramp spaces. It has also provided alternative means of transportation that help Cornell commuters drive an estimated ten million fewer miles each year (about 8,500 miles per year per commuter). This reduction in commuting translates to a savings of about 417,000 gallons of gas and prevention of 6.7 million pounds of carbon dioxide from being released into the atmosphere.[12] "If…every campus reduced carbon dioxide emissions by only one-tenth of what Cornell University has achieved through its transportation demand management programs, colleges and universities would prevent emissions of over 2.4 billion pounds of carbon dioxide into the atmosphere."[13] More current information states that through two demand-reduction programs, Cornell University has actually reduced the number of required parking spaces by 2,250.[14]

Use of campus site and landscape

Significant research exists on the environmental impacts of landscape, siting, and site planning, providing a number of enduring principles for site and landscape design.

Preserving the integrity of the site does not mean that nothing can be touched or changed. However, where possible, campus projects should preserve and enhance the natural features of the campus site and ecosystem. Many campuses have covered up such features, for example, by putting streams into culverts. Doing so may detract from the unique charm of the place—as well as adding expense to the project.

The plan for the Wake Forest University Health Science's Piedmont Triad Research Park in Winston-Salem, North Carolina opens Bath Creek, which long ago had been put into a culvert, making it a central amenity of the new biotechnology research park. Exposing the creek not only adds real-estate value to the project but also helps clean the water and provide natural habitat.

A field of wildflowers replaces
traditional lawn at Loyola
Marymount University

Environmentally sound campus landscape principles include:

· *Working in harmony with local environmental assets, such as wind, sun, geology, water, and native plant materials.* Using indigenous plant materials rather than exotic plant species, for example, increases the likelihood that operating costs will be reduced, because exotic species must be tended more carefully, may require more water, and may have to be replaced more often. Using native materials also enhances the sense that the campus belongs to and is rooted in a place.

· *More effective use of outdoor lighting.* Lighting levels can often be reduced without compromising safety on campus. Many older or decorative outdoor fixtures direct light up into the sky or at nearly horizontal angles. From an environmental standpoint, the generation of the extra electricity needed to provide this useless light contributes needlessly to pollution on the planet. Worse—light radiated up into the sky contributes to "light pollution"—the brightening of the night-time sky and concomitant invisibility of all but the brightest stars.

· *Reducing the acreage of high-maintenance lawns and manicured land.* Manicured lawns require mowing, fertilizing, and periodic treatment with pesticides. They may also be watered. In addition to their significant ongoing costs, these activities use nonrenewable fuel and water resources and poison the ground. Institutions should consider whether there are some areas of their manicured lawns that could be maintained as lower-maintenance landscapes.

· *Use of trees and other planting to ameliorate both the inside and adjacent outside environments of buildings, lessening energy consumption.*[15] *Urban Land* magazine reports a study by the American Forestry Association that shows that a single tree can annually save seventy-three dollars in air conditioning costs as well as seventy-five dollars in erosion and stormwater control. But the ecological benefits of trees go beyond cost savings. Reducing energy use in air conditioning and heating also reduces the amount of carbon emissions by utility companies. A single mature tree absorbs forty-eight pounds of carbon dioxide per year and releases enough oxygen to support two human beings.[16] Trees also absorb carbon monoxide, sulfur dioxide, and a number of other pollutants.

Mature trees shade a courtyard at Pepperdine University

· *Use of water resources to mitigate pollution and to reduce heating and cooling costs.* Always a pleasant visual amenity, ponds and streams on campus can be used to help manage stormwater runoff or for air-conditioning systems instead of cooling towers. Pools and fountains may also provide a natural cooling effect in hot, dry climates.

Overall, the environmentally sound use of the campus landscape will save the institution money in energy cost and landscape maintenance, and will create a beautiful, enduring campus that is in harmony with its region.

Principles of building siting and design for sustainability

Some siting and design actions that are environmentally effective are also simple and inexpensive. These include environmentally sensitive building siting and orientation, use of fenestration to maximize natural light and reduce heat gain, and good building ventilation. Buildings incorporating these features may be no more expensive to build initially than conventional buildings—perhaps less—and they save money operationally as soon as they are occupied. Not to incorporate some environmental features into every new building on campus makes no sense.

On the other end of the continuum are sophisticated—and perhaps expensive—buildings incorporating state-of-the-art technical systems that reduce the amount of energy a building requires. Even with low operational costs due to energy savings, the high initial investment may push the payback period for some of these buildings into decades, or longer. The decision to build such a building is not an economic one, but for other reasons it may still be a good one.

Louise and Erskine Wood Sr. Hall, Lewis and Clark University Law School

Each institution has to evaluate its willingness and ability to invest in making each new or renovated building green. As a minimum, every institution should be taking those actions that don't cost anything and may save money. Areas of building design and construction that have ecological impact include:

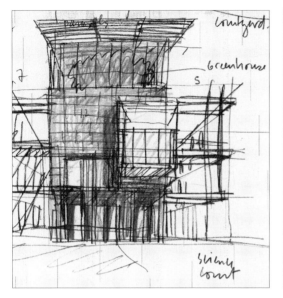

Overall building orientation, spacing, and massing

A building should be designed to minimize the environmental impact to the site. Siting of buildings should always take advantage of the unique conditions of the location, including solar orientation, wind patterns, and topography. Given a particular climate and topography, proper building orientation can provide significant lifecycle savings, cutting operating costs by up to 60 percent. With such savings and little if any additional cost, proper building siting should be the highest priority in planning for sustainable design.

Lay out functions and uses to support reduction of energy use and application of natural energy sources

The building design should locate functions with similar energy requirements together, so that the heating, cooling, ventilation, and lighting of each part of the building can be optimized.

The outdoor areas of the building should be designed to encourage community and to serve some functions. Outdoor "rooms," for example, can be used for some class meetings, for performances, and for informal meeting spaces. Covered porches allow students to be outside even during wet months as long as the temperature is reasonable. In some climates, usable outdoor spaces can reduce the need to build heated and air-conditioned indoor spaces.

Sustainable approach

A sustainable approach follows several principles that also contribute to
creating memorable buildings and spaces:

· Build for the long term while maximizing building flexibility
  for reuse
· Reduce maintenance requirements
· Strive to minimize the full life-cycle costs of the materials used
· Use materials with low environmental impact

Following these guidelines generally leads to the use of durable, high-quality
materials and of indigenous materials. They suggest good workmanship
and an attention to detail. Some institutions have found that they can
reuse materials from buildings taken down elsewhere, or from a building
being renovated. Such materials often have nostalgic value, contributing
to a sense of place. The University of New Hampshire's renovation of
Nesmith Hall, for example, used furniture and fixtures that were dis-
carded from other buildings. Reused items included the doors to every
office as well as the front door of the building. In its C. K. Choi Building
for the Institute of Asian Research, the University of British Columbia
reused 50 percent or more of the building materials. Much of the heavy
timber structure was reused from a demolished building across the street;
the building's exterior red brick is reused material from old Vancouver
city streets. Overall, the university completed the building within a budget established without regard to special recycling or energy-efficiency
measures, and achieves notable operational savings every year.

This approach has the potential of saving the university money over the long term, of minimizing harm to the environment, and of creating buildings that age gracefully, growing in character as the years pass and contributing to the quality of the campus physical environment.

Initiatives for sustainable environmental actions on campus

More and more universities and colleges are explicitly connecting their institutional missions with their commitment to teaching responsible environmental citizenship and their sustainability practices on campus. Their campuses reflect their commitment to educate students to nurture and care for the environment. While using their sustainability efforts to educate students, they are also finding ways to reduce facilities costs and enhance community on campus.

At these institutions and others, practicing sustainability is not a frill. It is fundamentally interrelated with other aspects of enhancing community on campus. Every institution has an opportunity to practice some form of environmental sustainability on its campus and to reap benefits of cost savings, educational leadership, greater community, and more beautiful campuses.

Specific initiatives would do well to include the following guidelines to provide good value for the institution.

Look on every campus project as an opportunity

· Some environmental initiatives may present themselves only when looked for.

· Many campus environmental initiatives make good sense in promot-ing community and collegiality and in providing opportunities for both academic and social learning. Many campus building and land-scape projects also provide opportunities to steward the environment.

· When investing in their campuses, institutions can frequently find ways to make each project serve multiple purposes and therefore reap many benefits.

Evaluate the costs and benefits fully

Each project at every institution should be evaluated from an environmental perspective as well as a financial and an academic one. Some environmental initiatives cost less—or at least do not cost more—than alternatives that do not address environmental issues.

The greatest value for money spent is not necessarily the least expensive. In determining the value of new facilities, institutions should find a way to balance short- and long-term costs, maintenance, material life-cycle cost, and environmental costs of producing, using, and ultimately removing materials. They should also find ways to factor in less tangible value, such as educational opportunities and the creation of memorable, unique places.

Use elements with reasonable payback, not just lowest initial cost. Institutions have a right to demand a reasonable payback on their projects and to keep project costs within bounds. However, the project with the lowest initial cost may not be the optimal-cost project, when taking all cost implications into account. A seemingly inexpensive project may create additional costs not considered in the project itself, such as extending infrastructure to a remote site; it may also require more expensive ongoing maintenance, such as the need for frequent repair of less durable exterior cladding materials. Some projects with low initial costs may have a shorter life cycle than others with higher initial costs, but still require more money in the long run. For example, developer-built housing may be designed to last only twenty-five to thirty years, requiring demolition and new construction at the end of that time. This shorter life reduces the value of the original investment, uses more resources, and creates more waste.

Integrate physical resources with educational programming

When planning building or landscape projects, institutions should involve students and other users as much as possible. Many institutions find it possible to offer course credit for this involvement. In addition, buildings and plants that incorporate sustainability concepts can be used as instructional laboratories.

Institutions with strong astronomy programs have taken the lead in the dark-sky movement, but all institutions can use the resulting principles of safe lighting design. With less night-sky pollution, other institutions may find it possible to add or improve astronomy offerings.

Institutions that have large land resources can and should integrate them with their educational programming. Sweet Briar College, for example, was originally managing its 3,000 acres as a revenue-generating resource, but not as a resource for academic programs or co-curricula activities. However, they have now set up a ropes course and team-building area for freshman, and they are using some of their land as a biological laboratory for their biology classes. They are monitoring the bee population in the fields and are considering establishing a working orchard.

Campuses' natural environments can be used for learning

Even a smaller land resource can have great educational value. The University of Wisconsin-Madison maintains 325 acres of open space known as the Campus Natural Areas (CNA), comprised of woods, open fields, beaches, a marsh, and restored prairie/savannah. It states as the CNA's mission:

> The Campus Natural Areas (CNA) are a place where the campus community can experience the aesthetic and intellectual benefits of nature. They provide biologically significant areas of natural plant and animal communities for teaching, research, outreach, and environmentally sensitive use. The CNA are as essential an element of the university as its lecture halls, laboratories, and playing fields. They contribute a strong sense of place to the UW campus as a whole and foster a mutually beneficial relationship between humans and the rest of nature.[17]

Institutionalize sustainability

To achieve energy savings and efficiency in its projects, an institution must work within a planning and project-management framework that supports this objective. Establishing an institutional framework for sustainability practices will have greater effects, over the long run, than conducting individual sustainable building projects. Institutions have approached this in a number of ways. Some have created and funded a sustainability office. The University of New Hampshire, for example, has a sustainability office supported by a $12.8 million special endowment. This office provides leadership and visibility for environmental programs on campus. The University of Kansas has an Office of Environmental Ombudsman. The Environmental Council at Middlebury College has student, faculty, and staff representation. Brown University has hired a coordinator for its well-published "Brown is Green" program. This program, in addition to working toward sustainability on campus and providing a model for the environmental program of the state of Rhode Island, also works with students in environmental-studies classes to conduct research leading to further change.

Create and work within a sustainable development plan

Some of the institutions that have been most successful at environmental stewardship have created a formal sustainable development plan that provides guidelines to promote sustainable development. These plans provide project management standards that promote sustainable development, and they provide specific, measurable performance standards that must be met.

For buildings, some institutions specify compliance with the Leadership in Energy and Environmental Design (LEED) Standard, published by the U.S. Green Building Council (USGBC). The LEED program is a voluntary national standard for high-performance, sustainable building design. Over 460 projects have registered their buildings with the USGBC, indicating an intention to obtain LEED certification; over sixty-five of these are college and university buildings.[18] As of May 2003, more than eighty buildings on American campuses had been either registered or certified.

Other institutions provide specific standards of their own. The Sustainable Design Guide of the University of Minnesota, for example, provides step-by-step diagrams and instructions for each phase of the building life-cycle. Each phase is broken down into steps, and performance indicators and scoring forms are provided for each step. The scoring forms allocate points based on the extent to which a building project meets sustainability goals appropriate to the phase. This lucid document provides clear principles and guidelines, along with measurable outcomes.

One institution with a far-reaching commitment to sustainability is the University of Oregon. In 1997, the university created a Comprehensive Environmental Policy Statement affirming its commitment to environmental responsibility. Pursuant to this policy, the University's Sustainable Development Plan states as its purpose: "The University will strive to become a national leader in sustainable development. All development, redevelopment, and remodeling on the University of Oregon campus shall incorporate sustainable design principles including existing and future land use, landscaping, building, and transportation plans. Sustainable endeavors will support the University's missions of teaching, research, and public service." The plan provides performance standards for the entire range of development on campus, including the planning and design process used; land use and transportation; sites and landscaping; water and energy; materials and resources; and indoor environmental quality. It specifies that the campus development process provide educational opportunities, ensuring user involvement in land use development and building design, and encouraging participation of students through class projects.

Creating a management structure for sustainability is no longer in the domain of only a few, select institutions but is becoming an operating reality for many. The good news is that there are now many successful models and a good support network for institutions moving on the road to sustainability.

thirteen
Taming the Automobile

Possibly the single largest contributor to overall deterioration of the campus environment and loss of community and collegiality, the automobile seriously damages many institutions' ability to achieve their mission. Colleges and universities feel pressure from faculty, staff, and students to provide parking close to the front door of their residence halls, classrooms, and offices. These parking lots and the roads needed to serve them seem to dominate some campuses. No matter how much parking is available, many institutions find themselves under a barrage of pressure to build more. In fact, adding parking usually increases the demand. Sometimes, indeed, more parking is needed. But more often, when the costs and tradeoffs are truly understood, institutions can better serve their missions by *not* adding more parking on campus.

Each institution must consider its policies and practices regarding automobiles in the light of its unique location, situation, student and staff population, and mission. An urban university such as the University of Pennsylvania in dense West Philadelphia will necessarily have a different approach from a suburban commuter-oriented institution such as George Mason University in Virginia. As of 2002, Boston College no longer issues permits for commuter parking to undergraduate students who live off-campus in areas served by public transportation lines. Despite planned growth, Vanderbilt University has resolved not to add more parking spaces in its core campus. As each institution evaluates its parking and traffic situation, it should take into account both quantifiable costs as well as the less quantifiable but perhaps more significant costs in destruction of quality of place, community, and a learning environment.

Don't it always seem to go / that you don't know what you've got till it's gone / They paved paradise / and put up a parking lot[1]

- JONI MITCHELL
Big Yellow Taxi

Impact of the automobile

As long as we continue to give priority to roads and parking over other active campus uses and open space, we will not be able to maintain the campus environments and vitality that we treasure and that are the hallmark of great American campuses. Through its destruction of the campus environment as a pleasant place to spend time and interact with people, and through the very door-to-door convenience that it promises, the automobile is a major factor in the erosion of community and collegiality on campus. It also contributes to many other problems plaguing campuses, including:

- Loss of green, pleasant, aesthetically attractive space in central campus areas
- Traffic with attendant driver and pedestrian injury on and near the campus
- Student health problems and unhealthy habits
- Environmental impacts
- Increased impact in neighboring communities

Loss of interaction on campus

Life once spent enjoying the richness of community on campuses is now increasingly spent behind the wheel of a car—commuting to campus, driving from one side of campus to another, and searching for a parking spot. Two individuals traveling to campus in single-occupancy vehicles are not likely to notice each other and pull off the road to have a conversation. More social forms of transportation such as walking or bicycling are much more likely to promote social interaction among individuals when it is possible to stop spontaneously and have a conversation.

As agents of isolation, automobiles can lead to a loss of a feeling of safety on campus. Large parking lots are generally not places to linger while coming or going from the car. With no one around, people feel unsafe and leave the area as quickly as they can, and the cycle of isolation grows worse. What suffers is community on the campus.

A former senior administrator at Florida State University described how the institution's plan—a number of beautiful old classroom buildings ringed by parking lots–created problems of community. Because they could park right next to their classroom building, the faculty would come in, teach, and then go home. They never had reason to walk on campus and seldom ran into students or colleagues. Many felt that this arrangement reduced the quality of education, led to cross-discipline issues among the faculty, and exacerbated community issues on the campus, especially at night.[2]

By contrast, many institutions in urban locations are characterized by a relative absence of convenience parking. When parking was banned in Harvard Yard some forty years ago, the Yard came alive with conversations and collegial pedestrian encounters.

Paving over our campuses

Every automobile on campus must be stored, and sometimes, if the car is used to get from a residence hall to and from class, more than one parking space per student must be provided. Each parking space paves over about two hundred square feet of ground, plus approximately one hundred square feet of roadway for access and travel, approximately three hundred square feet in all.

Christopher Alexander has observed, "Very simply—when the area devoted to parking is too great, it destroys the land…it is not possible to make an environment fit for human use when more than 9 percent of it is given to parking."[3] One might argue whether 9 percent is *exactly* the right figure, but clearly a campus where 30 or 40 percent of the land is given to parking has gone too far. Yet many campuses have given over large percentages of their core area to just this function. The authors' experience at Sasaki Associates indicates that an average of 15 percent—and in some cases as much as 40 percent—of the developed land at these institutions is in parking lots and roadways.

In fact, many institutions are devoting more of their land to parking. Newer campus areas show this trend more clearly than old, and as a result often feel like barren parking lots instead of like friendly campuses where community might burgeon. Because people want to park near the front door of each building, the amount of parking often forces the buildings and their uses apart. The result is often that distances become too great for most people to walk, increasing the demand for parking in an endless vicious cycle.

Even on older campuses, sometimes courtyards and quads have been paved over to provide close-in parking. Green, attractive spaces in central campus areas are threatened. Where there is no more room for surface parking, institutions constrained by land are building garages. Structured parking provides the benefits of allowing more parking nearer to central destinations while using less land, but it is also expensive—an expense not generally recouped by fees.

New campuses and old, in the center or on the fringe—too much space devoted to parking harms the campus more than it helps.

Street through the middle of the
Keene State College campus
Left: Before
Right: After

Traffic

Vehicles hitting pedestrians cause one in every seven vehicle-related deaths each year. A recent nationwide study by the Surface Transportation Policy Project showed that automobile-related deaths are most likely to occur with sprawling development patterns where roadways are designed to favor the car over pedestrians.[4] Campuses have not been immune to this trend. Sprawling campus development patterns in areas outside the historical or urban core of campuses have made management of vehicular problems difficult. Roads whose design gives dominance to the automobile and allow cars to go faster increase pedestrian and bicycle safety issues.

Some schools have successfully closed roads or reduced vehicular traffic through their campuses, either eliminating automobiles altogether or reducing their access. Even when the need for public and handicapped access, delivery, and service makes elimination of automobiles in the core campus impossible, institutions can implement methods for controlling vehicular access and giving priority to pedestrians over automobiles.

Health

As part of their mission to educate the whole individual, institutions are becoming more aware of their responsibility to teach students about many aspects of health as a part of their overall education. This includes exercise as well as diet and other topics.

The 1996 U.S. surgeon general report, "Physical Activity and Health" concluded that a sedentary lifestyle is a primary factor in more than 25 percent of all deaths from chronic disease and 10 percent of all deaths in the United States.[5] Health scientists and practitioners are becoming increasingly aware of the connection between personal health and creating physical environments that support and encourage physical activity.

Parking court at Rollins College is shielded from pedestrians by a hedge

Simple routine activities like taking an average ten- to fifteen-minute walk to class from a residence hall or commuter parking lot can provide the opportunity to accumulate the thirty minutes of exercise at least five days a week recommended by the Centers for Disease Control and Prevention.[6] Promoting the health benefits of walking and bicycling on campus will reach many more people than the traditional approach of advocating structured physical activities such as sports, aerobics, or weight lifting. One way that campus administrators and planners can do this is by arranging parking, roads, and paths for pedestrians and bicycles to encourage walking and biking.

Environmental impacts

The American automobile is the single largest contributor to global carbon dioxide emissions.

> American vehicles consume the equivalent of 4 billion barrels of oil each year, 20% of the world's oil production, half the motor fuel produced on the planet; each year they produce 1 billion tons of carbon dioxide, as well as vast amounts of nitrogen oxides and chlorofluorocarbons (CFCs), the major global warming gases... Compared to the contribution of American automobiles and trucks to the greenhouse effect, the deplorable destruction of the world's rain forests is almost benign.[7]

Automobiles are the largest single source of pollution in the United States. A typical car produces 8.6 pounds of pollution on one ten-mile trip.[8]

In addition to air pollution, automobiles contribute to pollution of the waterways through roadway and parking lot runoff.

Colleges and universities are increasingly finding that providing education and leadership on environmental issues is central to their missions. Students have initiated many environmental programs at their colleges and universities, but more and more, the institutions themselves are taking a leadership role. Clearly, finding effective alternatives to counter the ever-increasing demand for more automobiles on campus would be a significant way to show this leadership.

Increased impact on surrounding communities

The automobile too frequently drives a wedge between a university or college and its surrounding neighborhood. In many places, the institution is the single largest generator of traffic in nearby neighborhoods.

Why is there such a demand for automotive access?

If parking and cars are so bad for our campuses, why does everyone seem to want more of them? As with our patterns of growth and automobile dependence in American cities, campuses have seen a shift from walking and biking to using the automobile. Three interrelated forces have changed transportation patterns on campus, creating this problem.

People are in the habit of driving

Most students, as well as faculty and staff, have been raised in automobile-dependent communities. Single-use zoning patterns, impractical or nonexistent public transportation, and low-density development in these communities make driving the only realistic mode of transportation. Dependence on the automobile has created behavior patterns that lead people to use the automobile even for short trips that could be easily walked in ten or fifteen minutes. Between 1975 and 1995, the number of trips the average American adult took on foot each year dropped 42 percent. Compared with over 50 percent of children a generation ago, only 10 percent of children walk or bicycle to school today.[9]

The majority of today's college students grew up being chauffeured everywhere. By the time they were high-school juniors or seniors, many students had their own cars and were accustomed to driving them to school. Sixty-nine percent of college students who participated in one recent survey owned a car.

On a number of campuses, the authors have interviewed students who confessed to driving from their dormitories to their classes even if the classroom building was only a five-minute walk away. They sometimes spent ten or fifteen minutes looking for a parking spot, if they thought they might get one near the front door. Some students told of traveling by automobile to their recreation centers, even though they were aware that it took longer to get to their cars, drive to the recreation center, and park, than it would have taken to walk. Ironically, they did not think about the value of walking as part of their exercise routine.

The facts are that cars are convenient; they are directly tied to many people's egos; and current policies encourage use of single-occupancy vehicles. The college environment may be our society's best and only chance to introduce new habits into our culture and to educate students on the benefits of not driving.

Institutions place a high priority on convenient parking

As a result of the pressure to provide convenient parking, and more of it, many institutions have accepted close-in parking and general vehicular access to every building as a standard for new campus facilities. Such a standard creates a vicious cycle that leads to a need for even more parking, as the resulting proliferation of parking lots necessarily spreads the buildings out to make room for the automobiles. The convenience of automotive access thereby causes campus facilities to be dispersed beyond reasonable walking distances. As a result, the need for more roads and more parking escalates until, on many campuses, students and faculty must drive in order to have access to facilities.

Convenient low-cost parking makes automobiles the transportation of choice

First-year economics students learn that when products and services become "free goods," demand increases almost limitlessly. Free goods are a bargain offered, if not for free, then for a discounted price that is significantly less than its actual cost. On most American campuses, parking is a free good—or at least a heavily discounted one. On-campus parking fees for faculty, staff, and students almost never cover the institution's cost of providing the parking. Usually, they don't cover even the costs of financing, design, construction, maintenance, and operations, much less the cost of land.

Active ground-level uses displaced by parking

Because parking is a bargain sold at less than its actual cost, market constraints are effectively absent. Most students, staff, and faculty will choose to drive. Any attempt to increase parking capacity will only increase demand, as users perceive the low cost and easy availability of parking. Furthermore, on most campuses, once a student or faculty or staff member incurs the out-of-pocket expense of a parking permit, the cost of parking does not increase with increased vehicle use. Lack of a use charge encourages driving. When market constraints are effectively absent, the only way to limit driving to campus is to limit the supply of parking, which is often politically difficult to achieve.

Conventional supply-side solutions to perceived or real parking shortages favor increasing the number of spaces at a real cost to the institution, rather than reducing demand, usually at a substantially lower cost. By simply adding more spaces, however, the institution is making driving more convenient and therefore encouraging more vehicles. The cycle can be endless, destroying the campus environment in the process. If we are to influence automobile use behavior, it is essential that all automobile owners understand the actual cost of parking and that we link appropriate parking fees to the cost and convenience or vehicle use.

The cost of parking

The cost of a parking space can vary dramatically depending on whether it is provided in a surface lot or in structured parking; if structured, whether above or below grade and on the efficiency of the layout; on whether the parking is on an urban campus or a suburban or rural one; on the specific locality; and on the overall quality of design and construction. For surface lots, quality can be expressed in features such as the treatment of curbs, the lighting, the type of landscaping and surface treatment, and method of stormwater collection. In spite of these variations, we can develop a reasonable model of the *average* cost of parking.

Costs comprise capital cost and operational cost. Capital cost further comprises the cost of land, site preparation, and construction. In year 2000 dollars, the construction cost of a parking space in a surface lot ranges from $1,500 to $3,500. The construction cost of a space in an aboveground structured facility can range from $6,000 to $14,000.[10] Additional project costs, including design, surveys, testing, feasibility studies, financing, and so on, can add 25 percent over the construction and land costs. Parking structures are typically financed over twenty years; parking lots, ten years.[11]

Operating costs for parking may include management and administration costs, security, utilities, insurance, supplies, routine maintenance, structural maintenance, snow removal, and other expenses. Assuming no taxes and no attended revenue collection, but including security and administration, the operating cost of a single parking space in a surface parking lot is approximately $250 per year (1999). The approximate operating cost of a space in a parking structure is about $400 per year.[12]

Most institutions do not charge enough for parking permits to recover the cost of owning and operating surface parking. Not considering the cost of land, surface parking space with a construction cost of $2,000 financed at 5 percent over ten years, with an annual operating cost of $250, costs the institution $564 per year. A structured parking space with a construction cost of $10,000 financed at 5 percent over twenty years, with an annual operating cost of $400, costs the institution $1,392 per year.[13]

In addition to its hard costs, providing parking incurs intangible costs that are harder to quantify. Loss of community, health issues, pollution, loss of green space, and the impact on campus aesthetics have been described above.

Parking fees

In a 1999 survey covering thirty institutions, mostly large, public universities, the highest parking fees were charged for reserved faculty and staff parking spaces, with a high of $1,000 per year and a low of $100 per year. The lowest parking fees were generally for student commuter parking, with a high of $600 and a low of zero. While rates varied greatly from institution to institution, few of the institutions surveyed charged enough to cover the cost of surface parking, much less structured parking.

For every thousand parking permits where a dedicated space is required (reserved faculty and staff parking), the median institution is losing $237,000 per year for surface parking and $1,065,000 per year for structured parking. Slightly fewer than one space per car is required for on-campus student resident parking, but the financial situation is worse. The median institution is losing almost $400,000 per year per thousand spaces for surface parking and over $1,200,000 per year for structured parking.[14]

At most public institutions, parking is an auxiliary unit whose cost must be funded through permit fees and ticket revenues. Given the shortfall in parking fees to cover costs, most institutions balance their costs and revenues by averaging the cost of parking already amortized or funded through other sources with the cost of new parking, and by covering some expenses by other income sources.

At most private institutions, the gap is greater than the numbers shown here, with many charging little or nothing for parking. A review of the parking rates charged at a number of private institutions shows a typical rate of about $40 or $50 per *year* for a parking permit—far less than one-tenth the annual cost.

The portrayal of the university by Clark Kerr, former chancellor of the University of California system, as "a series of individual faculty entrepreneurs held together by a common grievance over parking" is as sadly valid today as ever. At a roundtable discussion during the 2002 annual meeting of the National Association of College and University Business Officers, the authors had the opportunity to ask a number of campus financial leaders why they do not charge the full cost for parking. The immediate answer, amid a burst of laughter and agreement, was, "Cowardice!" Faculty and staff want reserved spots and vocally resist increases in charges. Business officers perceive that students and their parents, already paying a high tuition charge, also would resist increased parking charges. Some, with campuses in urban areas, note that increased parking charges might drive more students and faculty to park in the neighborhood, increasing already strained town-gown relationships. At some institutions, the capital costs of parking—but not the cost of the land—are shown in college and university budgets, but the operating cost of parking is not broken out from other building and grounds maintenance costs. Who would want to tell the faculty that they have three fewer faculty positions because they built a garage? "You pick your battles," one chief business officer commented frankly, "It's just the cost of doing business." Another agreed, adding, "Some things are sleeping dogs."

Equity issues

Does charging parking fees that represent only a small percentage of the cost of providing parking mean that parking is free or inexpensive? Not at all! The costs of parking not recovered in fees are buried in the university's budget and charged to all students—drivers and non-drivers alike—as a part of their tuition. If parking is subsidized, then everyone is paying for the subsidy.

Some institutions express concern that recapturing all parking costs will drive fees so high as to create a hardship for needy students or for lower-paid employees. The concern is both thoughtful and just. However, the remedy is not to ask all students and all employees—needy and not—to subsidize the poorer ones. Institutions have at their disposal a number of ways to provide for those who need parking but can't afford it. These include providing incentives for carpooling, vanpooling, or taking transit; providing lower-cost or free parking at remote lots with shuttle service; providing parking subsidies on the basis of need for students; including parking subsidies in cafeteria-style benefits for employees; and so on.

It doesn't have to be so

When the full costs and impacts of letting the automobile dominate campus environments and patterns of interaction are identified, the communities on many campuses are motivated to take back their campuses from the automobile in favor of environments and life styles for human interaction. Eliminating *all* parking is neither desirable nor possible. The main remedy for the harm done by automobiles to health, community, vitality, economics, and ecology is to limit where possible automobile intrusion on the core campus.

Collectively, institutions of higher education are perhaps our best chance to educate future leaders about issues of increasing automobile dependence. A recent survey by the National Wildlife Federation found a significant minority of campuses of all types and sizes and from all regions of the country teaching and demonstrating sustainability in practice. Many of these practices had to do with alternative means of transportation. Initiatives like those described below can provide experiential learning opportunities for students as well as faculty and staff, foster good public relations with host communities, reduce costs, and set important examples for other institutions to follow.

- In line with its policy decision to reduce the use of automobiles on campus, the University of Oregon in Eugene dedicates less than 10 percent of its land (23 of 280 acres) to parking and roadways. With over 17,000 students and an additional 1,400 faculty, the university boasts only 3,270 parking spaces, but an impressive 4,600 spaces for bicycles. The university also provides a free bus pass to anyone who studies or works on the campus.

- By promulgating alternatives to single-occupancy vehicles, Cornell University[15] estimates that it avoided construction of 1,200 new parking-garage spaces at a construction and project cost of $12 – 16,000 each. These alternatives included a bus-pass system and a carpooling initiative. The annual cost savings over the six-year period 1991 – 1997 was calculated to be over $3,000,000. The effort has also reduced traffic in the neighborhood around the campus. A later estimate raised the number of spaces avoided at 2,250.[16]

Policies and strategies

The process for planning new parking and transportation policies and systems should ensure participation by students, faculty, staff, and the local community. A plan for communication and education is imperative for the success of the program. Constituencies should be educated on the cost, use of resources, environmental impacts, and on what it all means for them. In effect, ongoing communication should be provided through a marketing budget for alternative transit programs. "The successful campaigns at University of Colorado, University of Washington, and Cornell all had at least 2% of their transit budget allocated for marketing transit services."[17]

In addition, universities and colleges should work with the cities and towns where they are located to ensure that any new policies implemented on campus do not have an adverse impact on the city or town. Many college communities, for example, ensure that campus parking does not spill over into the neighborhood by instituting resident parking permit systems.

Parking management

Parking management to reduce demand by single-occupancy vehicles is one of the most effective traffic reduction strategies. Findings from several surveys reported by the University of Waterloo indicate that increases in parking fees at Queen's University by 25 percent would result in a 15 percent reduction in drivers. A 100 percent fee increase at the University of Waterloo would result in a 43 percent reduction in parkers.[18] Reduced parking demand can mean that an institution can reuse close-in parking for building expansion, or to accommodate parking generated by increased enrollment without construction of new spaces.

Politically, it may not be possible to change the parking fee structure all at once, but an institution can set a goal of raising the parking fees over time to reflect actual costs as closely as possible. Pricing strategies should furthermore include incentives to promote desirable behavior (such as carpooling) as well as disincentives for undesirable behavior (such as the use of single-occupancy vehicles to drive from door to door). Thus, parking fees should reflect the proximity to desirable locations, the time-of-day demand, and the full cost of providing the parking.

The policies of each institution should reflect an understanding that a subsidized parking strategy will cause an increase in demand for parking. Some institutions may determine that they would like to subsidize some parking under certain circumstances. One university president, for example, expressed a reluctance to make fees too high for lower-income students to afford. However, by keeping parking prices low, that university is effectively forcing the non-driving students subsidize the drivers. A better strategy might be to add some portion of the parking costs into the financial aid package of needy students.

Where parking is a necessity for commuting students, some institutions may decide to offer lower parking fees for commuters. When they do so, however, they should understand fully that they are offering a subsidized service built into the cost structure for all.

Other parking subsidies, however, can be used to further an institutional strategy of reducing the automotive presence on campus. Universities might consider establishing flexible permitting for occasional drivers and should provide subsidized parking for car- and vanpooling. For example, the free parking program for carpoolers at the University of Washington has reduced purchases of single-occupancy vehicle parking permits by 23 percent over ten years.[19]

Many employers, as well as states and cities where they are located, are finding creative ways to offer direct incentives to people for not driving to work. Nontaxable benefits for employees who do not drive may include transit passes, vanpool benefits, and cash in lieu of a parking space. In Minnesota and Southern California, for example, some employers offer a $2- to $3-a-day cash incentive for employees not to use their parking space at work. One of every eight employees who used to drive is now getting to work by another means.[20] California has passed a law that requires employers to offer to non-drivers the cash equivalent of the amount they subsidize driver parking—the difference between the employer's cost of parking and the amount the employer charges employees when they provide parking to them.[21] As large employers, institutions can implement similar incentives rather than adding more parking.

Many residential colleges don't allow freshmen to have cars on campus, or limit freshman use of cars. Some of these institutions feel that they don't have the space or the money to provide parking, or want to reduce the impact of automobiles on campus; others find the use of automobiles on campus inconsistent with their goals of building community and retaining students. These institutions want first-year students to develop habits of staying on campus and participating in campus life. Surveys show that students who become engaged in campus life during the first semester of their freshman year are much less likely to either drop out or transfer. Institutions that take this approach need to let prospective students and their parents know that a car is not a necessity on campus, as other transportation options exist.

Transportation demand management

In conjunction with pricing and other policies for managing parking demand, institutions should provide a transportation demand management program to provide attractive and viable alternatives to single-occupancy vehicles. Such a program requires a multi-modal transportation system that includes, where possible, pedestrian walkways, bicycle paths, carpooling, vanpooling, and convenient transit options.

Walking

Walking is the healthiest transportation option, and the one most conducive to enhancing the experience of community on campus. A pedestrian-oriented campus should be arranged so that students and faculty can walk from any classroom to most others within the normal ten-minute class interval. Frequent destinations should be close to their normal origins; for example, the recreation center should be close to housing, and housing close to the academic core.

Vanderbilt University

In areas where pedestrians must share spaces with automobiles, pedestrians should have the clear priority. There should be a sense that the automobile is intruding on pedestrian space rather than the other way around. Traffic calming techniques can be used slow vehicles, give pedestrians priority, and improve pedestrian safety. These include narrow lanes, "speed tables" (raised crosswalks), and "neckdowns" (narrowing of the road) at crosswalks. Parallel parking on a street also slows traffic, and it gives pedestrians a buffer from moving cars.

Bicycles

Colleges and universities can encourage bicycle use and improve the quality of the bicycling experience by providing bikeways and convenient bicycle parking. If a regional bicycle network exists, the university bike system should connect to it. Most will not find themselves in as bicycle-friendly geography as Davis, California, but much can still be learned from the University of California at Davis. UC Davis and the city of Davis have worked together to encourage the use of bicycles. With a flat terrain and a total population of 58,000, the city is home to 24,000 students and over 50,000 bicycles. Between them, the city and the university maintain fifty-nine miles of bike paths that are entirely closed to cars and another forty-seven miles of bike lanes on roads. In a single day, as many as 15,000 to 18,000 bicyclists may travel on the UC Davis bike paths.

Some institutions might want to explore the possibility of a campus/community-owned bike program like the one created by the University of New Hampshire. With a goal "to greatly decrease one-person car trips on campus,"[22] the University of New Hampshire runs a bicycle loan program known as the "Yellow Bike Cooperative." For a fee of five dollars, students receive a key that they can use to unlock any of fifty yellow bikes. They can use these bikes to go anywhere on campus, leaving them in a convenient bike rack when they reach their destination.

Carpools and van pools

Many institutions have been successful in providing incentives for vanpooling and carpooling. In addition to offering transit incentives, for example, the University of Washington has implemented a comprehensive U-Pass program that has been effective in encouraging carpooling and discouraging use of single-occupancy vehicles. While non-carpoolers pay $177 per quarter for parking (and receive a complimentary U-Pass), carpoolers can park for free—and vanpool riders and drivers can receive up to a $40 subsidy for their vanpool fares. To reduce the perceived inconvenience of carpooling, the university has implemented a program through which faculty and staff who miss their carpool home can be reimbursed for 90 percent of taxi fares up to fifty miles per quarter. This system has reduced the number of permits for single-occupancy vehicles by 24 percent, while carpool permits are up by 75 percent since the inception of the program.[23] According to Peter Dewey, the transportation systems manager at the University of Washington, "The program has allowed us to minimize the use of our parking facilities. We currently have 12,000 spaces, fewer than in 1983, despite 8,000 additional people. Without vigorously managing our parking and providing commute alternatives,

RONALD MOORE

the University would have been faced with adding approximately 3,600 parking spaces at a cost of over $100 million. With fewer cars on campus since the inception of U-PASS, the University has created opportunities to make capital investments in buildings supporting education instead of structures for cars."[24]

Many institutions and corporations use intranet matching to assist faculty, staff, and students to find carpool partners. Some institutions that are outside large urban areas also use intranet matching to assist students to find long-distance rides home for holidays and vacation. This assistance can help counter the argument that students need a car at school to get home for the holidays.

Transit

Increasing transit ridership is a proven strategy for reducing the number of vehicles on campus. Colleges across the country are doing so in a variety of ways. One method adopted by over seventy colleges and universities in North America is to provide a free or reduced-price transit pass to students, faculty, and staff. Universities that provide transit passes can offer employees a nontaxable benefit while at the same time decreasing automobile dominance and air pollution on campus.

The University of Colorado[25] has had remarkable success with its innovative student bus-pass program. Funded by a student-voted tax, the program has made local busses free to students and avoided the need to construct some 750 new parking spaces at a cost of $8,000 to $12,000 each. From 1991 to 1997, student rides on busses quintupled to 1,500,000 rides per year. Approximately 30 percent of these trips replaced travel in single-occupancy vehicles. The annual cost savings of the program is estimated to be $1,000,000.

Many campuses run shuttle busses to serve high-volume destinations on or near campus. Rice University has extremely limited parking within the inner core of its campus. Instead of adding parking lots, the university runs a well-organized and frequent shuttle bus system. Three different loops, all of which connect the academic inner campus and student center, remote parking lots, and student residential colleges, run as frequently as every eight minutes. One of these loops runs to off-campus graduate student housing; on Saturdays, this loop also connects the graduate housing to a nearby shopping center. Shuttle busses are free—and air-conditioned.

Begun as a student-initiated grassroots effort in 1972 and still largely run by students at the University of Maryland, Shuttle-UM has a mission to provide safe and dependable transportation to University of Maryland students, faculty, and staff, and to facilitate learning and involvement for student success and development. The system is supported in part by student fees and employs approximately 180 students, as well as eight full-time university staff. Student employees may apply their experience to coursework. Shuttle-UM transports over one million passengers each year between locations on campus and many of the area's apartment complexes and neighborhoods, shopping centers and entertainment, transit connections, and other destinations.

Other transit strategies include coordinating the routing of existing transit lines to better serve the institutional community. The University of Arkansas receives partial federal transit funding to run the public transit system in Fayetteville, Arkansas. The system also serves student trips to campus. The university has also received federal funding for a parking garage and transit center located in the heart of the campus.

Key to the success of these on-off-campus transit systems is to know where students live off-campus and to design a user-friendly system that encourages them to take transit to campus.

Land use, density, and on-campus housing

The location and arrangement of uses on campus can greatly affect travel behavior. If campus buildings serving a variety of uses are located conveniently close together, then more facilities and services are reachable by walking or bicycling. Even when the entire campus is so large that walking from one area to another is not realistic, if each area provides a mixed-use selection of on-site services for students, faculty, and staff, people may not have to get into their cars to reach those services.

On campus after campus, students express a preference for on-campus housing if it is near the core of the campus, safe, and affordable. Increasing on-campus student housing also provides an opportunity to promote alternative modes of transportation, including walking, bicycling, and transit. With proper design and planning, increasing the amount of on-campus housing can be a cost-effective way of reducing the demand for parking and traffic on campus.

All three of these strategies—mixing uses, increasing density in the core, and locating housing near the campus core—can be accomplished at little or no additional cost compared to alternatives, and can be significant contributors to reducing on-campus parking and traffic.

On-street parking at
Boston College

Key initiatives to taming the automobile

The automobile poses a complex problem whose solutions lie along a number of dimensions, from policy through design. They include:

Review policies. With knowledge of the costs and benefits in their financial, geographic, and social circumstances, institutions should, in whatever ways work best, provide subsidies and incentives for other means of transportation that can lower single-occupancy automobile use, including walking, bicycling, use of remote lots, carpooling, vanpooling, mass transit, and other kinds of shared transportation. The goals of these incentives are to:

· Provide more movement options: move people—not cars!
· Enable the highest and best uses of resources—land and capital

These goals can be realized through policies and management strategies, and through campus design.

Review pricing structures. Having decided to reduce vehicular traffic on campus, institutions can proceed along a number of fronts. One method is to use parking fees to reflect as closely as possible the full cost and impact of providing parking and having automobiles on campus. This method is particularly effective when combined with ensuring that attractive and economical alternative means of transportation are readily available. A more long-term, but ultimately most effective, strategy is to build or expand campuses with an appropriate density and mixture of uses so that most destinations are within walking distance.

Encourage other modes of transportation. An effective transportation demand management program will put into place incentives that encourage other modes of transportation, including walking, bicycling, car- and van-pooling, and mass transit.

Create a pedestrian-friendly environment in the core campus. A pedestrian-oriented campus provides an efficient and safe network of pedestrian pathways. Landscaping, shade trees, arcades, and good lighting after dark can all enhance the quality of the pedestrian experience, as will a chance to see and be seen by others. People will happily walk fifteen to twenty minutes if the experience is pleasant.

Mitigate the visual impact of parking. When adding or modifying parking, institutions should follow good design practices to mitigate the visual impact of parking on the quality of the campus environment.

The automobile too often has a direct, negative impact on central institutional goals such as recruitment, retention, community, and collegiality on campus; and its requirements can distort priorities for scarce financial resources. Tackling the issues of the automobile's impact on campus is not easy, but it can have great rewards. A number of mission-driven institutions are providing leadership in reducing the impact of the automobile on campus—and they are saving money in the process.

fourteen

Architecture

A framework for creating buildings on campus

Buildings provide space in which necessary institutional functions—such as classroom learning, administrative work, and indoor recreation—take place. Reflecting this priority, programs for buildings normally focus on how many offices, how many square feet of classroom space, and so on, are required.

Typically, not as much attention is given to the other vital roles that buildings play, some of them perhaps even more important than providing functional space. Buildings are a major component of the framework of the campus as a whole; they contribute to the overall life, learning, and vitality of the campus; and they are a key element of institutional identity.

First things first—the role of buildings in the campus framework

A cohesive campus expresses an overall vision and plan. Examples of historical campus and buildings conceived as one include Rice University, Sweetbriar College, Stanford University, and the University of Virginia. What these campuses have in common is a sense of place created by the plan and the buildings working together to define space and establish identity.

First and foremost, buildings are a part of the larger plan and vision of the campus. All buildings, whether intended as bold centerpieces or as collaborative structures, must contribute to the total campus structure—to the master plan and urban design framework. Every campus is the sum of its parts. As each individual part contributes to the whole, each building

> Campus buildings should be like the courses that make up a curriculum. Each may be valuable on its own, but they must also work together to create a larger vision.[1]
>
> - CHARLES LINN

Buildings define the campus framework at the University of Illinois, Champaign-Urbana

plays a role in the bigger scheme of the campus. Buildings help define the campus framework and open spaces—or, conversely, if located or designed without consideration of the greater framework, can damage its great places.

The landscape and open space structure create the memorable and enduring impressions of most campuses. When we think of the great campus places, we think of Harvard Yard, of the lawn at the University of Illinois, of the main quadrangle at the University of Colorado at Boulder. By framing and defining those spaces, individual buildings play a major role in creating an impression of a great campus.

Both its open spaces and the buildings that frame them define the physical character and quality of a campus; therefore, the best campus environments are created when these two elements are designed to work together. Building design should take advantage of opportunities to frame open spaces and define pedestrian paths on campus, and to increase interpersonal interactions. The frequency and location of buildings' entrances, for example, can often determine the success of the spaces these buildings define.

Buildings reinforce the vision and identity of the campus by establishing character and providing focal points. They establish character by common architectural scale, materials, and other features, creating a fabric and "feel" of the campus just as regional building styles establish the unique character of the region. They provide focal points to the extent that they have noticeably distinct features, such as through use of contrasting materials or through readily identifiable elements such as porches, bell towers, or spires.

The campus plan should include guidelines for appropriate functionality and siting of buildings serving different roles. The challenge is to create buildings that reinforce the intent of the plan, respond to their unique functions and sites, and contribute to the overall campus identity. When creating buildings, institutional leaders should keep in mind that they are not just filling an immediate need for a specific function; they are also creating a legacy.

The collaborative role of architecture on campus

All campus buildings should play a collaborative role on the campus to maintain the campus as a coherent, connected whole. In their collaborative role, buildings tie the campus together; create a sense of unity of character; and frame outdoor spaces. This doesn't mean that the buildings have to be all the same. Each can—and should—have its own unique features. But when looked at together, they should be seen as belonging together and contributing to an overall sense of the whole.

From the perspective of the overall campus structure and site, new collaborative buildings take their design cues from their planned context on campus, including:

- *Location.* Relative to the master plan framework and to geographical features (such as hills, valleys, and views to be protected or framed).
- *Scale.* Appropriate height, scale, and massing for the site and surrounding structures, streets, and public ways that are adjacent to them.
- *Building orientation.* Contribution to the adjacent buildings, open spaces, streets, and pedestrian ways.
- *Building context.* The ways in which new buildings relate to and affect existing campus buildings.

Buildings that are not one of a kind, such as residence halls and classroom buildings, are typically good candidates for a mainly collaborative role.

A few American campuses, such as Rice University, Carnegie Mellon University, and Stanford University, stand out as models of the ways in which a compelling and memorable plan has been reinforced over time by the architecture of its buildings while still embracing contemporary architecture. At Rice University, the Ralph Adams Cram General Plan of 1910 is significant for the way the plan, landscape, and architecture all collaborate to set the framework for the campus from the beginning. Rice is a model among historically significant American campuses for the consistency with which the original vision has been adhered to for almost 100 years. This can be attributed to the strength and clarity of the plan with its central axis and cross axis, and also to how the plan is reinforced by simple rectangular building shapes that reinforce and define the main spaces and courtyards. Because the plan—the combination of spaces created by reinforcing landscape architecture and architecture—is so emotionally compelling, successive generations of Rice's board have insisted that modern architecture retain and reinforce the original principles of the General Plan. Rice presents a model of the ways in which twentieth-century architecture has reinforced a plan while also expressing the identity and culture of the current period.

Top: Rice University
Bottom: University of Virginia
Right: Charleston, South Carolina

Landmarks and gateways

Landmark buildings can be used to create a physical representation of institutional mission and values, especially those occupying a unique location or serving a unique and visible function, such as a library or theater complex. Like the churches on New England town commons or the White House in Washington, D.C., such buildings embody communal meaning and a unique community function. They should stand out in some way, occupying a special location on campus.

Locations such as the end of an axis or a special intersection may justify a special building, such as a library or chapel. At the historic core of the University of Virginia, the library was designed as a special building both because of its function as the intellectual heart of the institution and because it had an axial relationship to the great lawn.

Some buildings, by virtue of their location at an entryway of the campus, serve as gateways—a particular type of landmark building. They represent the campus as a whole to the neighborhood and to visitors. Even if they serve a function that is not unique, such as classroom buildings, they may be designed as special buildings because of their location at the entrance to the campus. An excellent example is the new Ray and Maria Stata Center at MIT. Like many buildings at MIT, the Stata Center houses research and laboratory facilities. But the Stata Center redefines the entry to the MIT campus nearest to bustling, entrepreneurial Tech Square and the vast public/private research-and-development zone of Kendall Square. As a gateway, it comprises approximately 50 percent public space. Although the building reflects Frank Gehry's unforgettable use of materials and free-form facades, it extends and ties into the MIT campus with its unique use of interior corridors to connect its buildings.

To create landmark buildings, some institutions are commissioning "signature" structures by internationally acclaimed architects. Some people have likened the trend of colleges to hire famous architects to design new buildings on campus to commercial retail branding. Many of today's students grew up with familiar brands like "GAP" and "Abercrombie & Fitch"; why not have brand-name architects? And if there are brand-name architects, why not hire the best?

The performing arts center at Bard College

"We are the beneficiaries of the enormous explosion of interest in his work," declared Leon Botstein, president of Bard College, about Frank Gehry's new performing arts center on campus, "but in the long run it forces us to put a program in there that vindicates the promise of the building. When you do something of this scale, you raise expectations. His work puts an enormous burden of inspiration on our students, and on the college."[2]

Signature buildings set new levels of expectation for institutional identity. Even the elite are not immune. Harvard has its red brick, and Princeton has gray Gothic revival, but both institutions are hiring internationally recognized architects to enhance their identity—to create, or to satisfy, an image as a leading-edge university or college.

Every new building worth doing has some risk. Although there can be much to gain, hiring star architects to create landmark buildings also has particular risks that must be foreseen and addressed. These include:

· *Loss of campus continuity and coherency.* Buildings stand out precisely because they are different, because they go against the grain in one way or another. To have noteworthy buildings that play key, central roles on a campus is laudable. But if every building stands out, then none of them stands out in particular. The architecture is simply a jumble of conflicting styles and statements, saying nothing overall. The campus as a whole loses meaning. Unique statements should be reserved for buildings in unique locations or playing unique roles. The Stata Center at MIT, discussed above, is a good example. But what added roles can a signature dormitory, such as MIT's Simmons Hall, play?

· *Discontinuity with region or neighborhood.* Bard's undulating-roofed Performing Arts Center, discussed above, is a centerpiece and an inspiration for the college. But it was originally located off the center of the campus near an historical landmark structure. Its discontinuity with the historical style of the region provoked sufficient neighborhood controversy that the college had to change its planned siting for the building. The new site has been a great success with all constituencies, including the architect.

· *Longevity.* While many colleges are "struggling with a '60s legacy of ugly, wasteful, and outdated buildings,"[3] others are creating a new legacy of heroic buildings of the early twenty-first century. Is this a legacy that others, in turn, will have to struggle with? Materials, forms, and architectural elements that are "in" today may be "out" tomorrow. Will today's hot new building become precious as it ages, or will it become simply dated?

· *Cost.* Most icon buildings require budgets significantly above average, and many overrun even these generous budgets. Simmons Hall at MIT, for example, at a cost of over $250,000 per bed, may be the most expensive residence hall ever built. On the other hand, additional money can often be found to meet the high costs of landmark, noteworthy buildings.

Each institution, applying the principles set forth above, must decide what is appropriate for each of its buildings. Institutions have to decide on their values and how they want to express them, because the style of the buildings will express a set of values, whether it is the one intended or not. How do the institutional values of the mission want to reflect themselves in the style of the buildings?

Campus identity and character

Architecture establishes an impression of the character of an institution and reflects its values and mission. The identity of the institution is written in its buildings. Professor Dietrich Neumann from the Brown University Department of Art and Architecture, commenting on Brown University's buildings, noted, "The character of Brown's educational goals and commitment to diversity is reflected in its architecture."[4]

The issue of image affects every college and university. Each institution has to establish a process to determine which fundamental values will be reflected in its buildings, and how it can ensure that it gets what it wants.

Every new building on a campus is an opportunity to embody the regionally distinct physical and cultural characteristics that represent the specific environment of the institution. Advantages of having a building respond to its regional setting can include environmental sustainability, establishing a unique identity grounded in authenticity, and cost savings. Regional influences on building design include color, materials, forms, climatic responses, and cultural patterns.

Proposed neighborhood student and faculty housing at Rhode Island School of Design

Each institution should establish guiding principles for the character of the campus architecture and make sure that its buildings reflect this vision and institutional values. If an institution does not do this consciously, then the buildings will frame a campus identity by chance and by whim. Institutional values that buildings express can include sustainability or brand image.

Princeton University, for example, has been engaged in a dialogue on how its building style should represent its values. The university has established a policy for the campus architecture to reflect the institution's values and identity. The university has decided to be both Ivy League and forward looking; it has established two architectural zones, with more traditional architecture in the older, upper part of the campus and more modern, avant-garde buildings in the other parts of the campus. This approach has been the subject of some debate both on Princeton's campus and in the architectural profession. For Princeton itself, the collegiate Gothic style can signify the important role of history and tradition to Princeton while contemporary architecture can reflect the sense of freedom and an open society it has embraced in the 21st century.

Further, Princeton has recently decided that all new residential construction in the core of the campus will be in the Gothic revival style—despite the fact that building in this style will take longer and cost more than other, more contemporary styles. When this style was first adopted by the university in 1896, its then-president, Woodrow Wilson, wrote, "By the simple device of building our new buildings in the Tudor Gothic Style we seem to have added to Princeton the age of Oxford and Cambridge; we have added a thousand years to the history of Princeton."[5] Clearly, the university's image is at the heart of the decision—both then and now.

Each campus should have, or work toward having, its own unique character—whether expressed by materials, scale, style, or whatever is particular and cherished for the campus. The scale of the buildings and architectural elements such as materials, rooflines, and fenestration are the memorable and defining elements on many campuses. A consistent, complementary building character can be a key attribute in establishing a sense of place and identity of the campus as a whole. Where there is a distinctive predominant vocabulary of materials on campus, this can be reflected in new buildings to enhance a sense of place. Where the architecture of a campus has details and distinctive fenestration, new buildings can achieve a similar richness in their facades to give to the campus cohesiveness and a unique appearance. Architects should be encouraged to explore and expand on the cherished vocabulary of the existing campus buildings.

Right and Top: University of
Colorado at Boulder
Bottom: Dartmouth College

The University of Colorado is a good example of an institution that has consistently built according to a set of common principals. The ensemble of campus architecture produced by the original architect, Charles Z. Klauder, established a palette of elements, including scale, massing, forms, and a consistent vocabulary of materials; careful stewardship has allowed successive generations of architects latitude for reinterpretation while maintaining continuity of identity on what is widely recognized as one of America's most beautiful campuses.

When a controversy erupted on campus over the design of a new building that many felt did not fit in, Dartmouth College embarked on a community-wide process of creating design parameters for new buildings, essentially articulating its values for a "sense of place" for Dartmouth. The design dialogue helped the community come to agreement on what physical elements made the campus special. From the dialogue evolved a consensus: While the Dartmouth campus is home to buildings of a variety of styles, the Georgian influence embodied in the central Baker Library is dominant, and certain common architectural elements in the built environment contribute to a coherent whole that is important to the institution. Those elements include red brick buildings in Flemish bond, white multi-paned windows, masonry (granite and limestone) accents on buildings, pitched roofs in copper, and three- to five-story buildings of modest length.[6] From this consensus, Dartmouth developed a set of guidelines whose intent is not that new buildings duplicate all these characteristics, but that such buildings participate in some way in this campus vocabulary to maintain a coherent whole.

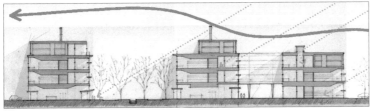

Winter

Building design takes advantage
of seasonal differences in sun
angle and prevailing winds

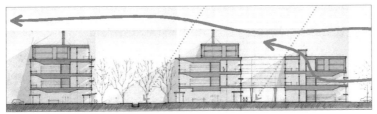

Spring and Autumn

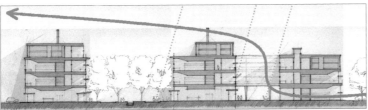

Summer

Sustainable buildings—something for everyone

Sustainability is the topic of much discussion today, but the term encompasses many things. Those institutions whose missions include educating responsible citizens are frequently finding that they must lead by example. Institutions that consider themselves leaders want to show their leadership in this area too. Especially institutions with substantial environmental programs find that not considering sustainability in building design would be academically inconsistent. It is therefore not surprising to find that the number of educational institutions seeking some level of LEED certification for new buildings has increased. Even without LEED certification, many institutions find they are considering environmental issues in their construction projects. Institutions not considering some level of environmental sustainability in new and renovated buildings are going to find themselves left behind—especially considering that environmental designs can be cost-saving designs—and that environmental action on a shrinking planet is the right thing to do.

Proposed library using sustainable technology at Morgan State University

Designing for sustainability encompasses a wide range of actions. Some environmentally effective features are simple and cost little or no money. These actions include proper building siting and orientation, use of fenestration to maximize natural light while reducing heat gain, and good building ventilation. Buildings incorporating sustainable-design features may be no more expensive to build initially than conventional buildings—perhaps less—and they save money operationally as soon as they are occupied. Not to incorporate such environmental features into every building possible makes no sense.

The spectrum of possible sustainable-design features ranges from these tried-and-true actions that are good for the environment and also save the institution money to complex buildings that may cost much more initially than conventional buildings but make a statement and create an image of environmental commitment. To what extent sustainability is a goal for each building project should be on the checklist of issues to reflect on as an institution. Students increasingly demand environmental consideration, and are often in the forefront in making environmental projects real. Many institutions now have or are planning to develop policy statements on environmental action.

Three important approaches in order by relative cost are discussed below.

The common sense approach

Common-sense design approaches that are environmentally sound should be applied to every new building. Energy-saving massing, orientation, use of natural light and fresh air, and other principles are cost effective both in construction and in ongoing operation.

The building should be oriented on the site and designed to minimize the environmental impact to the site. Further, views and connections to the natural environment should be preserved. Proper building orientation can provide significant operational savings, sometimes as much as 60 percent. Siting of buildings should always take advantage of the unique conditions of the location, including solar orientation, wind patterns, and topography.

In addition, institutions should consider multiple use of space when determining value. Marist College, for example, designed a large entry area for Fontaine Hall, its new building for the School of Liberal Arts, Marist College Institute for Public Opinion, and Office of College Advancement. Rather than minimizing this unprogrammed space to reduce cost and meet efficiency ratios, Marist College recognizes that at only a marginal additional cost they have gained an art gallery and a reception area.

The Buntrock Center at St. Olaf College unites tradition and contemporary technology

Some institutions are now planning teardown buildings for housing, partly on the grounds that students' tastes change. Purposeful creation of teardown buildings is bad policy on principle. Even with reuse and recycling of demolished materials, tearing down and rebuilding wastes energy and contributes unnecessarily to landfills. Instead, institutions should think of their buildings as permanent—and then plan to reinvest in them over the years. Durable buildings are made from durable materials with quality workmanship and attention to detail. They are built to be adaptable, rather than disposable, as needs change. Though durable buildings may seem to have higher initial costs, this appearance is typically false. Over a life-cycle of a few hundred years, there will be much less demolition and reconstruction than with buildings designed to last only a few decades.

Buildings should be adapted to the people who live, work, and study in them. In addition to their environmental soundness, a number of building features can save money in the building's operation and help create places that are conducive to work and study. Where people are comfortable, healthy and safe, absenteeism is reduced and performance is improved. These features include:

· Natural light
· Operable windows
· Good indoor air quality
· Noise containment
· Nontoxic materials

Top: San Francisco State University
Middle: St. Olaf College
Bottom: Charleston
Maritime Center

Materials and energy conservation

Energy-reduction methods that should be evaluated for use in the design of new buildings and, as appropriate, in building renovations include:

- Designing the building envelope for thermal performance.
- Considering the use of thermal mass to avoid extremes of heating and cooling.
- Selecting efficient lighting, equipment, and appliances, and, where possible, place them on electronic controls for automatic shut-off when not needed.
- Providing passive cooling and ventilation where possible.
- Making sure that the heating, ventilating, and air-conditioning equipment is properly sized. Given other energy economies in the design, less powerful equipment may be justified and substantial savings realized.
- Consider the use of alternative energy sources such as solar or wind-power as may be appropriate in particular circumstances.

In addition, considering the entire lifecycle of a building may lead to a willingness to invest more initially in order to reduce ongoing maintenance. Again, the use of enduring materials is an important factor. High-performance components and systems should be considered.

Through reuse and careful design, institutions should look for opportunities to minimize the amount of new materials needed. The selected materials should be durable and long lasting. Recycling materials whenever possible is not only environmentally sound but also cost-effective. As with all materials used on campus, where possible, building materials should be reusable, recyclable, and biodegradable.

Locally grown or manufactured materials are preferred for environmental reasons to avoid the impact of transportation. They have immediate benefits to the institution as well. By its appropriateness to the building vernacular of the region, use of local materials contributes to the sense of the institution's belonging to its place and geography. Local materials are frequently less expensive than exotic materials, and they don't go out of style. In addition, they can be operationally cost effective in local climate and conditions.

Some universities might be open to considering the innovative use of materials that can reduce overall environmental impact. The use of grass roofs, for example, is now gaining hold on both sides of the Atlantic. Loyola Marymount University in Los Angeles has a parking structure that provides a grassy playing field on its roof.

Consideration should be given to the environmental impact of the selected materials over their entire life cycle, from manufacture to disposal. The United States Department of Energy distributes free of charge decision-support software known as BEES (Building for Environmental and Economic Sustainability). By measuring the environmental performance of hundreds of building products, this tool can help select products that are both cost effective and relatively environmentally sound. Less expensive materials are not necessarily worse for the environment, nor more expensive ones better.

Showcase buildings and systems technology

A number of buildings across the country have been designed and built to operationally showcase sustainable design and construction. In some cases, such as at Oberlin College and Catawba College, these buildings are intended as working educational laboratories for sustainable practices, a fact that, together with projected operating savings, may justify otherwise high building costs. In other cases, such as at Northland College, useful environmental and educational goals were met within traditional building budgets.

Either way, the use of sophisticated—and perhaps expensive—state-of-the-art technical systems reduce the amount of energy a building requires. Depending on the expense involved, the lowered operational costs due to energy savings may still require decades to pay back higher initial cost. Such buildings are not for everyone, but the colleges and universities that invest in these buildings are paving the way to make some of their features more advantageous in the future. They are also reaping other benefits in educational opportunities and the prestige of leadership.

Merrimack College:
Architecture can serve as a
campus gateway or provide
a beacon at night

Building sustainably may still be a different way of thinking—but it is one that can have both immediate and long-term financial paybacks as well as other, more intangible benefits. In a world where resources are clearly limited, constructing buildings that don't reflect sustainable principles is becoming unacceptable. Institutions of higher education have the opportunity to play a leadership role in creating sustainable buildings and in the education of the responsible citizens of tomorrow.

Contribution to campus life

In addition to a role in the fabric of the campus, each building provides important functionality within its walls and in the spaces it makes. Buildings and the spaces they make, along with other elements of the physical environment, contribute significantly to the outcome of the educational experience. The traditional primary measure of a building's success is how well it provides the functions it is designed for. How well it contributes to the life and mission of the campus as whole is often a secondary consideration or not valued at all. Much has been written about good and bad principles for functional programming and interior design of buildings. Here, we touch upon how buildings contribute as elements of the larger campus environment and enhance learning on campus.

As significant campus places, buildings can support community on the campus by providing informal places for people to meet and interact. These informal meeting spaces should be just as important to the building program as classrooms and labs and should be true program elements. One impediment to meeting the goal of interaction and community is that campus facilities departments and state regulating agencies often set stringent standards for the building's efficiency—the allowable ratios of a building's net square feet to gross square feet.[7] These formulas seldom allow for the gathering spaces near lobbies or along corridors, where much of the informal learning and out-of-class discussion take place. Building programmers, administrators, and educators often underestimate the impact these spaces can have on influencing learning behaviors. Fundamentally, learning is a social activity, and the building program should provide opportunities that encourage collaboration and improve interactions—with peers, faculty, staff, and the campus community. Enlightened institutional leaders often find they continually need to educate legislators, governing board members, and donors that these types of spaces are integral to maximizing learning and social development.

The importance of common community space became apparent to the architect designing the Neuroscience Research building at the University of California, Irvine, when the placement of the coffee break room became a major consideration for the building's future occupants. The researchers who were going to occupy the building realized that most of the important interdisciplinary conversations between researchers happened in the break room; therefore, centrality of the room was a critical concern.

Colorado College:
New student housing commons

Every building has the opportunity to contribute to the abiding quality of the campus. Institutional buildings—unlike most commercial ones—are appropriately designed and built for a long lifespan, perhaps of centuries rather than decades. The last century has seen marked changes in functional needs. We have no reason to believe that the next century will remain static. "The purpose of campus planning and building," states Stefanos Polyzoides, Associate Professor of Architecture at the University of Southern California and co-founder of the Congress for the New Urbanism, "is not the making of individual buildings, however brilliant they may be and for however long they might be brilliant, but really a fabric of continuous building over time…Use is an important first cause in the making of buildings, but it is formed over time, and the ability of reusing form over time is the glory of most great buildings and most great cities."[8] Clearly, taking a long view of a building's lifespan implies ensuring that it will be flexible in supporting uses perhaps unseen when it is first built. Techniques for increasing building flexibility include use of structural systems that allow later changes in room and corridor sizes; regular fenestration rather than unique fenestration for each room; and standardization of interior spaces.

Buildings can contribute in many ways to the liveliness of the external environment. The outdoor areas of the building should be designed to encourage community and to serve some functions. Outdoor "rooms," for example, can be used for some class meetings, for performances, and for meeting spaces. Where possible, these exterior spaces can be included in the formal building program. The design of the building itself can

ameliorate its immediate environment against uncomfortable environmental conditions, such as by shielding against a cold prevailing wind in winter. Overhangs can protect against strong summer sun.

Building entrances are often meeting, gathering, and social spaces and should be designed to be visible, accessible, and to encourage interaction. Where buildings front on public streets, they should have inviting public entrances that activate the street edge; these entrances should be clearly visible at night as destinations. Such entrances provide great opportunities to encourage intellectual and social exchange.

Arcades and porches also offer opportunities for extending the life of a building into the outdoors. If oriented to respond to solar exposure and prevailing winds, arcades and porches can provide inexpensive protected space for programmed or informal use during much of the year. Covered porches allow students to be outside even during wet months as long as the temperature is reasonable. At some colleges, like Rice University, Stanford University, and Washington and Lee, arcades have become a hallmark identity of the school.

To the extent compatible with the programmed use, the activities within the building should be visible to the outside environment. Windows placed to provide views to the activities going on inside buildings could also add security and interest for occupants of adjacent open spaces, walkways, and streets. Since much of campus life occurs at night, "lantern buildings" with many windows can become landmarks on campus. If designed properly, building windows and entrances can also contribute to the life and activity of campus.

A framework for campus architectural decision-making

Prior any new building initiatives, institutional leaders should make sure that they establish for the campus both an overall campus plan as well as campus-wide guiding principles for the identity and character of architecture that are consistent with the institution's values and image. Then, when planning a new building on campus (or an addition to an existing building), leaders should take into account the following:

Evaluate the role of the building in the overall campus plan. How can the building contribute to the overall plan or vision of the campus? Can it be used to frame an important open space, to define a significant view, or to contribute positively to the campus edge?

Clarify and define the building's architectural role on campus. What will its collaborative role be in terms of location, scale, orientation, and context? Should it be a gateway or landmark building? What is its role in reinforcing the character of the campus and identity of the institution?

Ensure that the building follows overall campus architectural guidelines. In what ways must it conform in materials and vocabulary, and how much variation is acceptable?

Consider the building's ecological role. How can it support the values of sustainability and environmental education?

Identify the ways in which the building can contribute to the overall life of the campus in both design and program. What informal social and learning spaces and usable outdoor spaces should it provide? How can it contribute visually to the vitality and activity of the surrounding areas of the campus?

Most institutions have as part of their mission the goal to educate students to be good citizens. We educate them partly by example. Preparing students to be literate about the impact of the built environment on the quality of our lives is one thing they can learn through their experience in higher education. Institutions need to not only talk about the quality of the built world we live in but also to also demonstrate by example their commitment to this quality.

Entry pavilion at
St. George's School

fifteen

Technology, Learning, and Place

Not for the first time, the traditional definition of the learning environment is changing. In the middle ages, the cloister was the place of learning. This evolved, as we have seen, to the campus with its many types of buildings and classrooms. Now, we are moving toward communities of learning, some of which do not even have a physical campus. In one way or another, almost every college and university is engaged in pedagogical innovations involving computer and Internet technologies. In changes ranging from subtle to total, technology is affecting every aspect of higher education.

> Success in the new economy will go to those who can execute clicks-and-mortar strategies that bridge the physical and the virtual worlds…the benefits of integration are almost always too great to abandon entirely.[1]
>
> - HARVARD BUSINESS REVIEW

· Campuses are becoming wired (and wireless); and some campus administrators observe that the amount of time resident students spend in their rooms on computers seems to inhibit social interactions on campus.

· Commuter students are being offered classes that require them to come to the campus less often; and their connection to the community on campus—in some cases already tenuous—may be threatened.

· A growing enterprise for many institutions, distance learning is also an opportunity for people whose remote locations or other circumstances would not normally allow them access to higher education. But if learning is a social activity that best occurs in a community, and if community can best be created in a vibrant physical setting, what can we say about the quality of the education we are providing to distance learners?

In a wired world, the role of place will evolve to adapt to the changing nature of education—sometimes in surprising ways. But place will continue to play a key role in learning.

Computers on campuses

Internet use is now fundamentally a part of most college students' academic experience. According to the Pew Internet & American Life project, 79 percent of traditional college students say that Internet use has positively affected their college academic experience:

- Almost half the college students in the study have a class that requires them to use the Internet to contact other students.

- Two-thirds of the students subscribe to one or more academically oriented mailing lists that relate to their studies.

- Almost three-quarters reported using the Internet more than the library for information searching, while only 9 percent said that they used the library more. Most of the students used the library less than three hours per week. Even when using computers at the library, most of the students did not use online library resources that were available to them, preferring commercially available search engines and various Web sites.

- Well more than half of the students use email for classroom administrative purposes—reporting absences, setting up appointments, clarifying assignments, or discussing or finding out grades.

- Astonishingly, almost half of the students in the study reported that they could use email to express ideas to a professor that they *would not have expressed in class.*[2]

Isolation or community?

Picture this true story. The dorm room is quiet. Or maybe it is filled with music. It's dark outside, but the room is lit by desk lamps and by the glow from two computer monitors. The computers are on. Two roommates are typing busily at their keyboards. One roommate is researching a number of Web sites while conducting an instant message dialog with his girlfriend who attends a university in a different state. The other is downloading some files, writing a paper, and checking his email. The first student receives an email from his roommate. "I don't think we should have a party in our room on Saturday night," it says. "I have too much work to do, and my paper is due on Monday." He hits the reply button and writes, "OK. I'll see if Jason will do it in his room." He sends the message, and sends a quick email to Jason as well. A few minutes later, he gets an email from his roommate. "Works for me." The two are sitting in the same room, but not a word has been spoken.

As ever, students on campus continue to pursue all the normal under-graduate activities. They research and write their papers, meet with teammates on group projects, question professors, line up next Saturday night's date, and have bull sessions at midnight on the meaning of life. But now they can do all this without ever leaving their desk chairs in their dormitory rooms.

Colorado State University environmental psychology professor James Banning, commenting on a survey of over one hundred university hous-ing officers, stated, "Universities are saying: 'Oh, my God, they're in their rooms. How can we ever build a sense of community in this building if they don't come out?'"[3]

Informal group learning environments are being redefined by technology

On the other hand, considerable evidence supports students' use of com-puters for social purposes. The Pew Internet & American Life project notes that much of the student use of computers in libraries and com-puter labs was not for research but for social activities including email and instant messaging. In fact, most use of computers outside of writ-ing and research is social in nature. Even the wide popularity of online role-playing games is due in large part to the ability to interact and share experiences with other people; one survey of players reveals that well over half felt that their online friendships were as good as or better than their real-life friendships.[4] Reflecting on the use of email at Vassar, one student commented, "People probably spend easily three hours a day sending and receiving messages. It's the No. 1 way that romances go on at colleges."[5]

"Because we're in communication every day," declared David G. Brown, the provost of Wake Forest University, discussing the use of email among students and faculty, "we feel that we're a group ready to help one another, not only over the network but in person."[6]

Public computers
Public computer terminals can be, in fact, one of the important loca-tions encouraging face-to-face student interaction. "A significant number of college students use publicly accessible computers on campus for social purposes even when they have their own computer at home or their dorm room…On a Friday afternoon when classes were ending for the week, students were often observed congregating in the computer labs in groups ranging from two to seven people. People sitting next to each other shared interesting Web sites they had found, scores for an online game they were playing, or pictures they had received via email of a sorority party they had attended together…."[7] When doing schoolwork in the computer labs, students often work at neighboring computers so that they can socialize while working, perhaps discussing assignments or comparing work. People working in team projects can be observed

Wireless technology is transforming how and where students study

grouped around a computer, with one person typing and the others offering comments, suggestions, and answers, or just socializing. Here indeed is a place to meet and socialize with old friends and to make new ones.

"If you visited any of the computer labs at our colleges and had some kind of Geiger counter to measure student energy, you would discover that the greatest student activity and energy is now occurring in computer labs," writes Ron Bleed, Vice Chancellor of Information Technologies at Maricopa Community College District.[8]

Clearly, the use of computers and in-person socialization are not mutually exclusive. Properly designed, the placement of computers can enhance campus vitality.

Wireless campuses: the wave of the future?

The distinction between cell phones, personal digital assistants (PDAs) such as Palm Pilots, and portable computers is blurring. Many institutions are now setting up their campuses to support wireless communications, and others plan to do so in the near future.

Evolution of technology changes communications habits. Is text messaging over digital telephones truly worse than voice communication? A century ago, many people refused to use telephones at all because proper communication was supposed to occur face to face. Today people can— and thousands of times a day they do—use their cellular telephones linked with a GPS system to broadcast text messages to people nearby (strangers), asking to meet and chat about topics of common interest. New friendships may follow. Online gaming and matchmaking using mobile phones and a wireless network is currently a reality. These environments are intensely interactive and frequently quite social. Surely, learning environments will also follow.

If placement of public computers can enhance the physical social experience on campus, will wireless networks, by allowing opportunities for instant messaging, email, and other Internet uses without the need to find a public terminal or even talk with a friend, subvert it? Or…are we looking at new opportunities, yet unforeseen, for social experiences of the future?

Campuses in computers

The richness of the Internet allows online users to create, inhabit, and explore virtual places as vividly realistic as any described in books. The places of one's imagination can be as profound and moving as real places. Can these be used to enhance the experience of community among residential, commuter, and especially distance learners? The technology currently exists on the Internet to create, inhabit, and share imaginary—but objective—physical spaces. And there's never a problem finding a parking space.

Pavel Curtis, the creator of one of the earliest synchronous online meeting places, describes them as follows: "A MUD (Multi-User Dungeon or, sometimes, Multi-User Dimension) is a network-accessible, multi-participant, user-extensible virtual reality whose user interface is entirely textual. Participants (usually called *players*) have the appearance of being situated in an artificially-constructed place that also contains those other players who are connected at the same time. Players can communicate easily with each other in real time. This virtual gathering place has many of the social attributes of other places, and many of the usual social mechanisms operate there...."[9]

One would rightly suspect that such environments would not be around for long before some professors would find ways to use them in their classes. "Kenneth G. Schweller, a professor at Buena Vista University, reaches his students everywhere these days. He talks with them by the drink machine in the student union and laughs with them while relaxing on the south quad. He even joined them at midnight in a deserted warehouse near the campus for what he calls 'a real bull session' on the meaning of life. Mr. Schweller may seem to be everywhere at once—but he has a trick: All of these interactions took place in cyberspace. The student union, the south quad, and the warehouse do not exist. They are virtual spaces...on an Internet site called CollegeTown."[10]

Institutions that have taken advantage of text-based place-making technology for one or more courses include the University of Texas at Austin and at Dallas, University of California at Berkeley, University of Florida, University of Toledo, Miami University, University of Toronto, University of Wisconsin-Parkside, University of Virginia, West Virginia University, University of Pennsylvania,[11] Salt Lake Community College, and many others. Diversity University, a nonprofit educational organization, has developed an entire campus used by diverse teachers, institutions, and businesses.[12]

As with any text-based medium such as books, the places described in MUDs are only as compelling and beautiful as they are written to be. For every memorable place, there may be many others that are only bad prose. The same guidelines of placemaking discussed in earlier chapters may apply as much to the campus of the MUD as to an institution's physical campus—for unlike computer-based learning alone, MUD technology can be used to create a feeling of a campus and a sense of place for the online university.

As computer interfaces become richer and more visual, another emerging technology goes even further. Like MUDs, Massively Multiplayer Online Role-Playing Games (MMORPGs) create spaces that can be inhabited by thousands of people simultaneously. But these spaces are created visually as well as in text. These lucrative pay-for-connect-time gaming environments create whole worlds to inhabit, explore, and socialize in. These worlds are evaluated by players on their interactivity, the kinds of activities they provide, and in part on the richness and interest of the physical place that they create. How many visitors to how many colleges and universities judge the institutions and their campuses in exactly the same way?

MMPORG technology appeals to a growing number of people. As of mid-2002, Sony's "EverQuest," one of the more popular games, has a base of over 450,000 users.[13] The average EverQuest player is about twenty-five years old and plays about twenty hours per week. Almost a third of the players are students.[14] The world seems "real" enough that in 2001, a survey revealed that some 12,000 people considered the world of EverQuest to be their permanent home. Using an exchange rate established by actual prices players are willing to pay for EverQuest currency and artifacts, an economic analysis of the society revealed a GNP per capita "somewhere between that of Russia and Bulgaria."[15]

What is the relevance to the field of distance learning of a game environment so addictive that some people choose to "live" there? Time and again, technologies developed for gaming (such as color monitors and sound cards) have found their way into business, education, and the home. MMPORG technology is already beginning to be used in education to create environments for some courses. Researchers at George Mason University and the Harvard University Graduate School of Education, for example, have put together a course that is intended to teach higher-order reasoning to middle-school science students. Students visit River City, a three-dimensional virtual town of the 1890s, whose citizens are becoming sick with an unknown illness. They can explore the town, talk with the citizens, and interact with one another in teams to gather information, form hypotheses, and test their theories. "To make the virtual landscape authentic, the simulation features photographs and objects provided by the Smithsonian Institution, another partner in the project."[16]

"AlphaWorld" is a large virtual world given over to placemaking. Users build features of the world, which as of August 2002 covers a simulated area slightly larger than the state of California. It seems almost inevitable that someone would use this technology to build online learning environments. In fact, Active Worlds, the company that created AlphaWorld, has also created the Active Worlds Educational Universe (AWEDU), which makes place-building technology available to educators. Institutions that have participated in AWEDU include the University of Colorado, University of California Santa Cruz, Cornell University, and others.

The Contact Consortium, a nonprofit organization dedicated to fostering "the development of human contact, community and culture in digital space"[17] sponsored in 1998 an architectural competition to design "TheU," "one of the first virtual universities to be built in glorious three dimensions using the new virtual worlds technology. TheU looks like a real, visual campus with buildings, green space, meeting places, and a whole range of services. In TheU, people (represented as digital avatars) move around campus, interacting with each other, learning and helping others to learn."[18]

We have been examining a vision of a university as near as the student's monitor and as tangible as his keyboard. Extending the principles of existing technologies such as MUDs and MMORPGs to the university, one thing becomes apparent. Even in cyberspace, the creation of memorable places is key to creating a sense of belonging to a community and a world of interaction and learning. Universities and colleges may find in time that their visual presence online is just as important as the physical beauty of their actual campuses. Indeed, the one can be used to evoke the other in students' minds.

Hybrid learning on campus

Any innovation that allows residential and commuter institutions to offer additional classes without requiring additional classroom space is potentially attractive, as long as the quality of education is not compromised. For this reason, some institutions have embraced computer-based learning (on the distance education model) even for their resident and commuter students. Fairleigh Dickinson University, for example, requires all students, even residents, to take at least one course online each year. This means that approximately 10 percent of their courses meet in classrooms seldom or not at all. The online courses, taught by "virtual faculty" members who live all over the world, are part of the university's overall strategy to give its students a "global education." In addition, these courses help students learn how to succeed in online courses, which are likely to be a major component of their continuing education as adults.

Hybrid learning environment at
Maricopa Community College

Many other colleges and universities are offering "hybrid" courses, which typically meet half the time in traditional classrooms and half the time online. These courses seem to provide benefits inherent in both the online and the in-person milieus. Teachers are able to maintain personal contact with students, while students can learn at their own pace and in their own way. The University of Central Florida began offering online and hybrid courses to alleviate a shortage of classroom space. Their research has shown that students in hybrid courses do as well as or slightly better than those in more traditional classes. In addition, the hybrid courses have lower dropout rates.[19]

A freshman composition course at North Carolina State University met half the time in a physical classroom and half the time on a virtual campus. "…This was, without a doubt, the best composition class I have ever taught," reports the professor; "the student writing was the best I have ever incited, and the students themselves were extremely diligent, self-organizing, and enthusiastic about the class, often running class sessions on their own and often meeting after hours to do small group work."[20]

The virtual campus itself had two parts—an "above-ground" portion comprising the institutional and academic facilities and classrooms, and a "below-ground" area comprising "rhizomic steam tunnels…where the students were free to build anything they wanted, create their own rooms, and connect those rooms in any manner they desired to any other room in the steam tunnels…Students did spend all hours of the night and day logged onto the campus, talking with one another, sometimes working on class materials sometimes not, sometimes programming useful objects for extra credit, but they spent most of that time below-ground."[21]

Hybrid courses can be particularly appealing to commuter students. The number of times they must drive to campus is cut in half, so what used to be required commute time can now be spent actually studying, being online with classmates, or engaging in other facets of their lives. The institutions also benefit since fewer parking spaces are required, reducing automobile traffic on campus and in the neighborhood, and providing an environmental benefit.

Some institutions, intending their online and hybrid courses for commuters and distance learners, have discovered that these courses are also popular with the resident population. "'What surprised us the most was how insistent our campus students were about wanting to take these Internet courses,' says Bill Pelz, coordinator of online courses at Herkimer County Community College. 'Our plan was to not even let the on-campus students take these courses.'"[22]

"In the '70s when I was creating a new-era library school [at the State University of New York at Buffalo]," writes Dr. Vincent Giuliano, "in the jargon a library was a physical space or building, period…Today, the largest and most usable and important libraries are to be found on the Internet…It is probably time for some key visionary to start proclaiming that the real campus is the combination of the real and virtual and both need to be co-planned together."[23]

Education planner Philip Parsons adds, "Hybrid learning will have significant implications for physical campus design. Campuses will need fewer traditional classrooms and more of the facilities and amenities that complement the online experience. These include informal meeting and study areas, and technology-equipped 'learning centers' where students can get face-to-face help from faculty or peers while studying online."[24]

Distance learning

To many institutions, the allure of distance learning lies in its potential for improvement of their position with regard to what Sir John Daniel, formerly vice chancellor of The Open University of Great Britain, calls "the eternal triangle of access, cost, and quality."[25] Technology holds particular promise in potentially lowering the cost of providing education; in improving educational quality; and in providing access to a larger number and variety of students, many of whom may have been unable to attend traditional colleges and universities.

No place

Although many distance-learning courses require at least one face-to-face meeting, some administrators, faculty, and students involved in providing or receiving distance learning doubt the need for a *physical* location at all in higher education. "The notion of a living-learning community is dead or dying on most campuses today," one article reports glumly.[26] Sir John Daniel has stated, "The Open University has saved the UK government the capital cost of building about ten campuses."[27]

Many aspects of distance learning seem to support this assessment. Most courseware developed to facilitate remote education focuses on the subject matter of the course. Typically, remote-learning courseware presents lecture texts and graphics, allows bulletin board postings, and provides real-time text dialog of various sorts between professors and students and among students, along with other computer-based features. MIT's OpenCourseWare project is a well-publicized example of the curricula that are provided online. These contain course plans, lectures, sources, assignments, and correct answers—everything needed to re-create a class but nothing to create anything like a class*room*, much less a campus.

What's important?

What would distinguish a Bachelor's degree from, say, Yale University obtained through distance education (if such were offered) from a Bachelor's degree from the same institution obtained through four years of on-campus study? Certainly not the transcript! Considering that the transcript is the enduring, formal record of the undergraduate experience, some people might wonder whether on-campus education is a combination of a course of study (reflected in the transcript) and a kind of a four-year educationally oriented adventure camp (reflected in the residency on campus). Distance learners have simply done away with the adventure camp. As Arthur Levine, president and professor of education at Teachers College, Columbia University, put it: "Four years of living in residence becomes a luxury few can afford."[28]

"Fewer than one in six of all undergraduates fit the traditional stereotype of the American college student attending full-time, being 18 to 22 years of age, and living on campus."[29] Students at Walden University, an institution that has granted degrees through distance learning since 1970, range in age from 25 through 80, with an average age of 45.[30] With busy lives, houses, families, and jobs, these people are in a life-situation very different from that of the 18- to 25-year-olds comprising the majority of residential students. Perhaps the on-campus experience is unnecessary and inappropriate for them. Indeed, some institutions offering courses and degrees through distance education might decide that the experience of a physical community is not something that they, with their particular missions and cultures, require in order to grant a degree.

Who can say this is wrong? Research studies as well as anecdotal evidence generally indicate that online learning is at least as effective as classroom learning. "I teach a course over the Web with students everywhere in the world. It is as meaningful and as good as anything I ever teach in person," states Kermit Hall, president of Utah State University.[31] Many institutions of distance learning, such as Walden University, do provide opportunities for students to meet physically at least once per year to share an educational experience. But each institution that offers distance learning, considering its own mission and culture, must decide how best to engage in meaningful placemaking—if at all.

The limits of placeless learning

Some educators have argued that, because of the need for physical embodiment and presence, most forms of education cannot be effectively conducted over the Internet at all. Hubert L. Dreyfus, a professor at the University of California at Berkeley, points out that learning, especially mastery in a field, requires involvement of at least the emotions and sometimes other bodily attributes as well. An environment that is inherently disembodied can at best be only a partially satisfactory vehicle for higher education; physical presence is a necessity.[32] *The New York Times* reports that "the American Federation of Teachers…critical of the sterility of distance learning, noted, 'All our experience as educators tells us that teaching and learning in the shared human spaces of a campus are essential to the undergraduate experience.'"[33]

Certainly, skills like learning to drive a car, mastering concert-level piano, and surgery seem best taught in person. Distance learning will have some inherent limits on courses offered. But many other subjects are more amenable to distance learning. Here the challenge in making distance learning successful will not be in the subject matter itself but in conveying engagement, enthusiasm, and excitement—the emotional overtones that turn a career into a passion—and in creating a warm and vibrant community among faculty and students.

The Internet does provide more possibility for emotional involvement than some educators may acknowledge. About one in five college students have formed a relationship online before meeting in person.[34] Thousands of people have met love partners in chat rooms or received a groundswell of support from an online community when a child was seriously ill. If enthusiasm can be communicated over the Internet, why not enthusiasm for learning? And if communities can be built, why not communities of learning?

What else is there?

With or without placemaking, there is more to a good secondary education than just courseware, however good. Even older students feel it. A middle-aged husband studying remotely for a degree in law finds his imagination passionately aroused by his class. He has to talk with someone about it in person! His online class does not offer enough opportunity for this.

> [My husband] Ross says online college offers lifelong learning to anyone with a working mind and a working computer. Here is what I'm learning: We must hide from Ross after he has attended an online class with his professor, or after he gets a quiz back. My daughter Melissa and I listen for the voices to stop while he is "in a class" on his computer, and then we try to make ourselves scarce…It doesn't matter. He comes searching. He comes knocking. He finds us.[35]

What's missing here, of course, is community. Education isn't just assignments, readings, tests, and grades. It's also the interaction of a learning community—a way for students and faculty to be involved together in their interesting coursework. A person may be able to learn a particular portion of knowledge through isolated computer-based training, but the experience of gaining a degree is also fundamentally one of interacting with faculty and other students, and growing in this process. Regardless of how they achieve it, a sense of community is as important an aspect of education for distance learners as it is for on-campus learners. Maybe even more so.

Good programs of distance education encourage community on line. The Open University, for example, creates computer "conferences" for many of its courses—some 16,000 of them in 2001, engaging some 110,000 students. When a course has no official conference, the student association organizes one. "Every day, 150,000 messages fly around such virtual conference rooms…the communications greatly reinforce the sense of community among students and the effectiveness of the student association."[36]

One American student participated in a team visual-design project called Omnium, offered by the University of New South Wales. "Omnium v1.0 linked fifty design students from eleven countries all around the world in a process of dialogue and design for ten weeks. Participants existed in an online space that embraced, rather than became concerned with, the differences of time, geography, culture and experience of the participants. Students rubbed shoulders with leading practitioners in an online design studio; they began to learn how people behaved when collaborating together and discussed issues of design process."[37] Although the curriculum did not require synchronous communication, most of the teams wanted it. They needed to create a feeling of community and to get to know their teammates, and they were willing to go to some lengths to do so. Nearly reversing her normal sleep schedule, the American student went online at about 4 A.M. when her French teammate became available. They would "chat" and work through design issues for a while until their Australian and Philippines teammates came on after class. Together, the five students worked into the morning. The American student spent time with her family at breakfast, and then went to bed. Evaluating the experience, she commented, "Socially I think the virtual experience is close, and in some ways better [than face-to-face design teams], but there are still loopholes. It is the only group project I've had where I got to know my group mates as well as I did."[38]

The law student who dogged his wife and daughter needed online community too. He started an online bulletin board/chat room that now boasts over three hundred members. "It's obviously better to be able to associate a face to a posting," he admits, "but I have a number of good friends whom I haven't yet had the pleasure of meeting." He continues, "As far as the communication goes, the online chat rooms and email and phone make a significant connection for me…With some teachers I've engaged in ongoing debates about various topics. Much more access than in a fixed facility school."[39]

The technology used to facilitate team interaction in several of these cases was freeware—AOL Instant Messenger, ICQ, and Yahoo groups—along with standard email. These and other currently available software programs and Internet facilities may be sufficient to create a satisfactory sense of community in some courses and for some institutions that offer distance education.

Hybrid places for distance learning

Many distance learners may benefit from combining physical presence with distance learning. Even beautifully designed virtual spaces may not be enough. No matter how good the text and pictures, no matter how extensive the email and instant messaging, they fall short of physical presence. No matter the frequency and depth of interaction with a friend or colleague, it's nothing like seeing that person's real face. Even most institutions of remote learning provide, in one way or another, the intimate contact of a real physical place.

Distance learning on campus

If an institution of distance learning also has access to a campus, finding a way to use the campus can bring a number of benefits. Even those institutions that primarily provide distance education feel a need to create opportunities for face-to-face contact. Walden University, for example, conducts a three-week summer session on the campus of Indiana University in Bloomington, Indiana. The Open University in Great Britain conducts weeklong courses on a number of campuses in Britain, France, Germany, and Spain, as well as graduation ceremonies in thirty different locations each year. The Omnium project at the University of New South Wales concluded with a live, real-time exhibition of the team project results in Sydney, which most of the students attended.

The leaders of other institutions—those that have created or want to create beautiful campuses because they find that place contributes to learning and to the college experience in all the ways described in this book—find that a sense of place can also add to the quality of the distance-learning educational experience. Many are already experimenting with ways to use computer-learning tools on campus and with ways to create a campus experience for distance learners.

Learning at a distance from campus

As alternatives to existing campuses, many institutions are finding ways to set up satellite locations for remote learners. Argosy University, formed in 2001 by the merging of the American Schools of Professional Psychology, the Medical Institute of Minnesota and the University of Sarasota, has over a dozen campuses and branch locations from Washington, D.C., to Honolulu, from Tampa to Seattle. Headquartered in Bellevue, Washington, the private nonprofit City University offers its programs in twenty sites in Washington, California, Canada, and three locations in Central Europe. Many corporate universities are using educational facilities set up by Sylvan Learning Centers and others as branch locations to teach some courses.

Even where a formal branch location does not exist, students sometimes find ways to create one informally. In places as distant as St. Louis, Missouri and Cambridge, Massachusetts, the authors have seen and heard of Starbucks coffee shops populated largely by students quietly reading, working on their computers, or studying in small groups. In response to this use and use by others working on computers as well, many Starbucks locations now support customer Internet use.

Bricks and clicks

The adoption of technology in higher learning in many ways parallels its use in the retail industry. "Thirty years from now the big university campuses will be relics," predicts Peter Drucker succinctly.[40] Other futurists share the sentiment. But then, some pundits were also eager in the 1980s to predict the demise of retail stores because of the rise of remote (catalog, TV, and Internet) purchasing channels. "By now," one article states, "stores were supposed to be as obsolete as black-and-white television."[41] Some retailers, such as Egghead Computers, closed stores to focus on online sales.

No one would argue that the Internet has not substantially transformed the retail industry. In addition to streamlining its ability to warehouse and deliver products through supply-chain management and other operational technologies, the retail industry has created an online presence that represents a growing part of its business. The parallel between "e-tailing" for "brick and mortar" stores and distance learning for campus-based institutions is intriguing. What can be learned? A look at what has happened with retailing may illuminate the subject for institutions of higher education.

A 2004 research report by Cisco Systems and the University of Texas showed that the Internet economy reached over $270 billion in only the first two quarters of 2000 (projected to be $830 billion for the year).[42] But the brick-and-mortar storefront has been hardier than the pundits predicted. "Retailers came back by figuring out how to compete with other forms of selling. Instead of convenience, they had to give shoppers the one experience that technology could not replace—indeed, the experience that technology almost eliminated in our time. That is, to give *the pleasure of physically being somewhere* [emphasis ours], of going to a place that was bigger, grander and in every way more exhilarating and more energizing than anything the customer could experience at home."[43]

A symbiotic relationship continues to evolve between a retailer's physical presence and its presence online. The ability to deliver through an in-store Internet connection style, size, and color combinations that are not available in that particular store, for example, allows retailers to complete sales while maintaining low inventory levels and distribution costs.

Concept stores—a blend of retail and entertainment, focusing as much on brand recognition as on sales—"can generate 60% more merchandise sales per square foot than a traditional store of the same size."[44] "The idea of Niketown," says Howard Lichter, art director of Nike Inc. USA, "reflected our desire to give the brand a physical face."[45] Kathleen Seiders, marketing professor at Babson College, agrees. "These aren't so much stores as Nike museums. Niketown is not about profitability. This is about brand image. Nike invests in stores the same way they invest in advertising."[46] The Niketown store in Chicago attracts over a million visitors annually and is one of the biggest tourist attractions in Chicago.

Storefront windows at the Gap advertise gap.com online shopping. Bank customers in New York and Philadelphia can sip cappuccino while conducting online banking transactions at ING Bank. Developments such as these suggest that "the value of physical space is not going away but is evolving in its nature and purpose…We are increasingly buying through the electronic medium (Internet) once used principally for advertising, while, conversely, the physical retail space is increasingly stressing brand experience (marketing)."[47]

The parallel situation of the campus and its ability to draw prospective students is undeniable. The experience of retailing suggests that, even as more consumers (students) may choose to purchase their goods (receive their education) online, the brick-and-mortar store (physical campus) will always be important as the symbol of what the retail (educational) institution is—its "brand experience."

In addition to its uses to enhance the quality of education while lowering costs and providing access for more people, technology may provide colleges and universities with an unparalleled opportunity to increase awareness of their identity and "brand" as an institution.

Where do we go from here?

Technology is changing education in one way or another at most American institutions—and it is changing it rapidly and in many ways. We can begin to see some of the implications for the physical (and virtual) places on campus:

Institutional leaders need to think strategically about where computer work areas are located on campus, and how they can use public computer areas to foster social activities and community as well as learning. The increase in use of technology both for academic and other purposes has increased, not decreased, the need to create and to occupy spaces designed for social interaction. To promote interactions, computer work areas should be placed where they are visible and easy to get to. Rather than putting computer labs in converted classrooms that are typically in out-of-the-way locations, institutions should consider putting public computer work areas in central, public places. In addition, computer workspaces should be flexibly designed to accommodate work done in teams and small groups.

With the increase in wireless access, the whole campus is more than ever a potential learning environment. To create a learning area for students, institutions should think about creating settings that are wired, that are social in nature, and that provide food. Some of the old distinctions may vanish. A café-library-lounge might become a popular place.

Community is as important an aspect of education for distance learners as it is for on-campus learners. Whether through chat rooms or online environments, Starbucks-like local spaces or annual on-campus events, institutions must make sure to encourage and meet this need for community.

Hybrid learning environments seems to offer a rich potential in their many forms. Classes that meet sometimes in the classroom and sometimes online may help institutions make more of their limited classroom space, while virtual places may provide social opportunities for group learning.

The retail experience may offer lessons for institutions of higher education. Retailers have learned how to conduct their enterprises partly in physical environments and partly in virtual ones. Both environments have changed as a result of the experience. Clearly, through whatever experimentation lies ahead, institutions will have to find ways to coordinate the sense of identity and sense of place that they project in both worlds.

sixteen

Creating a Vital Neighborhood

Whether an institution is located in a small town, a suburb, or an inner city, a relationship that is mutually beneficial to both the institution and its neighbors can be elusively hard to achieve. The consequences to the institution can be devastating. One college located in a major city, seeking zoning approval for new buildings, was forced to deal with a neighborhood coalition still burning from the impact of previous expansion. To gain the approvals it needed, the college had to agree to an enrollment cap, violation of which required the institution to cease all new building anywhere on campus.

Typically, the town or neighboring community resents the tax-exempt status of the institution, whose non-taxed land is increasing every year. Most academic institutions, especially in confined cities and towns, are on a constant quest for space and land, a threatening reality to most neighbors. Pressures are constant: Student housing saturates the abutting neighborhood districts; parking and traffic congest the city streets; the public must pay to police nighttime student activities. Any community will describe endlessly the negatives while the positives receive little, if any, press.

Often there are negatives from the college's point of view as well. An unattractive or hostile neighborhood environment can have an impact on recruiting top students and faculty. And when the college community experiences a lack of safety in the neighborhood, students worry about going out into the city. The university faces the dilemma of how much to emphasize security with fences, gates, and guards, and how much to identify with and join in the larger urban community in order to gain the understanding and cooperation of community residents, thereby reducing the risk of hostile incidents.

Unless you're in what's perceived to be a vibrant and vital community, you're at a distinct competitive disadvantage to others.[1]

- JACK SHANNON

Many institutional leaders have found that they need to take the lead in building a healthy community. Those institutions that have achieved enduring symbiotic relationships with their neighboring communities or city districts are conscious of, and cultivate, the benefits that both the institution and the city or neighborhood can realize from this relationship.

As with the institutional community, physical places play a pivotal role in engendering a sense of community with the neighborhood and city. Planning and implementing change to the physical environment can be a powerful vehicle for turning a negative community relationship into a positive one, and for addressing the concerns of both the institution and the town. The institutions that are the most successful in creating a positive relationship with their communities work with their neighbors in many ways—from instituting policies of buying products and services locally to acting as developers in their areas. Focusing on the use of physical place, this chapter lays out six general principles followed by the most successful institutions:

- · Living in the neighborhood
- · Setting boundaries on growth
- · Creating a vital edge
- · Handling traffic and parking
- · Respecting the physical character of the neighborhood
- · Leveraging community partnerships through reciprocal planning

Living in the neighborhood

Most colleges and universities prefer that their faculty and staff live in nearby neighborhoods. Faculty who live nearby are more likely than those with longer commutes to spend time on campus when not teaching. Further, employees are more likely to use a means other than the automobile to commute to the campus, reducing traffic congestion. Staff and faculty living nearby strengthen positive ties with the community; and the availability of nearby appealing, affordable housing helps attract desirable new faculty and staff.

All else being equal, most faculty and staff share this preference for short commutes and nearby housing. Unfortunately, all else is not always equal. People do not want to relocate to neighborhoods that are rundown and that feel unsafe. If they have young children, they want the neighborhood schools to be good ones.

Some colleges and universities offer financial incentives to faculty and staff who buy homes in nearby areas. Yale University started such a program in 1994. "As of February 21, 2003," its Web site stated on the

Left: Penn State neighborhood district
Above: Design for new faculty housing
in Cambridge, Massachusetts near
Harvard University

following day, "534 Yale faculty and staff have participated in the Home-Buyer Program representing a financial commitment by the University of over $12 million toward home purchases of more than $63 million."[2]

Ohio State University, through a nonprofit group it created with the city of Columbus, Ohio, is acquiring and rehabilitating more than 1,300 substandard homes in an adjoining run-down neighborhood. In addition, the university encourages faculty members to move into the neighborhood by giving them $3,000 loans at no interest that will be forgiven over a five-year period. Improvements in home ownership in the neighborhood are being made along with a major redevelopment of a commercial street bordering campus. This redevelopment replaces some thirty-two businesses, many of them bars, with a mixed-use development comprising "five buildings with 250,000 square feet of retail space, 70,000 square feet of offices, 200 apartments and parking for 1,200 cars." The university will lease the office space and about 70 percent of the housing. In addition to a Barnes & Noble bookstore, the retail space will include a mix of local, regional, and national chain stores.

Since starting its program in 1998, the University of Pennsylvania has helped provide housing in West Philadelphia in a number of ways. Between 1998 and 2001, at least 276 Penn faculty and staff purchased homes in the area, assisted by Penn's Guaranteed Mortgage Program. Under this program, the university guarantees mortgages on single and two-family homes in a wide area of West Philadelphia for up to 105 percent of the purchase price (to cover closing costs) or up to 15 percent of the purchase price to help pay for home improvements. For homes within a more restricted designated area, lump-sum assistance is provided. Employees who already live in the area are also eligible for financial help in making exterior home improvements. In addition, the university is proactive in providing rental housing. It has raised more than $50 million in capital to create a fund to protect an inventory of over 200 units of moderate-cost rental housing for students and community members, and worked with a private developer to create another 282 units of housing. In some cases where a seriously distressed property was blighting an otherwise stable block in its area, the university has purchased, renovated, and resold the rundown unit.[3]

But all of these housing incentives might not have been enough to encourage employees and faculty to put down roots in West Philadelphia. "Because quality public education is a key factor in where families choose to live, Penn's partnerships with the West Philadelphia community have long focused on improving the neighborhood's public schools. Over the past decade, more than 1,700 Penn faculty, students and staff have joined together with local educators and community members in more than 130 programs at 33 different West Philadelphia public schools."[4] Many other colleges and universities are also actively involved in community schools.

Colleges and universities located in expensive neighborhoods also hope that faculty and staff will be able to live nearby. Providing economic assistance under these circumstances is also challenging. Some institutions subsidize housing for some of their faculty to make it possible for them to live nearby.

Affordable, attractive neighborhood housing is often an issue both for the community and the institution. Whether the problem is the deterioration of the neighborhood or its gentrification, colleges and universities may be the entities best able to find win-win solutions that both support the neighborhood and create opportunities of nearby housing for faculty and staff.

Setting boundaries

When a college or university engages in a program or pattern of buying land in its neighborhood, it may unwittingly become a contributor to the neighborhood's decline. Some people may purchase property as a speculative investment rather than as a place to live. These people and others, even if they do live in their property near the institution, do not feel encouraged to invest in that property, knowing that the university is a likely buyer who won't care much about the condition of the property when they buy it.

This activity destabilizes the neighborhood.

Most neighbors can live with a certain degree of institutional expansion, but they want an explicit understanding about how much the university is going to grow, what kind of growth it will be, and where it will take place. To be good neighbors, to contribute to the quality of the neighborhood rather than to its decline, institutions must, in partnership with community groups or town governments, set limits to their community encroachment, and then plan to live within those limits.

A sometimes-unexpected side benefit to the institution is that limiting expansion may cause it to be more creative in infill development on campus, increasing the density of interaction and feeling of community on campus.

From time to time, an institution may want to engage in some kind of development outside its growth boundaries in the neighboring community. Such projects should be undertaken with care. In close partnership with the community, the institution may be able to meet its space needs in ways that also provide substantial benefit to the neighborhood.

Creating a vital edge

Until recently, a clearly defined edge, ideally with a fence, was seen as a desirable way of distinguishing a college or university from its neighborhood. Today, edges must be more porous, as institutions seek ways to be part of, rather than separate from, their neighborhoods. Treatment of the *edge* between the institution and the town is one of the most decisive actions an institution can take in building vitality in its neighborhood. Many colleges and universities, considering only the organization of functions within their campuses, ignore this opportunity.

They do so at their peril.

Schuylkill Gateway, Philadelphia, illustrative master plan

Schuylkill Gateway revitalizes
former rail yards and connects
the University of Pennsylvania
with the center of the city

Meeting parking needs with large lots and structures at the campus edge may work well in preserving an historic campus core, but may blight the surrounding neighborhood, starting a chain reaction of deterioration. Conversely, livening the edges of streets shared with the town by judicious placement of residential use and student activities may create enough liveliness that markets open for private shops, cafés, and development as well.

Depending on the nature of the institution and of the town, many types of lively and enlivening seams between the two exist. Institutions can contribute to the vitality of their towns and neighborhoods through commercial, residential, research, and cultural interfaces.

Commercial campus district

A college or university may anchor a commercial district in a larger town or city. The institution plays a central role in this district, such as Syracuse University does in the M Street area of Syracuse. M Street is not the main commercial area of the city, but rather a neighborhood center that grew up next to the university. College Hill in Providence, which serves Brown University and the Rhode Island School of Design, and College Town at Cornell are other examples. Small colleges and universities in small towns may bring zest and vitality to an adjacent small downtown area. Oberlin College (3,000 students) plays such a role in Oberlin, Ohio (population 8,000); to a lesser extent, so does Stetson University (2,000 students) in Deland, Florida (population 21,000). Were it not for the presence of the college or university, most likely those small rural communities would not exist as such vital town centers.

Residential interface

Bates College in Lewiston, Maine houses four hundred of its 1,700 students in college-owned houses in the surrounding neighborhood. Absorbing local housing stock to remedy short-term residential needs or control ownership of bordering properties, though done with good intentions, can be harmful to the neighborhood. Owners stop reinvesting in their homes, opting to capitalize on student rents or waiting for the institution to buy them out. Most facilities administrators also dislike dealing with home ownership. A single-family home adapted to house a dozen students can be difficult to maintain, and operation is expensive and energy inefficient because the structure is not connected to the college's utility system. Bringing these structures up to applicable code and ADA requirements is difficult and expensive as well. Nevertheless, residential living in neighborhood houses is cited by Bates' students as one of the most popular housing alternatives. Bates is planning to address these issues in part through the creation of new mixed-use residential buildings along Campus Avenue.

Iona College in New Rochelle, New York, owned housing that was difficult to maintain on the edge of the campus. The facilities staff wanted to tear down these buildings in favor of additional parking. Upon careful planning consideration, however, the college decided instead to replace the old buildings with new housing on the perimeter designed as a series of suites and apartments—more traditional university housing buildings that were more feasible to maintain and more sensitive to the adjacent residential neighborhood.

Research

Research conducted by American universities plays a major role in the advancement of regional, national, and world economies. On a worldwide scale, university research has contributed to the development of innovations ranging from penicillin to radar and to cultural shifts as profound as the Internet and telecommunications. Public-private research partnerships must rise to many challenges, but the opportunities that they provide to make a significant impact on society make them central to many universities' missions.

Because of their deep commitment to research, many universities are now involved in owning or developing research parks.[5] A survey conducted by the Association of University Research Parks in 2003 reveals the depth of university involvement. Most research parks have been established on completely or partially university-owned land (65 percent), and in most cases the university completely or partially owns the buildings as well (56 percent). The university provides financing in 26 percent of the cases.[6]

Development of a new research campus provides an opportunity to make a difference both to the university and to the adjacent town. Historically, research campuses such as Princeton Forrestal were conceived of as office parks. Buildings were dispersed, often developed on greenfields (formerly undeveloped farmland). Cornell University's research park is located near the airport, not near the university. The university was reluctant to establish the new development on or near the core campus, as it wanted to reserve limited core-campus land for potential future university core purposes. It was also concerned about bringing private enterprises into the core campus. Because of its distance from the campus, however, the research function doesn't work as well as it might. Professors and students perceive the drive to and from the research area as an impediment to their activities. Like the suburban office parks on which they are modeled, these research parks perpetuate our society's dependence on the automobile, with its attendant traffic and pollution problems. By pulling people and functions off-campus, they also harm rather than promote community on campus.

MIT's Tech Square in Cambridge, Massachusetts provides a dense urban research environment

MIT's urban Tech Square is in many ways a better model. It creates a vital, vibrant community directly adjacent to the institution. From an urban viewpoint, Tech Square might have been even livelier if more housing had been included.

In or near former industrial neighborhoods, some colleges and universities find that old industrial buildings offer a perfect space for research. They buy these industrial properties and retrofit them, in the process transforming the neighborhood from one of warehouses and underutilized factories to an active academic area. MIT is a classic example, with its expansion along Vassar Street and Main Street in Cambridge.

The challenges in creating an environment that nurtures productive research are noteworthy. Traditionally, academic departments have wanted to be separate, often "owning" their own facilities. Many campus environments still reflect this approach. But increasingly, success in cutting-edge research requires extensive communication and cooperation across disciplines. In addition, research often involves interaction with private concerns. The academic and business worlds do not always mix smoothly. For example, industrial concerns about security must be balanced against academic freedom and desire for communication. The most successful research institutions are those that give serious consideration to how they organize their buildings and their campuses, as well as the human organizations that occupy them, to meet these often-conflicting agendas.

Cultural activities

Campus theaters and other arts functions of universities or colleges are often located on the edge of the campus, primarily because of the university's awareness that a large percentage of the attendees of those

New public space at
MIT's Tech Square

events are from outside the college community, and that townspeople are more likely to attend cultural events than they are to attend classes. Especially in small towns, this function integrates the institution and the town. Cornell University's Schwartz Center for the Performing Arts, for example, which houses the university's primary performance spaces as well as its Department of Theatre, Film, and Dance, sits on the border between the Cornell campus and neighboring Collegetown. The primary performance space of the North Carolina School of the Arts is the Stevens Center, a restored neoclassical 1929 silent-movie theater in downtown Winston-Salem, North Carolina. The Stevens Center also houses a number of community-based performance organizations such as the Winston-Salem Symphony and the Piedmont Opera Theatre.

As many paths can lead to a vital community and neighborhood as there are institutions and neighboring communities to create them. Each one is unique—but there are common elements. In most of these paths, the physical space of the campus, especially the edges where it joins the neighborhood, plays an important role.

Handling traffic and parking

The worst of town-gown relationships many times center on automobile issues. In every city and town where we develop a college or university master plan, traffic and parking are almost always on the agenda. In many places, the institution is the single largest generator of traffic in nearby neighborhoods. Lessening the impact of traffic and parking on the town requires a cooperative strategy. The best solutions can strengthen the university's relationship with its town; the worst can destroy the neighborhood.

Impact on surrounding communities

Some universities have bought up land in surrounding neighborhoods—often areas where students and faculty as well as neighbors once lived—and have torn down housing to create surface parking for the campus. These barren parking lots can destroy neighborhood character, isolate the institutions from their host communities, and perhaps even cause neighborhood decline.

Universities that build parking lots along their border with the community are—wittingly or not—sending a message of hostility to their neighbors. To avoid this, the University of Washington, which works closely with its neighbors in its planning and development efforts, specified in its master plan for the West Campus area that abuts a mixed-use, residential-scale neighborhood, "Development in that area should avoid an inward focus and care should be taken that development not turn its back on the community...."[7]

In the end, the impact of the automobile in the neighborhood hurts the institution. Being surrounded by traffic and parking lots, perhaps in a declining neighborhood, does little to enhance the institution's image among its visitors, prospective students, and their parents.

Fixing the problem at its source

The best method for reducing automotive impact on the neighborhood is to reduce demand for driving. Many colleges and universities are motivated to reduce demand because of problems on campus, particularly in the core area. In this case, the neighborhood will also benefit.

The University of California at Davis and the city of Davis, California have worked together to provide an extensive network of bicycle paths and lanes that interconnect the city and the campus. The city now requires bikeways in all new housing developments.

Respecting the physical character of the neighborhood

In its developments in or near its neighborhoods, an institution should respect those neighborhoods' physical character. The 2001 Seattle Campus Master Plan for the University of Washington specifies as a land-use policy that "University land uses located outside the boundaries and on the campus periphery should be compatible in size and nature with the surrounding uses."[8]

Like many colleges and universities, Georgia College & State University recognizes the importance, both to the college itself and to its community, of its beautiful campus. More conscious than most, Georgia College & State University includes its campus as a premier element of its mission statement.

Opposite and Above: Proposed student and faculty residences for the Rhode Island School of Design

> Georgia College & State University is Georgia's designated Public Liberal Arts University, located in historic Milledgeville, Georgia, less than a dozen miles from the geographic center of the State. Milledgeville was the antebellum capital of Georgia and is a center of history and culture featuring beautiful antebellum homes and historic buildings. The University enhances the town's beauty with its architectural blending of majestic buildings of red brick and white Corinthian columns. Georgia's Old Governor's Mansion, one of the finest examples of Greek revival architecture in the United States, is the founding building of the University and remains central to the University's Mission.[9]

Lack of respect for a neighborhood's character can cause lasting problems. Neighbors sometimes have long memories. Harvard University is still feeling the repercussions of its 1960s-era decision to build high-rise modern student-housing towers in Cambridge's blue-collar residential Riverside neighborhood. The Peabody Terrace complex, largely admired among architects, is generally loathed by the neighborhood community. "It's a great little neighborhood, except that Harvard built these three ugly concrete towers," one neighbor is quoted as saying.[10] And, almost forty years later, a *Boston Globe* editorial vividly recalls the emotions that Peabody Terrace provoked. It describes the complex as "a hulking three-tower high-rise [that] swallowed up city streets, obstructed views and access to the river, and dwarfed the surrounding two and three-story clapboard houses. The towers cast an ominous, permanent shadow over the predominantly African-American neighborhood." "They just come in and wipe you out, and they expect you to go away because they have money and power," one protester is quoted as having said—back in 1970. All this emotional grief was marshaled 31 years later in an editorial that opposed Harvard's building of two museums on a nearby site today.[11]

Leveraging community partnerships through reciprocal planning

Universities and their neighborhoods often share the same needs. Actions that benefit one can also benefit the other.

Lehigh University

Lehigh University and its residential neighbors

Lehigh University is located on the southern edge of the South Bethlehem business district, a section of Bethlehem, Pennsylvania that has developed an image as a lower-class area. Traditionally, the university has grown away from, rather than toward, the city. It acquired six city blocks of land just north of the campus, demolished the buildings on these blocks, and created parking lots in part to provide a buffer between the campus and the city. Despite the beauty of its campuses, the richness of nearby housing stock, and the safety of the neighborhood, none of these measures was sufficient to overcome visitors' image of the university as being in a dangerous, unattractive area. And despite the diversity and liveliness of the community and the presence of many students in off-campus housing in the neighborhood, not one store was oriented toward students. In 1998, the university decided to look again at its long-range campus and facilities plans with an interest in revitalizing the neighborhood as an asset for students and an enhancement to its strategic marketing.

Lehigh's new plan emphasized improving the historic in-city campus and the university's border with the city. As part of the planning process, the university learned that the density of student rental housing on some

Lehigh University's
main quadrangle

| *Creating a Vital Neighborhood*

streets was a neighborhood concern, and that an important initial action, from the neighborhood perspective, was to create additional student beds on campus. The new master plan addressed this need by proposing to build new student housing in a style compatible with the neighborhood on university-owned land adjacent to the town that it had previously converted to parking lots.

In addition, the university planned the addition of new academic buildings on the city street edge that would face outward as well as in, thereby providing a more open and welcoming face to the city. Construction has now begun on some of these projects.

Improvement of living conditions in two other neighborhood areas adjacent to the business area and to the university remained a concern to residents. In particular, they perceived a need for a strategy to "dedensify" certain streets and areas, encouraging the conversion of multifamily investment properties rented mostly to students back to single-family owner-occupied housing. In addition, neighborhood parks and play spaces, as well as local convenience stores, were needed. A new study by a nonprofit neighborhood development organization and funded partially by Lehigh, was undertaken to address these issues. A ten-year implementation period is envisioned and by 2001 was already partially funded.

Lehigh University and the South Bethlehem business district

The city of Bethlehem, Pennsylvania wanted to improve its South Bethlehem business district. To the south end of the district, Lehigh University provided some activity, but with the failure of Bethlehem Steel, many buildings on the north side had become vacant. Lehigh could have purchased these buildings outright for needed research facility expansion, but the university was sensitive to the city's concerns about becoming again a "company town" again, this time for the university. Rather than purchase and improve land on its own, Lehigh decided therefore to help fund a planning study that would be conducted by the city of Bethlehem. This study recommended the creation from the old Bethlehem Steel facilities a research and entertainment district and defined specific actions the city should take to integrate its revitalization efforts with those of the university. In addition, it specified policies and priorities for implementation.

In support of this plan, the university has currently leased space in the new research district, becoming its first, and prime, tenant. The city and the university together applied to the state of Pennsylvania for funding for street improvements. This funding—ten million dollars over a three-year phased approach—was approved in 2001.

Trinity College

Trinity College in Hartford, Connecticut is a distinguished school, but its poor-quality neighborhood put it at a significant disadvantage in student and faculty recruitment. Taking a leadership role in making changes, in 1996 the college announced a comprehensive revitalization initiative for the neighborhoods surrounding its campus, an initiative in which other organizations have joined. Broadly conceived, the initiative includes the development of a "Learning Corridor" linking Trinity with other institutions nearby and providing educational and recreational opportunities for the community, including a Boys/Girls Club, a Montessori Day Care Center, a middle school, and a charter school for the performing arts. In addition, "the initiative will generate over $130 million in new construction. Designed to increase owner occupancy throughout the neighborhoods, the initiative will weave housing rehabilitation, neighborhood retail businesses, streetscape improvements, job training, recreation, and family services into the fabric of the reinvigorated residential community, thus building widespread and deeply vested interest in maintaining the quality and vibrancy of the community."[12] Improvement to the physical quality of the neighborhood is only one part of the initiative—but a critical one.

"Trinity has assumed leadership of this effort because we have a profound sense of obligation to Hartford and we intend to honor it. And this obligation is not at odds with our fundamental educational mission. In fact, the two are closely aligned and complementary. It is vital to the College's future that our neighborhood turn itself around. We have led in this initiative because it is the right thing to do. It would be morally bankrupt for Trinity to teach the liberal arts on our campus and ignore what is happening across the street,"[13] stated Trinity's then-president, Evan Dobelle.

Themes and lessons learned

In many cities and towns, overall improvements in the neighborhoods near institutions of higher education should be good for the institutions, the cities, and the neighborhoods themselves. But often, these improvements are not possible without leadership and direct action by the institutions. Colleges and universities are emerging as significant players in urban revitalization. An institution working to improve its neighborhood can demonstrate its commitment through a variety of actions:

· Emphasizing in its own planning efforts the needed delicate relationships with the city and the surrounding neighborhoods

· Providing open communications to engender trust on both sides, ensuring that the city and neighborhood constituencies are involved in the planning process

· Understanding the needs and the viewpoint of the city and neighborhoods, which manifest the diverse cultures of their constituencies

· Responding appropriately to specific situations by playing the role that works best, at times by direct leadership, at others by background support, and when possible, by equal partnerships

· Above all, working with the city and neighborhood to create a bold and clear vision of the vibrant college town that the neighborhood is or could become

Part IV.
Conclusion

Making It Happen

Commitment to implementation makes the difference between a campus that supports the institution's mission and one that erodes it. Pressures to compromise the plan and physical vision of the campus are constant, and not always easily recognizable. Sometimes these pressures may present themselves as attractive alternatives—or even as logical extensions of the plan itself. The program manager might suggest that housing could be built for less money if it were built off campus, or the architect for the next building might maintain that it is a signature building and should be placed in the middle of the main quadrangle or blocking an important visual axis. Compromises to the plan may cause changes that in either radical or subtle ways obscure and then lose the vision. This chapter suggests some ways to stay the course.

> If society is paralyzed today it is not for lack of means, but for lack of purpose.[1]
>
> - LEWIS MUMFORD

Challenges

Providing leadership

People naturally tend to be vested in the status quo and in their own self-interest. A vice president for enrollment management, for example, is naturally motivated to do anything necessary to make the institution look attractive to prospective students. Not surprisingly, therefore, this officer and others may favor allowing freshmen to bring cars onto campus and providing plenty of free, convenient parking for them. Other campus constituencies lobby to reduce parking or at least limit its growth for reasons of aesthetics, environmental quality, and fostering an academic community of students and faculty on campus.

The president and the trustees are the people in the institution who look out for the institution as a whole, and who must therefore weigh the considerations of the different constituencies one against the other. Therefore, the president and the board are the natural source of leadership and vision for the institution. As leaders, they must create the vision in people's minds and then "sell" it—perhaps over and over—as the institution implements changes in the campus.

Competition for limited resources

Resources are limited. Pressure to keep higher education affordable limits the ability to raise funds by increasing fees, tuition, and room and board. Thus, capital improvements to the campus and facilities are in competition with many other needs, such as expanding research, adding new academic programs, supporting ongoing operations, and offering more financial aid.

One way to gain support for funding physical campus improvements is to communicate the linkage between a beautiful, collegial campus and other goals that the institution hopes to achieve. Unlike many other uses of funds, improving the campus can be highly leveraged. A beautiful campus is a major factor in attracting new students and faculty, in impressing donors, and in providing amenable spaces for students to study and learn.

Consistent follow-through

Lack of consistent follow-through in master-plan implementation has destroyed the fabric of some of America's great campuses. Master plans intended to guide growth for ten or more years may be compromised when the first new building is built. Architects, donors, and even newly inaugurated presidents sometimes have their own agendas and ideas and don't feel bound by an existing plan. But if every new building goes off in its own direction, ignoring the plan, then the campus as a whole is going nowhere.

The vision of the campus as a whole, as laid out in the plan, must be clear and explicit—and not just at the time it is conceived. Years after the plan is complete, each institution should still have a way to remember and respect the process it went through and the reasons why it made its planning decisions. The best way to ensure that this will happen is to empower someone or some group on campus to keep the vision in front of the campus constituencies. Ongoing relationships with planning consultants can also be highly effective in keeping an institution on course.

Leading the way

The single biggest factor in achieving quality in the campus environment is leadership that understands the relationship between the physical environment and achieving other institutional goals.

Visionary leaders articulate the linkages between the campus development plan and the resulting enhancements of the institution's essential characteristics, including:

- Unique culture and history
- Sense of place
- Academic programs and research initiatives
- Learning environment
- Interpersonal interaction and community

Many legislative bodies and governing boards are rightly focused on the mission of institutions to foster learning and pursue new knowledge. However, when this focus, in considering the physical campus, myopically favors teaching and research facilities—classrooms and laboratories—to the exclusion of other campus elements, it ignores the value of the entire campus as a learning enterprise and as a significant factor in attracting and retaining high-quality students and faculty. It is up to the institutional leaders to broaden this vision. They can do so by linking the campus development plan and each subsequent improvement to the cultural attributes, history, and regional identity of the institution. As stewards of the institution, college and university trustees must have confidence that physical planning ideas are linked to *their* unique and special place. In addition, making the connection between the vision of the physical campus—the campus plan—and the institution's strategic initiatives is a powerful tool in building broad support for overall facility improvements.

Vision alone is not enough. Some people may see the vision or plan as only a broad guideline and therefore don't understand that each project, with all its details, either supports or undermines that plan. Putting the vision aside in order to deal with a current crisis or take advantage of a current opportunity is always a temptation. Sometimes, during implementation, changes are proposed that modify the plan in some way without considering how much of the vision may be compromised. Sometimes, too, seemingly small decisions about physical changes have big or cumulative implications that are not immediately obvious. Institutional leaders have to be able to see in each decision the implication for the vision. Even small decisions can have impacts that cumulatively undermine the plan.

Shortly after completing its master plan, the University of Scranton found itself, because of overenrollment, in urgent need of more housing. The institution's existing housing was located on the side of the campus farthest from downtown. To enliven the core campus area and the downtown area close to the campus as well, the master plan prepared by Sasaki Associates identified a need for housing on the downtown side of campus. But this was a crisis situation—it was January, and the housing was needed by September. The university identified an immediately available piece of land on the far side of the existing housing. But before proceeding, they called the planners. Sasaki was able to identify three additional potential housing sites that were more in keeping with the long-range plan, and the university settled on one of them. To the delight of both the university and the city, new housing in a location supportive of the university's vision was ready for occupancy by mid-August.

The main quadrangle at Wesleyan College in Macon, Georgia, was open at one end. To complete the main quadrangle and create a more collegial and memorable central space, the master plan called for a new chapel to be built, with housing behind it. In the plan, the housing followed the grid established in the central campus, had a favorable solar orientation, and began framing a more intimate residential quadrangle behind the main one. When an architect was hired to design the housing, the master plan was ignored. The new design had no chapel and called for housing blocks at a forty-five degree angle, leaving the main quad open and ignoring the overall texture and quality of the existing campus. The college asked Sasaki Associates to review the first drawings for consistency with the plan. Based on Sasaki's review and articulation of the principles established in the plan, the college convinced the architect to make appropriate modifications to the design.

Commitment on the part of the president, governing board, and senior staff to sound planning and sensitive facility design is critical to plan implementation and maintaining stewardship of the long-range vision.

The president at Utah State University believes in the relationship of campus quality to the success of all his programs—research, academic, and recruiting. Despite huge (10 – 15 percent in 2002) budget cuts at the state level, he has been committed to a continuing program of campus improvements. He has Sasaki Associates intimately engaged in the strategic planning process with his board. As a result of his commitment to planning, he has been able to find private funding for a new arts complex and has obtained federal funding for a new research park.

Strategies to deal with resource challenges

Finding resources to meet needs for physical space on campus is a perennial challenge for most institutions of higher education. Getting more money from the legislature or receiving a gift from a donor are obvious ways to provide more facilities—but these methods aren't always easy or even possible. How can an institution meet its needs if these straightforward approaches are insufficient or impossible?

Institutional leaders, college and university boards, and state legislatures are always looking for creative ways to maximize what they can accomplish with the funds they have. Strategies include:

- Using existing facilities to the maximum
- Reusing and revitalizing existing buildings in preference to building new ones
- Accomplishing multiple objectives with each building project
- Finding creative funding opportunities
- Linking capital projects with larger institutional goals and strategies

Use existing facilities to the maximum

The best response to increasing space needs is to find ways to use existing facilities better—for a variety of reasons: Board members and state legislators want to be assured that their limited resources are being used to the maximum. More intensive use of existing space frees up capital resources for other investments and uses and reduces the amount of space that has to be maintained and operated. Furthermore, it is the right thing to do for environmental reasons.

One major area where consultants at Sasaki Associates consistently find underutilization is the classrooms and laboratories. We target utilizations of 75 percent and 60 percent, respectively, for these buildings. But at some liberal arts colleges, we have found rates as low as 23 percent. At public institutions, there can be government pressure to utilize facilities more; some states have instituted a standard use rate—typically around 60 percent—that must be met. Nevertheless, we sometimes find utilization rates at public institutions in the range of 40 percent.

Why is utilization so low? One reason reflects the lifestyle choices of students and faculty. Competition from extracurricular and co-curricular activities exerts pressure to schedule few classes after three or four in the afternoon. Many students and even faculty prefer to avoid early morning classes as well. In addition to avoidance of less desirable hours, many students and faculty prefer to avoid classes on Fridays, which has become a particularly dead day on most campuses.

To overcome these preferences takes determination on the part of the administration, especially the academic leadership. Acknowledging this trend—and responding as well to deep cuts in state funding, the University of Oregon offered tuition discounts to students who select classes offered in off-peak early morning, late afternoon, or early evening hours. As a result, Joe Stone, the Dean of Arts and Sciences reports, "We have actually had a better experience with classroom scheduling than in previous years."[1] In fact, some upperclassmen complained that they wanted to benefit from these savings but could not, since mostly large classes oriented toward first-year students were scheduled in the later hours, while smaller seminars for upperclassmen were not.

The recent rise in popularity of flexible scheduling also has a detrimental impact on classroom utilization because it limits which classes can be scheduled at which times in the same room. Especially on smaller campuses, flexible scheduling also has a negative effect on the feeling of campus community. When all classes are scheduled at the same times, the community sees itself collectively in the few minutes between classes; but when classes end and begin at different times, the number of people visible between classes can be substantially reduced, creating more of a feeling of isolation.

Another barrier to utilizing space efficiently rises when individual academic units control space. These units seldom have incentive to share their resources. Classrooms and lecture halls may go unutilized for days at a time, but departments don't want to give up the space for fear of losing it. Institutions that allocate space to individual academic units might want to work toward getting as much space as possible into a central inventory that can be controlled by the registrar to schedule classes. In institutions where academic units have controlled their own classroom space for a long time, a feeling that something is being taken away must be overcome. Many institutions find that they must provide some incentive to share.

These may seem to be difficult political and social problems to overcome. But the rewards are great. Even small to medium-sized institutions could find that an increase in utilization of existing academic buildings as small as 10 percent could eliminate the need to construct a new academic building.

Reuse and revitalize existing buildings

Campus buildings
Generally, institutions with older campuses don't hesitate to invest in and renovate buildings in the historic core. These buildings are often built to last for centuries and are treasured by the institutions. In addition, they may be of historic significance.

Renovating existing buildings rather than building new ones somewhere else can have important advantages. These buildings may be making a contribution to the fabric of the campus because of their location; and because of their historic value, they may be attractive to students, prospective students and their families, alumni, and potential donors. Revitalizing core buildings with high-traffic uses also helps to keep campus activities close together in the center.

Sometimes, institutional leaders may need to weave together the right story to raise money to renovate a building, since the immediate attraction of a named building is not available. Harvard University faced this issue when it decided to renovate two underutilized historic buildings on its Cambridge campus.[2] Memorial Hall, a fine example of American Gothic architecture from the Civil War period, was renovated into a freshman dining hall and student center. By stressing its importance in renewing commitment to undergraduate education, the university was able to inspire the imagination of a key donor. A nearby Georgian revival building by McKim Mead and White became the new humanities building. Although humanities are central to the Faculty of Arts and Sciences, the humanities departments were spread out in a number of locations, some off campus. By consolidating the humanities programs in a single location near the center of the campus, Harvard was able to physically demonstrate its commitment to "putting humanities back at the heart of liberal arts education." The capital campaign for renovation showcased the elegant old building's role in reshaping undergraduate education and reversed a previous decline in enrollment in humanities programs.

Freshman dining at Memorial Hall, Harvard University

While addressing deferred maintenance may not attract donor funding, giving an historic building a vital, contemporary purpose is always appealing. In addition to potential attractiveness to donors, reusing a building in a core location, even if renovations are extensive, has financial advantages because the site costs—utilities, roads, parking, and so on—have already been incurred. In addition, adaptive reuse can simultaneously address problems of deferred maintenance of these buildings. The same is true with open space. Often, institutions that reuse historic-core buildings find that by bringing more activity into the core, they can take advantage of an existing open space—perhaps a quadrangle that is inactive or underutilized—rather than building a new open space somewhere else. In addition, renovating existing buildings rather than building new ones is generally more environmentally sound.

Reuse includes adding on to an existing building in a way that will make the existing space more usable. For example, elevators might be added to an older building to make it more accessible. Or mechanical systems might be updated. An addition to an existing classroom building could

An addition to the campus center at Merrimack College (left) transformed an existing building (right)

supplement it with larger lecture halls that could not be retrofitted into the existing building. At the University of Scranton, a proposed addition to the existing campus center building in the heart of the campus addressed ADA and pedestrian access issues and also enabled the building to define two major pedestrian spines with active uses rather than blank walls.

At Merrimack College in North Andover, Massachusetts, the Gladys Sakowich Campus Center added on to an existing building to meet expanded program needs. The design also unified separate campus quadrangles with a diagonal travel path that created a "Main Street" social connector between the library and student housing. Three rooftop lanterns epitomize Main Street, filtering daylight throughout the campus center during the day and becoming beacons visible from across campus at night. Their strong visibility ties the campus center and the collegiate campus together, while a new, more transparent façade activates the adjacent plazas and lawns.

Buildings in the community

Some government agencies are becoming aware of the beneficial effect that a college or university can potentially have on a district needing revitalization. Through influence or through direct funding, these agencies and their associated institutions are finding creative reuse opportunities that provide needed space for the institution while generating life and vitality in the city or town.

Capital Community College in Hartford, Connecticut is a good example. Created in 1992 as the merger of Greater Hartford Community College (founded in 1967) and Hartford State Technical College (founded as the Connecticut Engineering Institute in 1946), the institution occupied two campuses until 2002, when it moved into a renovated, historic building in downtown Hartford. The city has gained a vibrant tenant, bringing some 3,000 students to its downtown area. And the college has gained a dramatic, compact "campus," occupying eleven floors, or 40 percent of this historic building. The state committed nearly $70 million in funds for renovations and equipment to make the move possible, while a private developer paid to renovate the other space in the building. The public-private partnership in sharing buildings is being studied as a possible model for other cities in the United States.

Accomplish multiple objectives with each project

Every building project on campus provides an opportunity to accomplish multiple institutional objectives. Leveraging building funds can not only supply needed academic or recreational space but also accomplish campus place-making objectives such as framing spaces, providing critical connections between uses, and activating a quadrangle or outdoor space. Other functions include providing a significant gateway to the campus and enhancing institutional image at a key location on the campus. Projects that can advance institutional objectives in multiple ways often have strong appeal to project sponsors and donors.

At the South Campus of Metropolitan Community College in Omaha, Nebraska, program expansion for library, learning center, and student services were incorporated into a new building that transformed the campus by meeting a number of important planning goals. These included providing an indoor pedestrian connection between the two existing academic buildings that were 550 feet apart. The project also provided a new library facility that was shared jointly between the university and the city, and a new transit hub, one of four citywide transit hubs being built by the Metropolitan Area Transit Authority. These new functions bring added life to the south campus. In addition, the new building with the two existing ones define a new campus quadrangle in a space that was previously used for surface parking. Overall, the development provides a new contemporary image for the college. Thus, one building accomplished many important objectives.

Look for creative funding opportunities

Partnerships

This section discusses partnerships related *primarily* to physical facilities and improvements on campus, rather than those related to business services, such as food services, even if some institutions have negotiated business service arrangements leading to help with developing physical facilities. Physical partnerships can take many forms and can be used to defray the costs of many things, including bookstores, sports and recreation facilities, food facilities, office space, transportation, and housing. In some partnerships, companies have built laboratories and then shared these with an educational institution.

Metropolitan Community College's South Omaha Campus expansion provides both a branch public library and a public transit hub

While partnerships may provide opportunities for creative funding, they usually also have restrictions and constraints. Some partnerships have been heralded successes. Others haven't worked at all.

Institutions should evaluate partnerships with open eyes. Though a proposed partnership can be tempting, it should not be done for its own sake, however financially attractive. Institutional leaders should place a priority on the physical change they desire, and then see whether a public or private partnership will further that change—or evaluate an offer in terms of how it meets their strategic physical objectives. Because the objectives of the institution and the developer or other partner are not likely to coincide, institutional leaders must be very clear about their objectives and their vision for the campus. If the proposed project does not bring the institution closer to its vision for the campus, leaders should be prepared to walk away from the deal.

The Metropolitan Community College development described above is an excellent example of a partnership in which the institution has successfully leveraged public money into a great physical transformation of its campus. The shared library facility reduces the amount of space that would have been needed for two independent facilities, and the city and the college shared this reduced construction cost. The city and the college library systems also share staff and operating costs. The transit hub was funded entirely by the transit authority and is designed so that its waiting area also serves as a satellite campus center, reducing the college's need to fund the campus center and allowing it to provide expanded food service both to students and to other transit users.

Funding for significant campus open spaces

Funding the creation of beautiful open spaces such as quadrangles is a particular challenge for many institutions. To control their expenditures many states have policies regarding which campus improvements they will fund. One common constraint is to limit funds only to site improvements within five feet of new buildings, leaving the institution to find other funding sources for campus open space. Such state funding policies are missing opportunities to support learning on all parts of the campus. In particular, the positive educational impact of outdoor green space close to classrooms has been proven.

Public institutions and many private ones find it difficult to take scarce resources from core programs and academic activities to fund open space, which some erroneously see as a frill. Many campus open spaces help define the image of the university as a whole and are therefore also an aid in recruiting and retention. The open spaces of a campus are essential to the overall creation of a learning community. When the elm trees in

Harvard Yard were dying, a visual simulation that showed what the Yard would look like without trees quickly attracted the funds necessary to replace the trees.

The best way to fund these vital open spaces is to link building projects with open space improvements when possible. They should be considered integrated projects: the quadrangle "belongs" to the building. Whether going for state money or a private donor—or even if there are multiple sources of funds—a building and its related open space ought to be thought of as one project.

The main quadrangle at Ryerson University is also the grass roof of the University's Recreation Center

Few institutions have the opportunity to design and build an entirely new campus. Most campuses are already partly or fully developed, and many times the landscape is not the asset that it could be. Finding the resources to restructure an existing landscape can be a challenge. The Ohio State University addresses this issue by reserving and protecting 2 percent of every project's budget for the "urban design component"—improvement to the landscape that goes beyond the immediate project's needs, such as making a space that provides a connection to another building.

In addition to open space and landscape, funding utility and infrastructure improvements can be a challenge. Some institutions impose a surcharge up to 10 percent on all building projects to fund general campus improvements.

Leveraging unusual funding opportunities

Sometimes an institution is offered an unusual opportunity, such as an outright gift of a building to help meet certain of its needs. Such opportunities may not fit within the framework of the physical vision of the campus, but may be too good to pass up. The Rochester Institute of Technology, for example, has made 170 upper-level undergraduate and graduate dormitory rooms in a donated historical Marriott hotel three miles from its main campus. To accommodate these students, the institution provides both free shuttle-bus service and preferred on-campus parking spots. Would that site have been their first choice for new housing if the building were not given to them?

Ithaca College had a goal of increasing its on-campus housing in order to enhance student engagement on campus. While working on a planning framework to accomplish this, the college was approached by the owner of an apartment complex adjacent to playing fields at the edge of the campus. These apartments were already primarily occupied by Ithaca College students. The owner offered to double the capacity of the development and proposed a financing mechanism that allowed the college to own the project at no cost over several years. With limited bonding capacity to build housing in its preferred location at the center of the campus, the college found this offer too good to pass up. However, pulling additional students away from the campus had the potential of undermining the college's object of activating the campus core. The Sasaki Associates planners suggested a number of interventions to better integrate this project with the campus, in support of the overall vision and plan. One major concern was that the students living in this housing might take their cars to class, thereby requiring two parking spaces each. But since, under the new arrangement, the housing comes under the management of student life, the university can limit these students' use of automobiles on the campus. The planners also recommended that the college encourage students to walk by improving the pedestrian connection with paths, lights, and security, and that it implement a shuttle bus system.

Institutions fortunate enough to receive such an offer may find, like Ithaca College, that even though the offer may not exactly match their plan, it is too good to refuse. In these situations, the institution must determine the best way to reconcile the offer to the vision and include the cost of the reconciliatory measures in its evaluation. While many offers are welcome, some may not be worth the cost.

Building institutional support for funding

Planned physical improvements on campuses are most likely to be realized when strategies for implementation are integrated into the planning and design process. Rather than create a plan, then put a price tag on it, and only at the end look at the institution's ability to implement, the planning team should integrate the funding strategy with the planning process. To accomplish this, the planning process must:

- Link capital projects with institutional goals and strategies
- Determine needs and issues through communication with the campus community, alumni, and outside stakeholders
- Identify financial resources and financing mechanisms, and build them into the plan
- Engage the institution's leadership—especially the president and governing board

Link capital projects with institutional goals and strategies

The strategic plan and mission for the institution must drive the physical plan. When the physical vision for the campus is linked with the strategic plan and mission of the institution, it carries much more power and greater validity, and is therefore more likely to be implemented. When the two are linked, then legislators, board members, and foundations can see the value of their investments in terms of the institution's long-term prosperity.

The barren main quadrangle at the University of South Florida in Tampa was transformed into the stunning Martin Luther King Plaza through use of creative funding opportunities

Oberlin College's Adam Joseph Lewis Center building, designed by William McDonough, provided a visionary setting for Oberlin's leading-edge environmental studies program—but at a very high cost per square foot. But the building clearly furthered Oberlin's objective to be recognized as a leader in environmental sciences and has gained a lot of recognition for the college's environmental studies program. Because of its mission-level importance (along with its modest size requirements overall), Oberlin was able to find new sources of funding for this building so that its other campus priorities were not compromised.

Even though institutions give priority to student and academic space most of the time, Ithaca College was able to get board and college support to give a high priority to a new administration building because one of the initiatives identified in its strategic plan was to improve the quality of work life.

The Florida university system has a special fund, created in part from fees paid by students, for projects intended to improve the quality of the student experience on campus. The University of South Florida had agreed with its students to allow the funds to accumulate in order to make meaningful campus enhancements. Through its master planning process, the university was able to articulate and focus its priorities for the application of these funds to infrastructure improvements that were not associated with new buildings. These improvements included closing off a major street that had bisected the core of the campus, creating instead a pedestrian mall and a greenway that included a central lawn and the Martin Luther King Plaza. This greenway stretched from the southeast corner to a large ecological preserve at the northwest corner of the campus, providing a counterpoint to the densification of the campus and restoring a more indigenous landscape. In addition, the university was able to gain state approval for a unified stormwater management system of ponds and waterways integrated with the greenway.

Determine needs and issues through communication with the campus community, alumni, and outside stakeholders

The planning and design process should engage all the constituencies in an organized fact-finding process. Students, faculty, staff, and neighbors all have things they want. The faculty, for example, may want a new classroom building; the student life organization may want a new field house; and the administration may want a new office building. They may all want more parking. These physical changes are all high priority for someone. When planners at Sasaki Associates create a plan, they do more than creating a shopping list of what everyone wants. They check the facts and the data, and they verify against standards as well as against the perceptions of other constituencies within the university. They create a process so that everyone can hear everyone else's concerns. The result is not just a wish list. It is a list of requirements that has been vetted against the facts to determine what is really needed and prioritized according to the urgency of these needs.

Board members want to know that the institution has gone through a process like this, and that projects are responding to true needs.

Identify financial resources, financing mechanisms and their limitations, and build them into the plan

Despite the advice of Daniel Burnham, the famous architect and planner, to "make no little plans; they have no magic to stir men's blood," there is no sense in planning a grand campus expansion that realistically could never be implemented. At the same time they do planning and design, planners and institutional leaders should integrate their understanding of the resources. For example, whenever the president of Philadelphia University reviewed progress on its master planning process, he always thought about costs and how much money he could raise. Thus, he was able to give the team important guidance on feasibility.

Sweet Briar College wanted to fund a major library addition and renovation, but upon completion of the plans, the projected budget for the project was about $30 million. The college's fund-raising base was such that it would take too long to raise this amount without too much loss of interest and momentum. Sweet Briar leadership knew that they couldn't reasonably raise funds for more than a $10 – 12 million project. In response, the designers were able to break the library project into three phases that the college could reasonably fund.

Keepers of the plan

To be successful over the long run, the planning and design process must engage the leadership of an institution and achieve their support. In fact, the best processes involve more constituencies that just the institutional leaders. The more the vision encompasses multiple objectives and is understood and supported by multiple constituencies, the more momentum is created to make it real. Metropolitan Community College, for example, has a process for annual board review of the campus plan. The board and the president, as well as the campus community, are fully engaged in the planning review process.

It doesn't take much for the plan or vision to get off track. As soon as a project sponsor or a donor comes along, reasons for the institution to do something not in the plan may arise. Sometimes the institution may not realize they have to give a copy of the plan to a new architect and insist on its being followed. Other times, the new architect may not understand what is consistent with the plan and what is not, unless he or she is given explicit guidance.

Vicious cycles, virtuous cycles

The problem with carelessly allowing even one project to deviate from the plan is that one bad decision can lead to another, slowly creating a "vicious cycle" that undermines community on campus. For example, a college may receive a gift of off-campus land and free student housing. But now more students drive to class. The college needs more parking lots close to the center, and better roads to connect to the new housing. The large parking lot makes the center feel inhospitable; so, fewer people hang around after class. The empty center begins to feel dangerous after dark. Clearly, the college needs more lighting—and it is beginning to wonder what has happened to community on campus. If all the ramifications had been considered, would the first decision have been made differently?

Similarly, decisions made with the vision and plan in mind can lead to more positive cycles such as the following: A university in an older, run-down part of town decides to regenerate an old city block it owns to create more student housing. Within a short time, the converted buildings are the most popular housing on or off campus, bringing more students back to the campus area. The campus feels livelier, and demand for nearby housing increases. So the university now plans to regenerate another block. University and town alike are on the way to recovery.

COURTESY OF SWEET BRIAR COLLEGE

Organizational structure

A structure or organization responsible for keeping the plan must be established. Ideally, this organization would have diverse representation from the university. In addition, it should have outside professional representation in the areas of planning, architecture, and landscape architecture, so that the keepers of the plan have the benefit of top-level objective professional input. Also, this outside participation helps to shield the keepers from internal political considerations. The keepers of the plan should have the immediate ear of the president.

After completing a master plan for the University of Colorado forty years ago, Hideo Sasaki helped set up a review board that is still active today. Because it reports directly to the president and because it includes many professionals of national standing, this board has considerable authority. Members are appointed for life, and the board is known to be professional and even-handed. As a result, it is highly respected across the country, and has been the model for many other universities' design review boards.

Inspired in part by the University of Colorado, the Ohio State University set up a design review board with guidelines and an organizational model that were recommended as part of its master plan in the mid-1990s and adopted, along with that plan, by the board of trustees. It includes faculty and student representatives as well as, at a minimum, two outside design professionals of national standing. The board is chartered to maintain the master plan in a broad sense, as well as design guidelines for individual projects that were set up in association with the master plan. Articulating how the master plan shapes decisions between individual projects

| *Making It Happen*

and university-wide principles such as circulation and open space, these guidelines specify for each project strategic criteria such as massing, materials, relationships with open spaces and other buildings, entry locations, and so on. Virtually all projects are subject both to formal reviews by the entire board and informal reviews by the planning and design staff of the university acting as agents of the design review board.

After finishing the master plan in 1997, Sasaki Associates recommended forming a design review committee that would be the keepers of the plan for the University of Arkansas. The university already had a design review committee comprised of faculty and staff—but since it reported only to the director of facilities, it was not seen to be effective. For example, when the Engineering Department put in a new building, everyone thought the building was a mistake but no one was willing to say so. The new design review board reports directly to the president. The board meets four times per year and uses the plan and the design guidelines as a basis for reviewing projects. Its members include the director of facilities, the vice president of finance and administration, and other faculty and staff, as well as paid professional advisors. They walk the campus once a year with the president to review how the campus is doing with respect to the plan.

Rather than creating or revising a master plan, the University of Missouri-Columbia meets with a planning consultant from Sasaki Associates once or twice a month to review what's going on from a planning perspective. This keeps the planning input in people's consciousness and provides a needed objective view of the planning implications of their campus issues.

Top: Presidential involvement at the University of Scranton was key to project success
Bottom: A student campus planning work session at Dordt College

There may be other models as well. Whatever model is adopted, a planning perspective must be integrated into an ongoing process and this role must be institutionalized to keep the principles that have been laid out in this book active.

Ultimately, creating a physical campus that reinforces the institution's mission and vision relies on the president and the board for leadership and for the staying power to make it happen. These top institutional leaders must create the vision in people's minds and "sell" it—perhaps over and over—as the institution implements changes in the campus. The only way that campus plans, landscape concepts, and building ideas can see reality and endure over time is with the full dialog and engagement of the college president, board, and senior staff.

o n e

Meeting Today's Challenges

1. Thomas A. Gaines, *The Campus as a Work of Art* (Westport, Connecticut: Praeger Publishers, 1991): 11.

t w o

A Changing Context

1. William Arthur Ward, "To Risk": http://www.appleseeds. org/to-risk_WAW.htm.

2. Thomas Snyder and Charlene Hoffman, *Digest of Educational Statistics 2000 NCES 2001-034* (Washington, D.C.: United States Department of Education, National Center for Education Statistics, 2001): 193.

3. William Leach, *Country of Exiles: The Destruction of Place in American Life* (New York: Pantheon Books, 1999): 136.

4. Laura Horn and C. Dennis Carroll, *Nontraditional Undergraduates: Trends in Enrollment from 1986 to 1992 and Persistence and Attainment Among 1989 – 90 Beginning Postsecondary Students NCES 97-578* (Washington, D.C.: United States Department of Education, National Center for Education Statistics, 1997): i.

5. Arthur Levine and Jeanette S. Cureton, "Collegiate Life: An Obituary," *Change* magazine (May/June 1998): 2.

6. Ibid: 8.

7. Thomas Snyder & Linda Shafer, "Indicator 24. College Costs," *Youth Indicators 1996, NCES 96-027* (Washington, D.C.: United States Department of Education, National Center for Education Statistics, 1996): 62 – 63.

8. Patricia Q. Brown, *Postsecondary Institutions in the United States: 1993 – 94 and 1998 – 99, NCES 2001-176* (Washington, D.C.: United States Department of Education, National Center for Education Statistics, 2001): 6.

9. Institute for Research on Higher Education, "When the Customer is Right: Market-Driven Accountability in Postsecondary Education," *Change* magazine (May/June 2000).

10. Council for Aid to Education Commission on National Investment in Higher Education, "Breaking the Social Contract: The Fiscal Crisis in Higher Education" (The Rand Corporation, April 1998; accessed December 23, 2000): http://www.rand.org/publications/CAE/ CAE100/index.html.

11. Patricia J. Gumport, et al., *Trends in United States Higher Education from Massification to Post Massification* (Stanford, California: Stanford University National Center for Postsecondary Improvement, 1997): 25.

12. Council for Aid to Education Commission on National Investment in Higher Education. "Breaking the Social Contract: The Fiscal Crisis in Higher Education." The Rand Corporation. Internet. http://www.rand.org/ publications/CAE/CAE100/index.html. Printed December 23, 2002.

13. "Colleges Brace for the Economic Downturn," *The Chronicle of Higher Education* (April 20, 2001): A10.

14. Harvey Kaiser, *A Foundation to Uphold: A Study of Facilities Conditions at US Colleges and Universities,* The Association of Higher Education Facilities Officers (APPA), 1996. Reported in Keith Covey, "Book Review: Fixing the Crumbling Campus," *Planning for Higher Education* (Winter 1997 – 98, Volume 26, Number 2): 42 – 44.

15. Alan G. Merten, Quoted in Sara Hebel, "In Virginia, Building Projects Halt While Enrollment Grows," *The Chronicle of Higher Education* (April 20, 2001): A11.

16. Florence Olsen, "Phoenix Rises: The University's Online Program Attracts Students, Profits, and Praise," *The Chronicle of Higher Education* (Nov 1, 2002): A29.

17. Anthony Carnevale, Presentation at the Annual Meeting of the American Council on Education (February 2002).

18. Jenna Russell, "On Campus Visits, Bid For High Marks," *The Boston Globe,* Volume 262 Number 69 (September 7, 2002): A1.

19. Mary Leonard, "On Campus, Comforts Are Major: Colleges Hope Perks Can Boost Enrollment," *The Boston Globe* (September 3, 2002): A1.

20. Joan Schmidt quoted in Leonard: A1.

21. Joe Agron, "Building for the Boom: The 27th Annual Official Education Construction Report," *American School & University* (May 2001): 24.

22. Andrew Cohen, "Rethinking College Recreation." *Metropolis Magazine* (August 2000): http://www.metropolismag. com/html/content_0800/ent.htm (accessed August 2000).

23. Ibid.

24. Joe Agron, "A Larger Scale: 10th Annual Residence Hall Construction Report," *American School & University* (July 1999): 50a – h.

25. National Center for Educational Statistics, "Enrollment in Degree-granting Institutions, Projections of Education Statistics to 2013": http://nces.ed.gov//programs/projections/ ch_2.asp (accessed May 7, 2004).

26. Kaiser: 42 – 44.

three

Linking an Institution's Mission and Its Place

1. Le Corbusier, quoted in Thomas A. Gaines, *The Campus As a Work of Art* (Westport, Connecticut: Praeger Publishers, 1991): 49.

2. Washington University in St. Louis, "University Mission Statement": http://www.wustl.edu/university/mission.html (accessed January 5, 2004).

3. Auburn University's Commission to Restructure the University, "Texas A&M University," included in "Documents from the May 8, 1998 Meeting of the Commission": http://www.ag.auburn.edu/commission/51198/mission/texas.html (accessed February 19, 2004).

4. University of Miami, "The University of Miami Mission Statement" (October 9, 2003): http://www.miami.edu/UMH/CDA/UMH_Main/1,1770,2472-1;23-3,00.html (accessed March 1, 2004).

5. Duquesne University, "The Duquesne University Mission Statement": http://www.mission.duq.edu/. 2002 (accessed January 16, 2004).

6. Marlboro College, "About Marlboro: Philosophy": http://www.marlboro.edu/about/philosophy.html (accessed January 16, 2004).

7. James J. Duderstadt, *A University For the 21st Century* (Ann Arbor, Michigan: University of Michigan Press, 2000): 39.

8. Thomas Jefferson to M. A. Jullien, 1818, quoted in Lipscomb and Bergh (editors), *The Writings of Thomas Jefferson, Volume 15,* Memorial Edition (Washington, D.C.: 1903 – 04): 172.

9. Thomas Jefferson to William C. Jarvis, 1820, ibid: 278.

10. David Starr Jordan, quoted in *Stanford Facts 2000: Information for Visitors and Prospective Students* (Stanford University Office of Communications): 8.

11. Thomas A. Gaines, *The Campus as a Work of Art* (Westport, Connecticut: Praeger Publishers, 1991): 11.

12. In a survey conducted in 1996, the Higher Education Research Institute reported that 72 percent of college freshmen went to college in order to make more money. This is an 18-percentage-point increase from 1976. This information, from A.W. Astin, et al., *The American Freshman: Thirty year Trends,* is cited in Arthur Levine and Jeanette S. Cureton, *When Hope and Fear Collide: A Portrait of Today's College Student* (San Francisco: Jossey-Bass,1998): 116.

13. Levine and Cureton: 116.

14. Ibid: 165.

15. Association of American Colleges and Universities, "Greater Expectations Project Overview": http://www.aacu.org/gex/overview.cfm. 2003 (accessed February 17, 2004).

16. Greater Expectations National Panel Report: Executive Overview: http://www.greaterexpectations.org/.

four

The Learning Campus – Enhancing Student Learning and Engagement

1. Terry O'Banion, "A Learning College for the 21st Century," *Community College Journal* (December/January 1995 – 96): 22.

2. NSSE 2001 Report, *Improving the College Experience: National Benchmarks of Effective Educational Practice* (Bloomington, Indiana: National Survey of Student Engagement, Indiana University Center for Postsecondary Research and Planning, 2001).

3. *Planning for Higher Education* (June – August 2003): 6.

4. Information in this section is summarized from the NSSE 2001 Report.

5. John Seely Brown & Paul Duguid, *The Social Life of Information* (Boston: Harvard Business School Press, 2000): 137.

6. Ernest Boyer, *College: The Undergraduate Experience in America,* The Carnegie Foundation for the Advancement of Teaching (New York: Harper & Row, 1987): 180.

7. Scott Carlson, "The Deserted Library: As Students Work Online, Reading Rooms Empty Out—Leading Some Campuses To Add Starbucks," *The Chronicle of Higher Education* (November 16, 2001): A35-A38.

8. C. Carney Strange and James H. Banning, *Education by Design: Creating Campus Learning Environments That Work* (San Francisco: Jossey-Bass, 2000): 138.

9. Ibid: 145-146.

10. Virginia Woolf, *A Room of One's Own* (New York: Harcourt Brace Jovanovich, First Harvest Edition, 1989):10 – 11.

11. See, for example, the following:

Kate Zernike, "The Feng Shui of Schools," *The New York Times* (August 5, 2001).

John B. Lyons, "Do School Facilities Really Impact a Child's Education? An Introduction to the Issues": http://www.coe.uga.edu/sdpl/articlesandpapers/lyons.html (accessed April 3, 2002).

C. Kenneth Tanner and Ann Langford, *The Importance of Interior Design Elements as They Relate to Student Outcomes:* http://www.coe.uga.edu/sdpl/research/SDPLStudiesIn Progress/criann02elem.html.

12. See, for example:

Heschong Mahone Group, *Daylighting in Schools: An Investigation into the Relationship between Daylighting and Human Performance* (Fair Oaks, California: Pacific Gas and Electric Company, August 20, 1999).

Patricia Plympton, Susan Conway, and Kyra Epstein, *Daylighting in Schools: Improving Student Performance and Health at a Price Schools Can Afford,* Document NREL/CP-550-28049 (Golden, Colorado: National Renewable Energy Laboratory, August 2000): http://www.deptplanetearth.com pdfdocs/nrel_daylitschools.pdf (accessed March 11, 2004).

C. Kenneth Tanner, "Essential Aspects of Designing a School" (Athens, Georgia: School Design and Planning Laboratory, The University of Georgia, April 2000): http://www.coe.uga.edu/sdpl/research/principlesofdesign.html.

See also:

C. Kenneth Tanner, *The School Design Assessment Scale: Validity, Reliability, and Weights,* paper presented at the Annual Conference of the Council of Educational Facility Planners, International, Baltimore, Maryland (November 1 – 5, 1999).

Extrapolation to the college environment is the authors' own.

five
Community on Campus

1. Carnegie Foundation for the Advancement of Teaching, *Campus Life: In Search of Community* (Princeton: Princeton University Press, 1990), quoted in Ray Oldenburg, "Making College a Great Place to Talk," *The Best of Planning for Higher Education,* George Keller, editor (Ann Arbor, Michigan: Society for College and University Planning, 1997): 90.

2. Neil Howe and William Strauss, *Millennials go to College,* American Association of Collegiate Registrars and Admissions Officers: 41.

3. Ibid: 54.

4. The National Center for Education Statistics, Beginning Postsecondary Students (BPS) Longitudinal Study. The current BPS Longitudinal Study is made up of people who first entered postsecondary education in the 1995 – 96 academic year: http://nces.ed.gov/surveys/bps/.

5. American Association of Collegiate Registrars & Admissions Officers (AACRAO), *Strategic Enrollment Management Monthly, Preview Issue* (November 2002): 2.

6. Arthur Levine, *When Dreams and Heroes Died: A Portrait of Today's College Student* (San Francisco: Jossey-Bass, 1980): xi – xii.

7. Arthur Levine and Jeannette S. Cureton, *When Hope and Fear Collide: A Portrait of Today's College Student* (San Francisco: Jossey-Bass, 1998): 93 – 114.

8. Howe and Strauss: 45.

9. Levine and Cureton: 102.

10. In her landmark book *A Room of One's Own,* Woolf describes how the gracious dinner in a residential dining hall at "Oxbridge" (a fictitious amalgam of Oxford and Cambridge Universities) is essential to conversation, learning, and community at an institution of higher education.

11. C. Carney Strange and James H. Banning, *Education by Design: Creating Campus Learning Environments That Work* (San Francisco: Jossey-Bass, 2000): 17.

12. Ref. Barker & Wright 1951, Wicker 1984 in Strange, et al.: 19.

13. Strange, et al.: 20.

14. George D. Kuh, John H. Schuh, Elizabeth J. Whitt, et al., *Involving Colleges: Successful Approaches to Fostering Student Learning and Development Outside the Classroom* (San Francisco: Jossey-Bass, 1991): 309.

15. William H. Whyte, "The Humble Street," *Historic Preservation* (January 1980): 34 – 41. Quoted in Norm Tyler, "William White's View of Downtowns": http://www.emich.edu/public/geo/557book/c113.whyte.html.

16. Ray Oldenburg, "Making College a Great Place to Talk," *The Best of Planning for Higher Education,* George Keller, ed. (Ann Arbor, Michigan: Society for College and University Planning, 1997): 90.

17. Howe and Strauss: 73.

18. Kuh, et al., quoting research by Moos and by Bickman and others: 110. (This research refers to small groups of people living together, not to small rooms.)

19. Strange, et al.: 143.

six

Neighborhood and Urban Community

1. Aristotle, quoted in Ted Goodman (ed.), *The Forbes Book of Business Quotations: 14,266 Thoughts on the Business of Life* (New York: Black Dog & Leventhal, 1997).

2. Henry James, *The Bostonians* (London: Purnell, 1886): 229.

3. Bill Archambeault, "Harvard Land Deal Puts Area Towns On the Defensive," *Boston Business Journal* (July 30, 2001): http://boston.bizjournals.com/boston/stories/2001/07/30/story7.html.

4. Susan Diesenhouse, "Harvard Ponies Up, At Least a Little," *Cityfeet.com Commercial Real Estate Listings and News:* http://www.cityfeet.com/news/newsarchivecontents.asp?local_news_id=724&lCityId=431 (accessed March 13, 2003).

5. Robert Gavin, "Study: Colleges Pump $7.4b Into Local Economy," *The Boston Globe* (March 8, 2003): C1.

6. Sharon R. Duhart, *The Economic Impact of University System of Georgia Institutions on their Regional Economies,* university system of Georgia Board of Regents Office of Economic Development (March 2002). Of the $8 billion, about $4.8 billion stayed in the state of Georgia, equaling almost 2 percent of Georgia's gross state product. The university system also collectively (directly or indirectly) accounted for over 100,000 jobs—2.8 percent of all the jobs in Georgia.

7. Brown University Office of Community and Government Relations, "Brown University: Global Reach. Local Impact," Brown University (June 2000): http://www.brown.edu/Administration/University_Relations/econ.shtml. Only 8 percent of Brown's approximately $327 million in annual revenue comes from sources within Rhode Island, but 68 percent of its $227 million in annual spending is in the state. In addition to Brown's expenditures, students and visitors spend more than $27 million in the Providence area. Considering both direct and indirect spending, Brown's overall economic impact in the area was nearly $400 million in 1998.

8. Columbia University Office of the Vice President for Administration, "Columbia University's Contribution to the New York City Economy, 1996": http://www.columbia.edu/cu/evp/nycecon.html (accessed March 12, 2003).

9. Richard M. Rosan, "The Key Role of Universities in Economic Growth and Urban Revitalization," PowerPoint presentation given at St. Louis University (April 10, 2002).

10. Mary Beth Marklein, "Come for a Diploma, Stay for Life: Cities Become Part of Campus Recruiting," *USA Today* (April 23, 2003): D1.

11. Ron Mason quoted in David J. Maurrasse, *Beyond the Campus: How Colleges and Universities Form Partnerships with Their Communities* (New York: Routledge, 2001): 22.

12. "Best Places to Retire," *Money* magazine (May 8, 2002): http://money.cnn.com/2002/05/01/retirement/bpretire_providence/.

13. Mary Shanklin, "The Senior Class Retirees Relocate to College Towns to Learn and Play," *Orlando Sentinel* (November 12, 2000).

14. Jack Shannon, then Managing Directory of Economic Development at the University of Pennsylvania, quoted in David J. Maurrasse, *Beyond the Campus: How Colleges and Universities Form Partnerships with Their Communities* (New York: Routledge, 2001).

15. Judith Rodin, "Common Cause: Investing in the Local Community," University of Pennsylvania (Spring 2001): http://www.upenn.edu/president/rodin/common_cause_01.html.

seven

Meaningful Places

1. J. Scott Odom, "My Place," *South Carolina Architecture,* The American Institute of Architects South Carolina Chapter (2003/2004): 88.

eight

The Plan Expresses the Big Idea

1. Tennessee Williams, *The Glass Menagerie,* (New York: New Directions Publishing Corporation, 1970): 63.

2. Martin Jischke, quoted in Linda Charles, "Land-grant Universities Born From Radical Idea," The Iowa *Stater* (February 1997): http://www.iastate.edu/IaStater/1997/feb/landgrant.html (accessed February 19, 2004).

3. Thomas Jefferson, quoted in Eyler Robert Coates, Sr., "Chapter 40. Publicly Supported Education," *Thomas Jefferson on Politics & Government,* University of Virginia Library. http://etext.lib.virginia.edu/jefferson/quotations/index.html (accessed February 2004).

4. "The Laws of the Indies," The Knight Program in Community Building, University of Miami School of Architecture: http://www.arc.miami.edu/knight/Resources/Laws%20of%20the%20Indies.html. 2002 (accessed January 24, 2004). This site contains an English translation of

the Laws of the Indies by Axel Mundigo and Dora Crouch, reprinted by *The New City* with permission from "The City Planning Ordinances of the Laws of the Indies Revisited, I," *Town Planning Review,* Vol. 48 (July 1977): 247 – 268. Text reference is to ordinances 112 – 122.

5. Paul V. Turner, Marcia E. Vetrocq, and Karen Weitze, *The Founders & the Architects:The Design of Stanford University* (Stanford, California: Department of Art, Stanford University, 1976): 25.

6. The discussion of this example is drawn from Sasaki Associates' document *Master Plan and Implementation Program for the Tampa Campus of the University of South Florida* (Watertown, Massachusetts: 2002).

7. The discussion of this example and all quotations are drawn from the Sasaki Associates' document *Submittal for the 2004 AIACC Awards for Regional and Urban Design* (Watertown, Massachusetts: 2004).

8. The discussion of this example is drawn from the Sasaki Associates' draft document *Hollins University Master Plan* (Watertown, Massachusetts: January 29, 2004).

n i n e

Creating Interaction Through Density

1. Kevin Lynch, *Site Planning* (Cambridge, Massachusetts: The MIT Press, Second edition, 1971): 33.

2. Ibid: 34.

3. FAR is the common metric that planners utilize to define how many total square feet of building are put on a parcel of land. The term is defined as the ratio of the total square feet of gross building floor space divided by the square feet of land that the building or buildings occupy. Building coverage is the area of building footprint (the area of building that touches the ground) on a defined parcel of land. For example, a 100- by 100-foot, two-story building provides 20,000 square feet of floor space on a 10,000-square-foot footprint. If this building is located on a 40,000-square-foot parcel of land, then the parcel has a .5 FAR and a 25% building coverage ratio. If 51 people work in the building, it provides close to 50 people per acre.

4. David Neumann, conversation with Dan Kenney and Ginger Kenney (February 12, 2002).

5. Lynch uses the ideas of *connections* and *intensity of use* in a similar way to proximity and centers of activity. See his

book *Site Planning* for more discussion on these and on character of space.

6. Christopher Alexander, *A Pattern Language* (New York: Oxford University Press, 1977): 59.

7. Ibid: 71.

8. Stephen R. Porter and Paul D. Umbach, "We Can't Get There in Time," *Planning for Higher Education* (Winter 2001-2002): 35 – 40.

t e n

A Mixture of Campus Uses

1. Jane Jacobs, *The Death and Life of Great American Cities* (New York: Random House, 1961): 152.

2. One such source is the Fort Lewis College Housing/Residential Life program; see "Residence Life and Housing," Fort Lewis College: http://www.fortlewis.edu/prospective_ students/housing/default.asp (accessed April 30, 2004).

e l e v e n

Landscape

1. Frederick Law Olmsted's 1865 "Preliminary Report on the Yosemite and Maripissa Grove," quoted in Joseph Engbeck's history of the park.

2. Stephen Fox, *The Campus Guide: Rice University* (New York: Princeton Architectural Press, 2001): 6.

3. Vassar College Admissions Web site: http://admissions. vassar.edu/visit_tour.html (accessed May 9, 2003).

4. "The main plaza is to be the starting point for the town… inland it should be at the center of the town. The plaza should be square or rectangular, in which case it should have at least one and a half its width for length…[The plaza] shall be not less that two hundred feet wide and three hundred feet long, nor larger than eight hundred feet long and five hundred and thirty feet wide. A good proportion is six hundred feet long and four hundred wide… Around the plaza as well as along the four principal streets which begin there, there shall be portals, for these are of considerable convenience to the merchants who generally gather there; the eight streets running from the plaza at the four corners shall open on the plaza without encountering these porticoes, which shall be kept back in order that there may be sidewalks even with the streets and plaza…The streets shall run from the main plaza in such

manner that even if the town increases considerably in size, it shall not result in some inconvenience that will make ugly what needed to be rebuilt, or endanger its defense or comfort." From "The Laws of the Indies." English translation by Axel Mundigo and Dora Crouch from "The City Planning Ordinances of the Laws of the Indies Revisited, I," *Town Planning Review,* Vol. 48 (July 1977): 247 – 268. Reprinted in *The New City* by the University of Miami School of Architecture. Found on the Internet at http://www.arc.miami.edu/Law%20of%20Indies.html (accessed January 21, 2004).

5. Cranbrook Schools: http://www.cranbrook.edu/archives/brief_hi.htm.

6. Jon Stemmle, "A 'campus garden…place of beauty' planned for MU." *Facilities Focus,* University of Missouri Campus Facilities (May/June 1998):" http://www.cf.missouri.edu/fm/comm/focus/1998/may-jun98/garden.html (accessed January 20, 2004).

7. Harold Shapiro, "The Beauty of the Campus," Princeton University President's Page (February 7, 2001): http://www.princeton.edu/pr/president/01/02-07-01.html (accessed January 20, 2004).

8. See discussion in Chapter 4 "The Learning Campus."

t w e l v e

Environment and Sustainability

1. David W. Orr, *Earth in Mind: On Education, Environment, and the Human Prospect* (Washington, D.C.: Island Press, 1994): 12.

2. Mary McIntosh, et al., *State of the Campus Environment: A National Report Card on Environmental Performance and Sustainability in Higher Education,* National Wildlife Federation (N.p.: 2001): 2.

3. Ibid: 21 – 24.

4. "The Environment: Risky Business," *The Wirthlin Report,* Vol. 9, No. 9 (McLean, Virginia: November 1999).

5. A 1999 survey asked whether the respondents thought the environment in the next century will be better, worse, or about the same as it is today. Among respondents over 64 years old, 21percent thought that it would be better, and 54 percent thought that it would be worse. But among respondents aged 18 to 29, only 12 percent thought that the environment would be better, and 68 percent thought that it would be worse.

6. University of Oregon, "UO Makes Top 'Green' Grades in US" (Eugene, Oregon: University of Oregon, March 31, 2002): <www.uoregon.edu/newscenter/greengrades.html>.

7. Warren Wilson College, "Making an Environmental Difference" (Asheville, North Carolina: Warren Wilson College): <http://www.warren-wilson.edu/environdiff/index.shtml>.

8. Zachary Block, "Pigging Out," *Brown Alumni Magazine* (November/December 2001): 19.

9. Elizabeth F. Farrell, "U. of Oregon Offers Discount on Late-Afternoon Classes," *The Chronicle of Higher Education,*(July 19, 2002): A33.

10. United States Department of the Interior, US Geological Survey, USGS Fact Sheet FS-068-98, "Materials Flow and Sustainability" (June 1998): <http://greenwood.cr.usgs.gov/pub/fact-sheets/fs-0008-98/fs-0008-98.pdf>.

11. United States Environmental Protection Agency, *WasteWise Update: Building for the Future* (Washington, D.C.: nd.): <http://www.epa.gov/wastewise/pubs/wwupda16.pdf>.

12. David J. Eagan and Julian Keniry, *Green Investment, Green Return: How Practical Conservation Projects Save Millions on America's Campuses* (National Wildlife Federation, March 1998): 16.

13. Ibid: 4.

14. Ronald G. Ehrenberg, *Tuition Rising: Why College Costs So Much* (Cambridge, Massachusetts: Harvard University Press, 2000): 213.

15. "Made in the Shade," *Urban Land* (October 1998): 20. This study shows that a single tree can annually save $73 in air conditioning costs, $75 in erosion and stormwater control, $75 in wildlife shelter, and $50 in air pollution control. This $273 in annual savings comes to over $57,000 over the 50-year life of the tree, when compounded at 5%.

16. Mike McAliney (ed.), *Arguments for Land Conservation: Documentation and Information Sources for Land Resources Protection* (Sacramento, California: Trust for Public Land, December 1993), as quoted in "Urban Forests/Trees," The Trust for Public Land Research Room (January 14, 1996): <http://www.tpl.org/tier3_print.cfm?folder_id=726&content_item_id=1103&mod_type=1>.

17. University of Wisconsin-Madison, "Mission and Overview," *Campus Natural Areas* (Madison, Wisconsin: University of Wisconsin-Madison: nd) http://gaia1.ies.wisc.edu/cna/.

18. The LEED standard is developed and maintained by the United States Green Building Council, a nonprofit organization. See http://www.usgbc.org/leed/leed_main.asp for more information.

thirteen

Taming the Automobile

1. Joni Mitchell, "Big Yellow Taxi," Ladies of the Canyon (Siquomb Publishing, 1970). All Rights Reserved. Used by Permission. Warner Bros. Publications U.S. Inc., Miami, Florida 33014.

2. Comment made during a roundtable discussion during the ACE Annual Meeting (San Francisco: February 2002).

3. Alexander: 121.

4. Richard E. Killingsworth and Jean Lanning, "Development and Public Health: Could Our Development Patterns Be Affecting Our Personal Health?" *Urban Land* (July 2001): 14.

5. Ibid: 12.

6. Ibid: 12.

7. Stanley I. Hart and Alvin L. Spivak, *The Elephant in the Bedroom: Automobile Dependence & Denial: Impacts on the Economy and Environment* (Boca Raton, Florida: New Paradigm Books, 1993): 4.

8. Ada County [Idaho] Highway District Commuteride, "Pollution Facts" (Garden City, Idaho: June 19, 2002): http://www.commuteride.com/justforfun/doyouknow/pollutionfacts.htm.

9. Ibid: 14.

10. Mary S. Smith, "Planning for Surface Parking," in Anthony P. Chrest, et al., *Parking Structures Third Edition: Planning, Design, Construction, Maintenance & Repair* (Boston: Kluwer Academic Publishers, 2001): 22. (In the practice experience of the authors of this book, a typical range for the cost of a parking space in an aboveground facility is $7,000 to $15,000.)

11. Ibid: 24 – 25.

12. Ibid: 26.

13. These figures do not take into account the cost of land, since most institutions consider the land a "given." Even if an institution already owns the land, however, the cost *should* be considered when tallying the cost of parking, since opportunities are lost for the institution to use the land for other, perhaps more central, purposes. At a land cost of about $30 per square foot ($1.3 million per acre)—a reasonable estimate for an inner suburb or city—for a three-story garage or $10 per square foot ($435,000 per acre) for surface parking, the revenue needed to break even rises to $1,044 per year for the space in the parking lot and $1,692 per year for the space in the garage.

14. Non-reserved faculty/staff parking and commuter parking turn over more frequently; therefore, to compute the shortfall, we apply a turnover adjustment factor of .86 to the cost of non-reserved faculty/staff parking spaces and .41 to the cost of student commuter parking spaces. For non-reserved spaces, the median annual shortfall is $400 and $300 for surface parking, and $1,230 and $1,120 for structured parking for these two types of drivers.

15. Smith: 16.

16. Ehrenberg: 213.

17. Tom Kelly, et al., "Sustainable Transportation Trip Report and Recommendations" (Durham, New Hampshire: University of New Hampshire, September 15, 1999): http://www.sustainableunh.unh.edu/promise/actions/trip_report.htm.

18. Emily Head, et al., "Getting There: A Transportation Demand Management Assessment of the University of Waterloo Community" (Waterloo, Ontario: University of Waterloo, May 1, 2000): http://www.adm.uwaterloo.ca/infowast/Transportation/720FinalFolder/720Final.html.

19. Ibid.

20. Michael Replogle, transportation director of Environmental Defense, quoted in Killingsworth and Lanning, *Urban Land*: 16.

21. Head, et al.

22. From "Top Ten Green Campuses": http://www.sustainableunh.unh.edu/ybcoop/about/index.html (accessed May 19, 2004).

23. University of Washington, "10 Years of Results" (Seattle, Washington: University of Washington, 2001): http://www.washington.edu/upass/news_and_reports/upass_reports/facts.pdf.

24. Peter Dewey, University of Washington Transportation Systems Manager, quoted in "U-PASS Program Celebrates 10 Years Of Reducing Campus and Regional Congestion" (King County, Washington: May 23, 2001): http://www.metrokc.gov/exec/news/2001/0523012.htm.

25. Ibid: 14 – 15.

fourteen

Architecture

1. Charles Linn, "Academic Buildings: Reeducating the Masses," Architectural Record (October 1998): 149.

2. Leon Botstein, quoted in Michael Melia, "Art for Arts: EMP's Gehry Moves On To Small College," *The Seattle Times* (May 19, 2002): http://seattletimes.nwsource.com/html/artsentertainment/134455423_wgehry19.html.

3. Scott Carlson, "Colleges Struggle With a '60s Legacy: Ugly, Wasteful, and Outdated Buildings," *Chronicle of Higher Education* (August 17, 2001).

4. Alex Carnevale, "Building Brown: A Walk Around Campus With Architecture Professor Dietrich Neumann," *Post Magazine* (Providence, Rhode Island: October 25, 2002): 6 – 7.

5. Robert Campbell, "When Building Becomes 'Branding,'" *The Boston Sunday Globe* (August 4, 2002): L5.

6. Nancy Kepes Jeton, Alumni Trustee, Dartmouth University, in an email to Dan Kenney dated September 10, 2001, and subsequent conversations.

7. The net square footage is defined as assignable space, such as classrooms, labs and offices, and everything else is classified as gross square footage.

8. Stefanos Polyzoides, "Success and Failure in Campus Design in the Post-World War II Era: An Historical View and Focus on California," presented at the forum *Designing the Campus of Tomorrow: The Legacy of the Hearst Architectural Plan, Present and Future* (Berkeley, California: February 10, 2000): Transcript from the Internet, http://sunsite.Berkeley.edu/uchistory/archives_exhibits/hearst/3_panel1_2polyzoides.html.

fifteen

Technology, Learning, and Place

1. Ranjay Gulati and Jason Garino, "Get the Right Mix of Bricks and Clicks," *Harvard Business Review*, Reprint R00313 (May – June 2000).

2. Steve Jones, *The Internet Goes to College* (Washington, D.C.: Pew Internet & American Life Project, September 15, 2002): http://www.pewinternet.org/.

3. James Banning, quoted in Trip Gabriel, "Computers Help Unite Campuses But Also Drive Some Students Apart," *The New York Times* (November 11, 1996): A12.

4. Nicholas Yee, *The Norrathian Scrolls: A Study of EverQuest*, Version 2.5. http://www.nickyee.com/eqt/report.html.

5. Abigail Butler, quoted in Gabriel: A12.

6. David G. Brown, quoted in Gabriel: A12.

7. Jones.

8. Ron Bleed, "A Hybrid Campus for the New Millennium," *Educause Review* (January/February 2001): 19.

9. Pavel Curtis, "Mudding: Social Phenomena in Text-Based Virtual Realities," Xerox PARC (March 3, 1992): 1.

10. Lisa Guernsey, "College 'MOOs' Foster Creativity and Collaboration Among Users," *The Chronicle of Higher Education,* Information Technology Section (February 9, 1996): A24.

11. Information about University of Pennsylvania's PennMOO, including classes offered there and in other university MOOs, may be found at http://www.english.upenn.edu/PennMOO/.

12. Information about Diversity University may be found at http://www.du.org/. This rather large virtual campus is rendered in ASCII text-based "graphics."

13. Jeff Harrow, "The Reality of the Game," *The Harrow Technology Report* (May 27, 2002): http://www.theharrowgroup.com/articles/20020527/20020527.htm.

14. Yee.

15. Edward Castronova, "Virtual Worlds: A First-Hand Account of Market and Society on the Cyberian Frontier," *The Gruter Institute Working Papers on Law, Economics, and Evolutionary Biology,* Volume 2, Issue 1, Article 1 (The Berkeley Electronic Press, 2001): http://www.bepress.com/giwp/default/vol2/iss1/art1.

16. Bonnie Rothman Morris, "Budding Scientists, Let Loose in a World They Can Save," *The New York Times* (June 6, 2002): http://www.nytimes.com/2002/06/06/technology/circuits/06NEXT.html.

17. The Contact Consortium, "About the Contact Consortium and its Member Services" (Scotts Valley, California): http://www.ccon.org/org/org.html (accessed September 27, 2002).

18. The Contact Consortium, "TheU Home Page" (Scotts Valley, California): http://ccon.org/theu/ (accessed September 27, 2002).

19. Jeffrey R. Young, "'Hybrid' Teaching Seeks to End the Divide Between Traditional and Online Instruction," *The Chronicle of Higher Education* (March 22, 2002).

20. John Unsworth, "Constructing the Virtual Campus," text of a paper delivered at the 1994 Modern Language Association meeting in Toronto (May 18, 1995): http://www.village.virginia.edu/~jmu2m/Virtual.Campus.html.

21. Ibid.

22. Young.

23. Vincent Giuliano, former Dean, School of Library and Information, SUNY, in email to Ginger Kenney (April 26, 2003).

24. Philip Parsons, former Associate Dean for Physical Resources at the Harvard University Faculty of Arts and Sciences, in written communication to authors dated April 23, 2004.

25. Sir John Daniel, "Renewing Universities for the New Economy," Presentation at the National Governors Association Winter Meeting (Washington, D.C.: February 28, 2000): http://www.open.ac.uk/vcs-speeches/Governors.htm.

26. Arthur Levine and Jeannette S. Cureton, "Collegiate Life: An Obituary," *Change* Magazine (New Rochelle, New York: May/June 1998): 1.

27. Sir John Daniel.

28. Levine: 10.

29. Ibid: 2.

30. Walden University Web site: http://www.waldenu.edu (accessed September 24, 2002).

31. Kermit Hall, statement made during roundtable discussion at ACE conference, Vancouver, British Columbia, February 10, 2002.

32. Hubert L. Dreyfus, *On the Internet* (London and New York: Routledge, 2001).

33. Gabriel: A12.

34. Jones: 16.

35. Mary E. Mitchell, "Living With an Online Student Is More Than a Marriage; It's an Adventure." Article posted to www.KaplanCollege.com on August 4, 2000.

36. Sir John Daniel, "Lessons From the Open University: Low-Tech Learning Often Works Best," *The Chronicle of Higher Education* (September 7, 2001): B24.

37. "Omnium Overview": http://www.omnium.unsw.edu.au/ (accessed September 8, 2002).

38. Elizabeth Aukamp, email to Ginger Kenney (September 7, 2002).

39. Ross E. Mitchell, emails to Ginger Kenney (September 5 and 8, 2002).

40. Peter Drucker, quoted in "Seeing Things as They Really Are," *Forbes Magazine* (March 10, 1997): http://www.forbes.com/forbes/1997/0310/5905122a_print.html (accessed October 27, 2002).

41. Paul Goldberger, "The Store Strikes Back," *The New York Times* (April 6, 1997): Section 6, Page 45.

42. Cisco Systems and University of Texas, "Measuring the Internet Economy" (report dated January 2001): www.internetindicators.com (accessed April 29, 2004). The source cited for the data is the Center for Research in Electronic Commerce of the Graduate School of Business, University of Texas at Austin, 2001.

43. Ibid.

44. SportsTrust, "Issue 33—Concept Stores," *Sports News You Can Use* (1998): http://www.onlinesports.com/sportstrust/sports33.html (accessed November 6, 2002).

45. Howard Lichter, "Adapt to Survive," Town Centre Management 3rd World Congress Report, Association of Town Centre Management (London: June 14 – 16, 2000).

46. Kathleen Seiders, quoted in Chris Reidy, "Equal Parts Entertainer and Vendor Niketown Is Latest in Trend That Has Stores Catering to Shoppers' Sense of Fun," *The Boston Globe* (July 20, 1997).

47. Horan: 48.

s i x t e e n

Creating a Vital Neighborhood

1. Jack Shannon, then Managing Director of Economic Development at the University of Pennsylvania, quoted in David J. Maurrasse, *Beyond the Campus: How Colleges and Universities Form Partnerships with Their Communities* (New York: Routledge, 2001): 33.

2. Yale University, "Yale University Human Resource Services—New Haven HomeBuyer Program Page" (February 21, 2003): http://www.yale.edu/hronline/hbuyer/hbuyprog.html.

3. University of Pennsylvania, "The Goal: Improving Housing and Home Ownership" (2003): http://www.upenn.edu/president/westphilly/housing.html.

4. University of Pennsylvania, "The Goal: Improving Public Education" (2003): http://www.upenn.edu/president/westphilly/education.html.

5. The Association of University Research Parks (AURP) defines a research park (or technology incubator) as "a property-based venture, which has:

   · Existing or planned land and buildings designed primarily for private and public research and development facilities….

· A contractual and/or formal ownership or operational relationship with one or more universities or other institutions of higher education, and science research.

· A role in promoting research and development by the university in partnership with industry, assisting in the growth of new ventures, and promoting economic development.

· A role in aiding the transfer of technology and business skills between the university and industry tenants." Association of University Research Parks (AURP), *University Research Park Profile 2003* (Rockville, Maryland: 2003).

6. Ibid: 10, 14.

7. University of Washington, *University of Washington Master Plan Seattle Campus,* final plan (September 2001): 13.

8. Ibid: 20.

9. Georgia College & State University, "The GC&SU Mission" (October 28, 2003): http://www.gcsu.edu/GCSU/gen/mission.html (accessed January 16, 2004).

10. Robert Campbell, "Urban Scrawl," *The Boston Globe Magazine* (January 12, 2003): 11.

11. Cob Carlson, "A Better Plan For Harvard," editorial in *The Boston Globe* (November 26, 2001).

12. Trinity College, "Trinity/SINA Neighborhood Initiative": http://www.trincoll.edu/pub/city/trinity_sina.html (accessed August 16, 2003).

13. Evan Dobelle, quoted in "Trinity, Its Neighbors, and Hartford": http://trincoll.edu/pub/heights/backcover.html (accessed August 16, 2003).

Making it Happen

1. Lewis Mumford, *The Culture of Cities* (New York: Harcourt Brace, 1938): 229.

2. Joe Stone, "The Dean's Letter," University of Oregon College of Arts and Sciences: http://cas.uoregon.edu/alumnidev/cascade/200305.dean.html (accessed May 5, 2003).

3. Philip Parsons, former Associate Dean for Physical Resources at the Harvard University Faculty of Arts and Sciences, in a private conversation with the authors on August 19, 2003.

Ada County [Idaho] Highway District Commuteride. "Pollution Facts." Garden City, Idaho. Updated June 19, 2002. http://www.commuteride.com/justforfun/doyouknow/pollutionfacts.htm.

Agron, Joe. "A Larger Scale: 10th Annual Residence Hall Construction Report." *American School & University.* July 1999.

———. "Building for the Boom: The 27th Annual Official Education Construction Report." *American School & University.* May 2001.

Alexander, Christopher. *A Pattern Language.* New York: Oxford University Press, 1977.

American Association of Collegiate Registrars & Admissions Officers (AACRAO). *Strategic Enrollment Management Monthly.* November 2002.

Archambeault, Bill. "Harvard Land Deal Puts Area Towns On The Defensive." *Boston Business Journal.* July 30, 2001. http://boston.bizjournals.com/boston/stories/2001/07/30/story7.html.

Association of American Colleges and Universities. "Greater Expectations Project Overview." 2003. http://www.aacu.org/gex/overview.cfm (accessed February 17, 2004).

Association of American Colleges and Universities. Greater Expectations National Panel Report: Executive Overview. http://www.greaterexpectations.org/ (accessed May 3, 2004).

Association of University Research Parks (AURP). "A Role In Aiding The Transfer Of Technology And Business Skills Between The University and Industry Tenants." *University Research Park Profile 2003.* Rockville, Maryland: 2003.

Astin, A.W., et al. *The American Freshman: Thirty year Trends.* Los Angeles, California: Higher Education Research Institute, UCLA, 1997.

Auburn University Commission to Restructure the University. "Texas A&M University." Included in "Documents from the May 8, 1998 Meeting of the Commission." http://www.ag.auburn.edu/commission/51198/mission/texas.htm (accessed February 19, 2004).

Aukamp, Elizabeth. Email to G. Kenney, September 7, 2002.

Bennett, Paul. "It Takes a Village." *Landscape Architecture.* October 1998.

"Best Places to Retire." *Money* Magazine. May 8, 2002. http://money.cnn.com/2002/05/01/retirement/bpretire_providence/.

Bleed, Ron. "A Hybrid Campus for the New Millennium." *Educause Review.* January/February 2001.

Block, Zachary. "Pigging Out." *Brown Alumni Magazine.* November/December 2001.

Boyer, Ernest. *College: The Undergraduate Experience in America.* The Carnegie Foundation for the Advancement of Teaching. New York: Harper & Row, 1987.

Brown University Office of Community and Government Relations. "Brown University: Global Reach. Local Impact." June 2000. http://www.brown.edu/Administration/University_Relations/econ.shtml.

Brown, John Seely and Paul Duguid. *The Social Life of Information.* Boston: Harvard Business School Press, 2000.

Brown, Patricia Q. *Postsecondary Institutions in the United States: 1993 – 94 and 1998 – 99, NCES 2001-176.* US Department of Education, National Center for Education Statistics. Washington, D.C.: 2001.

Campbell, Robert. "Urban Scrawl." *The Boston Globe Magazine.* January 12, 2003.

———. "When Building Becomes 'Branding.'" *The Boston Sunday Globe.* August 4, 2002.

Carlson, Cob. "A Better Plan For Harvard." Editorial in *The Boston Globe.* November 26, 2001.

Carlson, Scott. "Colleges Struggle With a '60s Legacy: Ugly, Wasteful, and Outdated Buildings." *The Chronicle of Higher Education.* August 17, 2001.

———. "The Deserted Library: As Students Work Online, Reading Rooms Empty Out—Leading Some Campuses To Add Starbucks." *The Chronicle of Higher Education.* November 16, 2001.

Carnegie Foundation for the Advancement of Teaching. *Campus Life: In Search of Community.* Princeton: Princeton University Press, 1990.

Carnevale, Alex. "Building Brown: A Walk Around Campus With Architecture Professor Dietrich Neumann." *Post Magazine.* October 25, 2002.

Carnevale, Anthony. Presentation at the Annual Meeting of the American Council on Education, Vancouver, British Columbia. February, 2002.

Castronova, Edward. "Virtual Worlds: A First-Hand Account of Market and Society on the Cyberian Frontier." *The Gruter Institute Working Papers on Law, Economics, and Evolutionary Biology.* Volume 2, Issue 1, Article 1. The Berkeley Electronic Press, 2001. http://www.bepress.com/giwp/default/vol2/iss1/art1.

Charles, Linda. "Land-grant Universities Born From Radical Idea." *The Iowa Stater.* February 1997. http://www.iastate.edu/IaStater/1997/feb/landgrant.html (accessed February 19, 2004).

City Place in West Palm Beach—Palm Beach County Convention and Visitors Bureau, "Palm Beach County, Florida," World Wide Web, 2000. http://www.palmbeach-fl.com/.

Coates, Sr., Eyler Robert. "Chapter 40. Publicly Supported Education." *Thomas Jefferson on Politics & Government.* University of Virginia Library. http://etext.lib.virginia.edu/jefferson/quotations/index.html (accessed February 2004).

Cohen, Andrew. "Rethinking College Recreation." *Metropolis* Magazine. August 2000. http://www.metropolismag.com/html/content_0800/ent.htm.

Columbia University Office of the Vice President for Administration. "Columbia University's Contribution to the New York City Economy, 1996." http://www.columbia.edu/cu/evp/nycecon.html (accessed March 12, 2003).

Contact Consortium. "About the Contact Consortium and its Member Services." Scotts Valley, California. http://www.ccon.org/org/org.html (accessed September 27, 2002).

The Contact Consortium. "TheU Home Page." Scotts Valley, California. http://ccon.org/theu/ (accessed September 27, 2002).

Council for Aid to Education Commission on National Investment in Higher Education. "Breaking the Social Contract: The Fiscal Crisis in Higher Education." The

Rand Corporation. http://www.rand.org/publications/CAE/CAE100/index.html (accessed December 23, 2002).

Covey, Keith. "Book Review: Fixing the Crumbling Campus." *Planning for Higher Education.* Winter 1997 – 98, Volume 26, Number 2.

Cranbrook Schools. http://www.schools.cranbrook.edu/Default.asp?bhcp=1.htm (accessed May 3, 2004).

Curtis, Pavel. "Mudding: Social Phenomena in Text-Based Virtual Realities." Xerox PARC. March 3, 1992.

Daniel, Sir John. "Lessons From the Open University: Low-Tech Learning Often Works Best." *The Chronicle of Higher Education,* September 7, 2001.

———. "Renewing Universities for the New Economy." Presentation at the National Governors Association Winter Meeting, Washington, D.C., February 28, 2000. http://www.open.ac.uk/vcs-speeches/Governors.htm.

Dewey, Peter (University of Washington Transportation Systems Manager), quoted in "U-PASS Program Celebrates 10 Years Of Reducing Campus and Regional Congestion." King County, Washington: May 23, 2001. http://www.metrokc.gov/exec/news/2001/0523012.htm.

Dibbell, Julian. *My Tiny Life: Crime and Passion in a Virtual World.* New York: Henry Holt and Company, 1998.

Dreyfus, Hubert L. *On the Internet.* London and New York: Routledge, 2001.

Duderstadt, James J. *A University For the 21st Century.* Ann Arbor, Michigan: University of Michigan Press, 2000.

Duhart, Sharon R. *The Economic Impact of University System of Georgia Institutions on their Regional Economies.* University System of Georgia Board of Regents Office of Economic Development. March 2002.

Duquesne University. "The Duquesne University Mission Statement." 2002. http://www.mission.duq.edu/ (accessed January 16, 2004).

Eagan, David J., and Julian Keniry. *Green Investment, Green Return: How Practical Conservation Projects Save Millions on America's Campuses.* National Wildlife Federation. March 1998.

Ehrenberg, Ronald G. *Tuition Rising: Why College Costs So Much.* Cambridge, Massachusetts: Harvard University Press, 2000.

"The Environment: Risky Business." *The Wirthlin Report.* Vol. 9, No. 9. November 1999.

Farrell, Elizabeth F. "U. of Oregon Offers Discount on Late-Afternoon Classes." *The Chronicle of Higher Education.* July 19, 2002.

Gabriel, Trip. "Computers Help Unite Campuses, But Also Drive Some Students Apart." *The New York Times.* November 11, 1996.

Gaines, Thomas A. *The Campus as a Work of Art.* Westport, Connecticut: Praeger Publishers, 1991.

Gavin, Robert. "Study: Colleges Pump $7.4B Into Local Economy." *The Boston Globe.* March 8, 2003.

Georgia College & State University. "The GC&SU Mission." October 28, 2003. http://www.gcsu.edu/GCSU/gen/mission.html (accessed January 16, 2004).

Giuliano, Vincent (Former Dean, School of Library and Information, SUNY). Email to Ginger Kenney, May, 2003.

Goldberger, Paul. "The Store Strikes Back." *The New York Times.* April 6, 1997.

Goodman, Ted (ed.). *The Forbes Book of Business Quotations: 14,266 Thoughts on the Business of Life.* New York: Black Dog & Leventhal, 1997.

Gragg, Randy. "Library: Law-School Addition Juts Into Forest, 'Interacts With Nature.'" OregonLive.com. (from The Oregonian newspaper.) Portland, Oregon: February 10, 2002. http://www.oregonlive.com/living/oregonian/randy_gragg/index.ssf?/xml/story.ssf/html_standard.xsl?/base/entertainment/10131729331471648.xml>.

Guernsey, Lisa. "College 'MOOs' Foster Creativity and Collaboration Among Users." *The Chronicle of Higher Education,* Information Technology Section. February 9, 1996.

Gulati, Ranjay, and Jason Garino. "Get the Right Mix of Bricks and Clicks." *Harvard Business Review,* Reprint R00313. May-June 2000.

Gumport, Patricia J., et al. *Trends in United States Higher Education from Massification to Post Massification.* Stanford University National Center for Postsecondary Improvement. Stanford, California: 1997.

Gussow, Mel, "A Polymath Selects Polymath to Direct Bard Arts Center." *The New York Times.* July 18, 2002. http://www.ninecircles.orghtml/press/levi_ny_times.html.

Harrow, Jeff. "The Reality of the Game." *The Harrow Technology Report.* May 27, 2002. http://www.theharrow-group.com/articles/20020527/20020527.htm.

Hart, Stanley I., and Alvin L. Spivak. *The Elephant in the Bedroom: Automobile Dependence & Denial: Impacts on the Economy and Environment.* Boca Raton, Florida: New Paradigm Books, 1993.

Head, Emily, et al. "Getting There: A Transportation Demand Management Assessment of the University of Waterloo Community." University of Waterloo, Ontario. May 1, 2000. http://www.adm.uwaterloo.ca/infowast/Transportation/720FinalFolder/720Final.html (accessed April 2004).

Hebel, Sara, and Jeffrey Selingo. "For Public Colleges, a Decade of Generous State Budgets is Over." *The Chronicle of Higher Education.* April 20, 2001.

Hebel, Sara. "In Virginia, Building Projects Halt While Enrollment Grows." *The Chronicle of Higher Education.* April 20, 2001.

Heschong Mahone Group. *Daylighting in Schools: An Investigation Into the Relationship Between Daylighting and Human Performance.* Pacific Gas and Electric Company. Fair Oaks, California: August 20, 1999.

Hibbard, Joe (principal, Sasaki Associates, Inc.). Notes from conversation with the authors, May 6, 2003.

Horan, Thomas A., Ph.D. *Digital Places: Building Our City of Bits.* Washington, D.C.: ULI—The Urban Land Institute, 2001.

Horn, Laura and C. Dennis Carroll. *Nontraditional Undergraduates: Trends in Enrollment from 1986 to 1992 and Persistence and Attainment Among 1989 – 90 Beginning Postsecondary Students NCES 97-578.* United States Department of Education National Center for Education. Washington, D.C., 1997.

Howe, Neil, and William Strauss. *Millennials Go To College.* Np: American Association of Collegiate Registrars and Admissions Officers (AACRAO). LifeCourse Associates.

Hughes, Ken. "The Plaza That Makes a Sense of Place." 2002 American Planning Association National Planning Conference Proceedings. http://www.asu.edu/caed/proceedings02/HUGHES/hughes1.htm (accessed February 27, 2004).

Illuminating Engineering Society of North America. *Lighting for Exterior Environments.* RP-33-99. New York: 1999.

Institute for Research on Higher Education. "When the Customer is Right: Market-Driven Accountability in Postsecondary Education." *Change* Magazine. May/June 2000.

International Dark-Sky Association. "Control of Outdoor Lighting at Wesleyan University." Information Sheet 27. February 1997.

Jacobs, Jane. *The Death and Life of Great American Cities.* New York: Vintage Books, 1992.

James, Henry. *The Bostonians.* London: Purnell, 1886.

Jeton, Nancy Kepes (Alumni Trustee, Dartmouth University). Email to Dan Kenney, September 10, 2001, and subsequent conversations.

Jones, Steve. *The Internet Goes to College.* Pew Internet & American Life Project. Washington D.C., September 15, 2002. http://www.pewinternet.org/.

Kaiser, Harvey. *A Foundation to Uphold: A Study of Facilities Conditions at US Colleges and Universities.* The Association of Higher Education Facilities Officers (APPA). 1996.

Kelly, Tom, et al. "Sustainable Transportation Trip Report and Recommendations." University of New Hampshire. Durham, New Hampshire, September 15, 1999. http://www.sustainableunh.unh.edu/promise/actions/trip_report.htm.

Killingsworth, Richard E., and Jean Lanning. "Development and Public Health: Could Our Development Patterns Be Affecting Our Personal Health?" *Urban Land,* July 2001.

Kuh, George D., John H. Schuh, Elizabeth J. Whitt, et al. *Involving Colleges: Successful Approaches to Fostering Student Learning and Development Outside the Classroom.* San Francisco: Jossey-Bass, 1991.

Kunstler, James Howard. *The Geography of Nowhere: The Rise and Decline of America's Man-made Landscape.* New York: Simon & Schuster, 1993.

Leach, William. *Country of Exiles: The Destruction of Place in American Life.* New York: Pantheon Books, 1999.

Leonard, Mary. "On Campus, Comforts Are Major: Colleges Hope Perks Can Boost Enrollment." *The Boston Globe.* September 3, 2002.

Levine, Arthur, and Jeanette S. Cureton. "Collegiate Life: An Obituary." *Change* Magazine. May/June 1998.

———. *When Hope and Fear Collide: A Portrait of Today's College Student.* San Francisco: Jossey-Bass, 1998.

Levine, Arthur. *When Dreams and Heroes Died: A Portrait of Today's College Student.* San Francisco: Jossey-Bass, 1980.

Lewis & Clark College. "Justice Scalia To Speak At Dedication." *L&C News.* February 10, 2002. <http://www.lclark.edu/cgi-bin/shownews.cgi?1013362200.1>.

Lichter, Howard. "Adapt to Survive." *Town Centre Management 3rd World Congress Report.* Association of Town Centre Management. London, June 14 – 16, 2000.

Linn, Charles. "Academic Buildings: Reeducating the Masses." *Architectural Record.* October 1998.

Lyons, John B. "Do School Facilities Really Impact a Child's Education? An Introduction to the Issues." http://www.coe.uga.edu/sdpl/articlesandpapers/lyons.html (accessed April 3, 2002).

Marklein, Mary Beth. "Come For A Diploma, Stay For Life: Cities Become Part Of Campus Recruiting." *USA Today.* April 23, 2003.

Markowitz, Frank, and Alex Estrella, "Campus Moves: Lively Experiments In Transportation Technology Are Crossing the Line Between Town and Gown." *Planning* Magazine. The American Planning Association. 1998. Also on the Internet at http://bap.ucsb.edu/planning/1.background.stuff/campus%20moves/campus.moves.html (accessed July 28, 2002).

Marlboro College. "About Marlboro: Philosophy." http://www.marlboro.edu/about/philosophy.html (accessed January 16, 2004).

Maurrasse, David J. *Beyond the Campus: How Colleges and Universities Form Partnerships with Their Communities.* New York: Routledge, 2001.

McAliney, Mike (ed.). *Arguments for Land Conservation: Documentation and Information Sources for Land Resources Protection.* Trust for Public Land, Sacramento, California, December 1993.

McIntosh, Mary, et al. *State of the Campus Environment: A National Report Card on Environmental Performance and Sustainability in Higher Education.* National Wildlife Federation. N.p.: 2001.

Melia, Michael. "Art for Arts: EMP's Gehry Moves On To Small College." *The Seattle Times.* May 19, 2002. http://seattletimes.nwsource.com/html/artsentertainment/134455423_wgehry19.html.

Mitchell, Mary E. "Living With An Online Student Is More Than a Marriage; It's an Adventure." Article posted to www.KaplanCollege.com on August 4, 2000.

Mitchell, Ross E. Emails to Ginger Kenney, dated September 5, 2002 and September 8, 2002.

Morelli, Sabrina, LEED Program Coordinator, US Green Building Council. E-mail to Allyson Solorzano dated June 4, 2003.

Morris, Bonnie Rothman. "Budding Scientists, Let Loose in a World They Can Save." *The New York Times.* June 6, 2002. http://www.nytimes.com/2002/06/06/technology/circuits/06NEXT.html.

Mumford, Lewis. *The Culture of Cities.* New York: Harcourt Brace, 1938.

National Association of State Universities and Land-Grant Colleges. Press Release: "State and Land-Grant Universities Are Powerful Engines for Economic Growth." Washington, D.C., August 23, 2001.

National Survey of Student Engagement, Indiana University Center for Postsecondary Research and Planning. *Improving the College Experience: National Benchmarks for Effective Educational Practic.* Bloomington, Indiana, 2001.

Nebraska Community College Association. "Community College Development in the United States." http://www.ncca.state.ne.us/system/Natlhistory.htm (accessed February 14, 2004).

Neumann, David. Conversation with Dan Kenney and Ginger Kenney, February 12, 2002.

O'Banion, Terry. "A Learning College for the 21st Century." *Community College Journal.* December/January 1995 – 95.

Odom, J. Scott. "My Place." *South Carolina Architecture—2003/2004.* South Carolina Chapter American Institute of Architects.

Oldenburg, Ray. "Making College a Great Place to Talk." *The Best of Planning for Higher Education.* George Keller, ed. Society for College and University Planning. Ann Arbor, Michigan, 1997.

Olmsted, Frederick Law. "Preliminary Report on the Yosemite and Mariposa Cove." 1865.

Olsen, Florence. "Phoenix Rises: The University's Online Program Attracts Students, Profits, and Praise." *The Chronicle of Higher Education.* November 1, 2002.

"Omnium Overview." <http://www.omnium.unsw.edu.au/> (accessed September 8, 2002).

Orr, David W. *Earth in Mind: On Education, Environment, and the Human Prospect.* Washington, D.C.: Island Press, 1994.

Parsons, Philip (former Associate Dean for Physical Resources at the Harvard University Faculty of Arts and Sciences). Conversation with Dan Kenney and Ginger Kenney, August 19, 2003.

Plympton, Patricia, Susan Conway, and Kyra Epstein. *Daylighting in Schools: Improving Student Performance and Health at a Price Schools Can Afford.* National Renewable Energy Laboratory. Golden, Colorado, August 2000. Document NREL/CP-550-28049. http://www.deptplanetearth.com/pdfdocs/nrel_daylitschools.pdf. (accessed March 11, 2004).

Polyzoides, Stefanos. "Success and Failure in Campus Design in the Post-World War II Era: An Historical View and Focus on California." Presented at the forum *Designing the Campus of Tomorrow: The Legacy of the Hearst Architectural Plan, Present and Future.* Berkeley, California, February 10, 2000. Transcript from the Internet. http://sunsite.Berkeley.edu/uchistory/archives_exhibits/hearst/3_panel1_2polyzoides.html.

Porter, Stephen R., & Paul D. Umbach. "We Can't Get There in Time." *Planning for Higher Education.* Winter 2001 – 2002.

Reidy, Chris. "Equal Parts Entertainer and Vendor Niketown Is Latest in Trend That Has Stores Catering to Shoppers' Sense of Fun." *The Boston Globe.* July 20, 1997.

Research Triangle Institute (RTI). Beginning Postsecondary Students (BPS) Longitudinal Study conducted for the National Center for Education Statistics (NCES). http://nces.ed.gov/surveys/bps/ (accessed March 26, 2004).

Rodin, Judith. "Common Cause: Investing in the Local Community." University of Pennsylvania. Spring 2001. http://www.upenn.edu/president/rodin/common_cause_01.html.

Rosan, Richard M. "The Key Role of Universities in Economic Growth and Urban Revitalization." PowerPoint presentation at St. Louis University, April 10, 2002.

Russell, Jenna. "On Campus Visits, Bid For High Marks." *The Boston Globe.* September 7, 2002.

"Seeing Things As They Really Are." *Forbes* Magazine. March 10, 1997. http://www.forbes.com/forbes/1997/0310/5905122a_print.html (accessed October 27, 2002).

Shanklin, Mary. "The Senior Class Retirees Relocate to College Towns to Learn and Play." *Orlando Sentinel.* November 12, 2000.

Shapiro, Harold. "The Beauty of the Campus." Princeton University President's Page. February 7, 2001. http://www.princeton.edu/pr/president/01/02-07-01.html (accessed January 20, 2004).

Simonds, John Ormsbee. *Landscape Architecture: An Ecological Approach to Environmental Planning.* New York: McGraw Hill, 1961.

Smith, Mary S. "Planning for Surface Parking," in Anthony P. Chrest, et al., *Parking Structures Third Edition: Planning, Design, Construction, Maintenance & Repair.* Boston: Kluwer Academic Publishers, 2001.

Snyder, Thomas, and Charlene Hoffman. *Digest of Educational Statistics 2000 NCES 2001-034.* United States Department of Education National Center for Education Statistics. Washington, D.C., 2001.

Snyder, Thomas, and Linda Shafer. "Indicator 24. College Costs." *Youth Indicators 1996. NCES 96-027.* United States Department of Education, National Center for Education Statistics. Washington, D.C., 1996.

SportsTrust. "Issue 33—Concept Stores." *Sports News You Can Use.* 1998. http://www.onlinesports.com/sportstrust/sports33.html (accessed November 6, 2002).

Stanford University Office of Communications, Stanford University. *Stanford Facts 2002: Information for Visitors and Prospective Students.*

Stemmle, Jon. "A 'campus garden…place of beauty' Planned for MU." *Facilities Focus.* University of Missouri Campus Facilities. May/June 1998. http://www.cf.missouri.edu/fm/comm/focus/1998/may-jun98/garden.html (accessed January 20, 2004).

Stone, Joe. "The Dean's Letter." University of Oregon College of Arts and Sciences. May 5, 2003. http://cas.uoregon.edu/alumnidev/cascade/200305.dean.html.

Strange, C. Carney, and James H. Banning. *Education by Design: Creating Campus Learning Environments That Work.* San Francisco: Jossey-Bass, 2000.

Tanner, C. Kenneth. "Essential Aspects of Designing a School." School Design and Planning Laboratory, The University of Georgia. Athens, Georgia, April 2000. http://www.coe.uga.edu/sdpl/research/principlesofdesign.html.

———."The School Design Assessment Scale: Validity, Reliability, and Weights." Paper presented at the Annual Conference of the Council of Educational Facility Planners, International, Baltimore, Maryland, November 1 – 5, 1999.

Tanner, C. Kenneth, and Ann Langford. *The Importance of Interior Design Elements as They Relate to Student Outcomes.* University of Georgia. Athens, Georgia. http://www.coe.uga.edu/sdpl/research/SDPLStudiesInProgress/criann02elem.html.

Thomas Jefferson Memorial Association. *The Writings of Thomas Jefferson.* Albert Ellery Bergh (ed.), Memorial Edition, Volume 15. 1909. www.constitution.org.

Trinity College. "Trinity, Its Neighbors, and Hartford." http://trincoll.edu/pub/heights/backcover.htm (accessed August 16, 2003).

Trinity College. "Trinity/SINA Neighborhood Initiative." http://www.trincoll.edu/pub/city/trinity_sina.html (accessed August 16, 2003).

Trust for Public Land Research Room. "Urban Forests/Trees." January 14, 1996. <http://www.tpl.org/tier3_print.cfm?folder_id=726&content_item_id=1103&mod_type=1>.

Turner, Paul V., Marcia E. Vetrocq, and Karen Weitze. *The Founders & the Architects: The Design of Stanford University.* Department of Art, Stanford University. Stanford, California, 1976.

Tyler, Norm. "William Whyte's View of Downtowns." http://www.emich.edu/public/geo/557book/c113.whyte.html (accessed April 2004).

United States Department of the Interior, U.S. Geological Survey. USGS Fact Sheet FS-068-98, "Materials Flow and Sustainability." June 1998. <http://greenwood.cr.usgs.gov/pub/fact-sheets/fs-0008-98/fs-0008-98.pdf>.

United States Environmental Protection Agency. *WasteWise Update: Building for the Future.* Washington, D.C., nd. <http://www.epa.gov/wastewise/pubs/wwupda16.pdf>.

University of Miami School of Architecture, Knight Program in Community Building. "The Laws of the Indies." Axel Mundigo and Dora Crouch (trans.). http://www.arc.miami.edu/Law%20of%20Indies.html (accessed January 21, 2004).

University of Miami. "The University of Miami Mission Statement." October 9, 2003. http://www.miami.edu/UMH/CDA/UMH_Main/1,1770,2472-1;23-3,00.html (accessed 1 March 2004).

University of Oregon. "UO Makes Top 'Green' Grades In US." Eugene, Oregon, March 31, 2002. <www.uoregon.edu/newscenter/greengrades.html>.

University of Pennsylvania. "The Goal: Improving Housing and Home Ownership." 2003. http://www.upenn.edu/president/westphilly/housing.html.

———."The Goal: Improving Public Education." 2003. http://www.upenn.edu/president/westphilly/education.html.

University of Texas at Austin. "Star Light, Star Bright: Mcdonald Observatory Completes Joint Project To Reduce Light Pollution, Cut Costs On Electric Bills; Program Could Serve As Model For Texas Cities." On Campus. Volume 27, number 17. July 27, 2000.

University of Washington, U-Pass. "10 Years of Results." Seattle, Washington, 2001. http://www.washington.edu/upass/news_and_reports/upass_reports/facts.pdf.

University of Washington. *University of Washington Master Plan Seattle Campus, Final Plan.* September 2001.

University of Wisconsin-Madison. "Mission and Overview." *Campus Natural Areas.* Madison, Wisconsin: nd. http://gaia1.ies.wisc.edu/cna/.

Unsworth, John. "Constructing the Virtual Campus." Paper delivered at the 1994 Modern Language Association meeting in Toronto, May 18, 1995. http://www.village.virginia.edu/~jmu2m/Virtual.Campus.html.

United States Department of Education. *Youth Indicators 1996.* "Indicator 28. School Completion."

Upgren, Arthur. "Conrol of Outdoor Lighting at Wesleyan University." International Dark-Sky Association, Information Sheet 27, February 1997.

Urban Land Institute. "Made in the Shade." *Urban Land.* October 1998.

Valen, Gary L. "Hendrix College Local Food Project." *The Campus and Environmental Responsibility.* David J. Eagan and David W. Orr, eds. San Francisco: Jossey-Bass New Directions for Higher Education series, Number 77, 1992.

Vassar College Admissions Web site. Http://admissions.vassar.edu/visit_tour.html (accessed May 9, 2003).

Walden University Web site. http://www.waldenu.edu (accessed April 2004).

Ward, William Arthur. "To Risk." http://www.appleseeds.org/to-risk_WAW.htm.

Warren Wilson College. "Making an Environmental Difference." Asheville, North Carolina: 2002. <http://www.warren-wilson.edu/environdiff/index.shtml>.

Washington University in St. Louis. "University Mission Statement." 2004. http://www.wustl.edu/university/mission.html. (accessed January 5, 2004).

Williams, Tennessee. *The Glass Managerie.* New York: New Directions Publishing Corporation, 1970.

Woolf, Virginia. *A Room of One's Own.* New York: Harcourt Brace Jovanovich, 1989.

Yale University. "Yale University Human Resource Services— New Haven HomeBuyer Program Page." February 21, 2003. http://www.yale.edu/hronline/hbuyer/hbuyprog.htm.

Yee, Nicholas. *The Norrathian Scrolls: A Study of EverQuest.* Version 2.5. http://www.nickyee.com/eqt/report.html (accessed April 2004).

Young, Jeffrey R. " 'Hybrid' Teaching Seeks to End the Divide Between Traditional and Online Instruction." *The Chronicle of Higher Education.* March 22, 2002.

Zamora, George. "New Campus Lighting Good for Costs, Astronomy." *New Mexico Tech.* New Mexico Institute of Mining and Technology. Socorro, New Mexico: 2001. http://www.nmt.edu/mainpage/news/2001/23mar02.html.

Zernike, Kate. "The Feng Shui of Schools." New York *Times.* August 5, 2001.